MOVIDA

SPANISH CULINARY ADVENTURES

FRANK CAMORRA & RICHARD CORNISH

MURDOCH BOOKS

CONTENIDO

CONTENTS

INTRODUCTION

It seemed that after the Second World War the youth of every western nation found its voice. For the Americans, it happened swiftly with the advent of 1950s rock and films like *Rebel Without a Cause*. The seminal moment for the British was Post-Punk New Wave. In Spain, a cultural movement hit the big cities in the decade after Franco's death in 1975. It was like a reawakening of the spirit of youth. It was called *La Movida Madrileña* or the Madrid Movement. It was a time of youthful hedonism and artistic expression. In Madrid, it became a way of life. The slang of the time, *cheli*, contained the expression '*¿dónde está la movida?*' — 'where's the action' would be the Australian equivalent. Bands and artists sprung up during this time, one of whom was the famous film director Pedro Almodóvar. A movement with such sheer enthusiasm for being young, Spanish and proud seemed the perfect title for the very first tapas bar I put my name to.

This is our second MoVida. Our first, MoVida Mark I, was in a funky 1970s pub in West Melbourne. We were there for 2 years before this central city location became available in 2003.

The idea for MoVida goes back to when I was studying to be an architect. I love form and function but swotting to build shopping centres just didn't gel. Something inside me said 'No!' I was born in Barcelona, Spain, and my parents decided to move to Australia in 1975. Mum is a brilliant cook and I remember watching over her shoulder as she made *roscos* (doughnuts). Dad is also a good cook. In Spain, men cook certain dishes, such as paella, and take as much pride in their cooking as Aussie blokes take in their cars or sheds. It was hard to turn my back on 5 years of study, but one day I bit the bullet and decided to become a chef. I worked with the Grossi family (at Florentino's Grill, Pietro's and Café Grossi) and trained with them, eventually becoming head chef. After working with them for 8 years my partner, Vanessa (also a chef), and I decided to work in Spain.

I had been back to Spain with mum and dad in the past where we were welcomed at large family dinners. My parents' families would come and everyone would get reacquainted and comment on how much my sister and I had grown. The cooks, both men and women, were eager to teach. I remember my father and my aunty's boyfriend arguing at my uncle's place in the Corridera Mountains about how they should cook the pancetta over the *barbacoa* (barbecue). It seemed that everybody had a different opinion on how to cook.

When I went back to Spain with Vanessa, I took her to meet my Aunty Pepa in the little town of Aguila de la Frontera. Aunty Pepa showed us her particular method of cooking a great *potaje* (a spinach and chickpea dish). It was so good and so renowned for being delicious that by the time she came to serve it the famished family were slavering like hungry Labradors.

In Spain, every cook prepares the same dish differently. My mum's *potaje* is different to my Aunty Pepa's. As the dish passes from one cook to the next, there's always room for improvement or a change of style. Vanessa and I learned this when we cooked for 12 months in a restaurant called Bodega de Pepe, in the Pyrenees mountains in Aragon, northern Spain. Aurora, the mother of the owner, was a hard taskmaster but very generous with her time. She taught us a great tortilla recipe, as well as a local speciality, lamb *chilindrón*.

This book is filled with those recipes. Recipes from my family, our friends and from the people we worked for in Spain. Some recipes we have adapted from traditional Spanish dishes and some we have simply made up. We have adapted recipes by substituting only very few of the ingredients where they are unavailable in Australia.

The recipes in this book come from a commercial kitchen, which works at a hectic pace, making dishes that range from humble tapas and slow-cooked braises to the heights of modern gastronomy. These recipes are made daily by a team who watch the produce come through the front door every morning and who come up with ideas to transform great raw ingredients into great little dishes in an intelligent, respectful and efficient manner, 7 days a week, in a tapas bar that is always under the hammer. We're constantly changing the menu, so even our regulars can expect novelty and because of that there's a tension that adds to the excitement.

And that sense of excitement and potential keeps a large corps of regular customers coming back for more. They understand that dining is not a passive consumer activity. They know that a good night in a tapas bar requires that they have to have the right disposition — if they're feeling up for a good night, they'll get one. Sitting at the bar is to be part of the night, part of the action, part of the theatre. And our food is only as good as our team can create it on that day with the produce we've got. We are not machines and there is beauty in imperfection. Like our hand-thrown stoneware tapas plates, each little morsel that we send out from the kitchen is a handcrafted work, created to appeal to all the senses. Every dish is slightly different from the next. We say to our customers, 'If you're looking for consistency above everything else then go to a chain restaurant'.

This book is about getting back to the roots of tapas and other Spanish food and allowing you to enjoy handcrafting some *empanadillas*, *croquetas* or making some great *pollo al ajillo* (garlic marinated chicken cooked in a sherry and onion sauce, see page 230) to share with family and friends.

The recipes in this book are meant to be shared. Some tapas dishes make great finger food for parties, while other dishes are perfect as part of a long, slow lunch or dinner. They have not been designed to be part of an entrée, main and dessert three-course meal. However, to help you determine how many recipes you'll need to feed a certain number of people, please follow the rough guides provided below.

TAPAS

Tapas comes from the word 'cover' and refers to the covering of bread that bartenders once placed on top of drinks in Spain to keep away the dust and flies. The meaning has since evolved to refer to hundreds of different bar snacks. A tapas is one piece of food, a bit like a canapé. So when you see 'tapas 24' you know that this makes 24 little snacks.

MEDIA RACIÓN

A *ración* is a serve from a shared plate. A *media ración* means a smaller portion of this. A recipe described as '*media ración* 8' means that if you served this at the table, eight people could take a small serve, roughly equivalent to an entrée-sized portion.

RACIÓN

As stated above, a *ración* is a serve from a shared plate. A '*ración* 6' portion in this book serves six people as a main-sized portion, if served with one or more accompanying dishes.

CONOCIMIENTOS BÁSICOS

CONOCIMIENTOS BÁSICOS
BACK TO BASICS

There are 40 million Spaniards and each one cooks differently. There is no one particular way of making any dish. A simple soup may change from region to region, from town to town and even from neighbour to neighbour. The one unifying tradition that binds Spain's cooks together is the belief in finding the best ingredients to make a dish to *their* traditional recipe. The beauty of living in Australia is we can cherry-pick the best Spanish recipes that suit our climate and lifestyle. The only danger with this is ending up with a soulless blend of recipes that have no sense of place or season. That is why we have a tacit manifesto at MoVida that gently guides us through the seasons and around the food fads.

Be led by the season and let the produce create the menu.
Find a source of inspiration from a region in Spain or a region in Australia. Consider the produce, climate and culture in each country, find the similarities and help them work together.
Create but remain true to the source of both the produce and the inspiration.
Explore and be curious with new techniques.
Reject pointless complication and embrace the beauty of simplicity.

Some ingredients that I learned to cook with in Spain are not available in Australia or just so different that I have had to localize the way I cook. I think it's important to pay respect not just to the original dishes but also to the produce of the country the dish is being cooked in. That's why we're always searching for the best produce that our farmers grow and fishers catch.

INGREDIENTS

ALMONDS — ALMENDRAS

Almonds are essential to Spanish cooking and therefore to the recipes cooked at MoVida. A meal in Spain may start with a few salted almonds, may continue with a wet rabbit dish thickened with ground almonds then finish with *Tarta de Santiago* — a rich tart filled with almonds and decorated with a cross made with dusted sugar (see page 332).

I am yet to find in Australia the same quality of almonds I cooked with in Spain. The flavour and softness are not the same. That said, there are some good nuts produced in the Riverland, South Australia, and parts of inland New South Wales and Victoria, and these are at their best when freshly harvested in the autumn. Try to buy these local almonds. Urban areas with a large Middle Eastern population have stores that sell quality nuts — a high turnover ensures that the nuts are always fresh. Almonds, like any nut, should be stored in a cool, dry place.

The recipes in this book call for raw almonds with the skin on. We also use some blanched almonds (almonds with the skins removed). If required, they can be roasted in the same manner as the method below.

ROASTED ALMONDS — ALMENDRAS TOSTADAS

Some dishes do require roasted almonds. Roasting brings out the nuttiness and changes the texture of a dish. To roast almonds, lay the required quantity of almonds flat on a baking tray and roast in a 200°C (400°F/Gas 6) oven for 10–15 minutes. The almonds should be nicely golden all the way through. Allow to cool a little before removing the loose skins by rubbing the nuts in a tea towel (dish towel) and then discarding the skin.

BEEF — CARNE DE BUEY

I was taught to respect every piece of meat on an animal, not just the most popular. My favourite cuts of beef are those with the most flavour. These are the ones closest to the bone — the lesser-loved cuts such as shin, oxtail and blade. They are so gelatinous and succulent. They make great slow-braised dishes such as *estofado* (beef shin braised with carrots, tomatoes, white wine and saffron — see page 265). A nice chunk of chewy chuck steak or shin will release a lot of flavour and texture into a *cocido* (chickpea and meat broth — see page 104). We braise the brisket with onions and red wine to make a stuffing for *piquillo* peppers. We also finely chop wagyu topside to make our *bistec alemán* (steak tartare — see page 257).

There is, however, a lot to be said for a piece of prime rib eye steak aged on the bone. Dense, meaty and with a hint of minerality, when chargrilled and rested this is the king of steaks. I buy a lot of beef from one farmer who breeds some of the best grass-fed wagyu cattle in Australia, a Japanese breed known for its marbling.

There is also the great 'grain-fed versus grass-fed' debate. Grain-fed beef can be more tender than grass-fed beef but, generally, grass-fed animals have more flavour.

What makes a big difference to meat is dry aging. All the meat we grill at MoVida is dry aged. This is a traditional process where whole, half or part of the carcass is aged just above freezing point in a controlled atmosphere. Enzymes break down the muscles and connective tissues, and sugars are transformed into lactic acid. The carcass can lose up to 20 per cent of its weight through moisture loss. The meat, although more expensive, has a lot more flavour and a cleaner, sharper finish. If you can find a butcher who dry ages beef, support them, because dry aging, sadly, is a dying art.

In general, I believe buying from a butcher is best. They'll have what you need and, if you smile, they'll go that little bit further to look after you.

BREAD AND BREADCRUMBS — PAN Y PAN RALLADO

Bread is to Spanish cooking what rice is to Asian cuisine and potatoes to the Irish. Bread fills people up, mops up sauces and it is an integral part of most people's diets.

The traditional Spanish bread is crusty on the outside and has a moist, dense interior. Sourdough bread is enjoyed but never used in cooking. Two-day-old bread and breadcrumbs, however, are used a lot. When using breadcrumbs to thicken a sauce or make a soup, you can use stale *pasta dura* — those big, round and dry Italian loaves. They can be bought in most good delicatessens, Italian bakeries and some good supermarkets. Bread labelled '*pasta dura*' from high street franchise bakers just doesn't cut the mustard. If you can't find *pasta dura*, substitute with another firm crusty bread.

At MoVida we also use Japanese panko breadcrumbs to coat food that will be deep-fried. They are light, dry and airy and available from Japanese food stores and good food suppliers. Alternatively, you can cut the crusts off a 2-day-old *pasta dura*, partially dry it in a moderate oven and then put it through a food processor. Either way, avoid using bread that comes in a plastic bag — in my opinion this is not real bread.

CHICKPEAS — GARBANZOS

To the Spanish, *garbanzos* (chickpeas) have been an integral part of cooking since the occupation of the Moors. Full of goodness, they have a deep, rich, nutty and earthy flavour that gives a sturdy background flavour to dishes in which they are used. I always use dried chickpeas, soaking them the night before cooking.

Australian chickpeas are generally of good quality and tend to be free of stones. I prefer the chickpeas grown in the Ord River region in Western Australia. There they get enough heat and water to allow the rich flavours to develop.

Chickpeas are sensitive little souls who react badly to any sudden changes in temperature. When dropped into boiling water they like to show their disdain by toughening up and refusing to become soft.

Tinned chickpeas are okay only in an emergency. Rinse them thoroughly under cold running water and don't use the liquid in which they are tinned, as it makes food taste dull.

TO COOK CHICKPEAS

The ratio to follow is that 1 kg (2 lb 4 oz) of dried chickpeas will give you about 2.25 kg (5 lb) of cooked chickpeas. Wash the chickpeas and remove any stones or discoloured peas. Cover with warm water and soak overnight (three parts water, one part chickpeas). Drain and gently place the chickpeas into a large saucepan of warm water (five parts water, one part chickpeas). Bring to the boil and add 250 ml (9 fl oz/1 cup) cold water to slow things down a little. Bring to the boil once more and cook the chickpeas until they are plump and soft. This should take approximately 2 hours. Remove from the heat and allow to stand until the water reaches room temperature. Keep the chickpea stock as this has a lot of flavour, adds a lot of texture and can be used in many other dishes. The chickpea stock can be refrigerated for a few days.

EGGS — HUEVOS

In Spain, egg dishes never fell from favour as they did in Australia, where eggs have now been relegated to breakfast-time toast warmers. Spanish egg dishes are held in high esteem and seem to have arisen from a bountiful supply of fresh eggs from back yard chickens scratching about and laying eggs with firm whites and buttery orange yolks.

All the recipes in this book call for free-range eggs. I'm not trying to make you feel guilty; I just know from experience that they simply taste better. At MoVida, we only use free-range eggs and I advise you to do the same.

All recipes in this book call for eggs weighing 59 g (2¼ oz) each and at room temperature.

FRUIT — FRUTA

When my family first arrived in Australia my father planted a fig tree. He wanted us all to know the deep, sweet flavour of a fig straight from the tree. He taught me that for every fruit there is a window in which it is at its best. Pick it before it's ripe and it won't be sufficiently sweet or complex; eat it too ripe and you've missed the prime of its life. We are lucky that we live in such a large country with each season producing a wave of ripeness, starting in the north and progressing south, the last of the fruit often coming from Tasmania.

Generally, spring and early summer is stone fruit season and summer is berry time. In autumn, look forward to apples, pears and quinces. Citrus hits its peak in winter — especially blood oranges. Your local greengrocer should put you on the right track as to when a particular fruit is at its best.

I also use a lot of dried fruit. I buy sultanas (golden raisins), raisins and currants from shops patronized by migrant families from the Middle East. These shops have a high turnover of stock and the produce is always of good quality. Some popular brands of dried fruit are sprayed with oil to prevent clumping. This oil can become rancid and affect the taste of the fruit.

GAME — CAZA

It is a well-known fact that the only people who love shooting more than Americans are the Spanish. General Franco set aside large tracts of land in Spain for game reserves, to which people would head out during hunting season. A day in the reserve once involved driving out to a wooded area, finding a nice picnic spot then shooting a few of the little birds and animals that lived there and making a paella with them. Most of the game reserves are now national parks but that has not tapered the Spanish love for game meat.

I used to hunt for rabbit with my dad out the back of Geelong, where I grew up. Wild young Australian rabbit is very good but is getting harder to buy. I like wild game animals because they have a wild vitality about their flesh that cannot be emulated by raising an animal in a cage or behind a barbed wire fence. In Spanish markets, whole animals are displayed in feather or fur, such as quail, pheasants, partridge, woodcock, rabbit, hare, boar, goat and haunches of venison.

We have a game industry here in Australia but almost all — with the exception of wild shot rabbit, hare, kangaroo, boar and wallaby — are farmed birds and animals. Because farmed game creatures rarely have to do anything more than walk from drinking trough to feed bowl, they have little chance to develop muscles, so are very tender and faster to cook than wild game. They also don't develop the strong gamey flavours of wild animals.

All the game recipes listed in this book have been tested using readily available farmed birds and animals. If you are lucky enough to have wild game you will have to accept that the animals will be a little more toothsome and may require longer cooking — but what you lose in tenderness you will gain in flavour.

Farmed game animals can be found in the central food markets of big cities. Wild shot kangaroo is also available in some large supermarkets. Wild game animals can be found living wild in the country — but you'll need a gun, a licence and be a very good shot.

GOAT — CABRA

For millennia, goat has been the most widely eaten animal on the planet but only quite recently has it re-emerged on Australian menus. It is lean, carries flavours very well and is surprisingly inexpensive. Older animals and males can have a strong flavour so we buy baby goats and use the whole animal in a variety of dishes. You can buy goat in markets or in butchers' shops in areas with large Indo-Chinese, Indian or Middle Eastern communities. Ask for cuts from smaller goats.

HAZELNUTS — AVELLANAS

My family is from Córdoba, the main hazelnut-growing area in Spain and, as a result, we were brought up always cracking our nuts as we needed them. Those who have had really good fresh hazelnuts will understand that they truly are little morsels of joy. Ready for harvest at the end of autumn, they are nutty but with no residual sensation of fat or oil and with just a little grip on the palate. To me, hazelnuts are a gustatory bright spot before the long grey winter.

Nuts in the shell have had less chance to oxidize and are difficult to crack. But this is the price we pay for having a love of fine food. Some hazelnuts, particularly supermarket hazelnuts, are not just stale — they are rancid. Middle Eastern shops and some nut specialists in the city markets have a good range of fresh nuts. Hazelnuts are also making a welcome appearance at farmers' markets in the southern states of Australia.

ROASTED HAZELNUTS — AVELLANAS TOSTADAS

Hazelnuts' flavour deepens and transforms after a little roasting. I lay them on a tray and roast until just golden inside. This takes 10–15 minutes in a 200°C (400°F/Gas 6) oven.

HAM, SPANISH — JAMÓN

Dad still cures his own legs of pork at home and they are very good, but it can never be the same as *jamón* from Spain. *Jamón* is the cured hind leg of a pig. The cured front leg is called *paletas* and the cured loin, *lomo*. The two main types of *jamón* are *jamón serrano* and *jamón ibérico*.

Jamón serrano makes up the great bulk of *jamón* made in Spain, and is made in large commercial quantities from crossbred pink pigs. It is a classic family snack food — particularly when served with *pan catalán* (Catalonian tomato bread, see page 67).

Jamón ibérico makes up only 10 per cent of the ham production in Spain but it is a truly wondrous food. It is made from Iberian pigs, which are an indigenous breed derived from wild boars. They feed outdoors on acorns in the great oak forests of Extremadura. The hind legs are salted for 3 months then hung to dry in *secaderos* (drying halls), where they dry for a further 3–7 months. During this time, moulds develop on the outside, imparting rich flavours. These moulds add flavour just as moulds add flavour to cheese. The legs are then transferred to cellars and aged for a further 9 months to over 3 years. During this process the *jamones* have lost 40 per cent of their original weight but have transformed almost miraculously in flavour. *Jamón* is hand sliced with a sharp knife along the length of the muscles into *lonchas*, translucent wafers of fat and flesh that melt on the tongue, releasing nutty and mineral aromas while pleasing the mouth with a smooth, round texture. We can now buy Iberian *jamón* here in Australia but it costs up to ten times the price of locally made *jamón*. Unfortunately, due to government restrictions, the bone is removed prior to shipping to Australia.

There are some good Australian made Spanish-style hams, generally cured by Spanish expatriates and these can be quite acceptable. If you can't find *jamón*, use very good prosciutto.

Jamón bones are required for a few of the recipes in this book. These are the bones that remain from locally made Spanish hams and are available from some delicatessens. Prosciutto bones can be substituted and, at a stretch, a ham bone could be used instead.

LAMB — CORDERO

Long before Australia rode on the sheep's back the Spanish had a global wool industry based in the Castilian regions. Great cheese and lamb have been the by-products of this industry for centuries. Milk-fed lamb is a speciality of Segovia in Old Castile. *Lechazo al horno* (roast baby lamb) is a sweet, succulent dish and the *chuletillas* (little baby lamb cutlets) are amazing. Australian lamb seems to smell more than the Spanish lamb that I cooked with, but I have found some really good lamb producers. We buy a lot of lamb from a biodynamic farm with geese, chickens, ducks, pigs, some really good wine and beautiful sheep — crossbred animals that are slaughtered when they are a little older, between 10–15 months. Milk-fed lambs are available in the markets from some speciality retailers.

My favourite cut of lamb is the old school forequarter. This is the front leg and shoulder. The shoulder is generally cut up and sold as diced lamb or sawn up into barbecue chops. But a whole forequarter makes the sweetest roast in the world. It's moist, juicy, gelatinous and — with the help of some salt — the skin roasts to crispy perfection.

Australian lamb is best in the spring. But I implore you to find a good butcher and shop with them. Once you're doing business with them they'll cut your meat to order and will generally give you a fair assessment as to when their lamb is at its best.

OLIVE OIL — ACEITE DE OLIVA

The Spanish use olive oil in every meal throughout the day — from frying eggs to drizzling on toast, making salads, soups, marinades and sauces to cooking meats and fish. They also use it like butter to shorten pastry. At MoVida we have taken this tradition into our kitchen and we too use a lot of olive oil.

There are two big differences between Spain and Australia with regard to olive oil. One is that Spanish oils are grown in regions like wine. Different Spanish regions grow different types of olive oil, which are used in specific dishes. We don't have that sort of regionality here in Australia. An oil sold here as 'robust' would be perfect for *alioli,* but for *remojón* (Grilled salt cod salad with blood oranges, parsley and smoked paprika, see page 156) you would ask for a 'mild' or 'fruity' olive oil. There are some good speciality olive oil shops in our capital cities and some very good growers of olive oil in southeastern and Western Australia. It really is a case of try before you buy. Keep the robust oils for hearty dishes and the softer oils to dress the more delicate dishes.

The other difference is that in Spain, a percentage of acidity on the label is an indication of the quality — the lower the acid the better the oil. In Australia we don't use that system yet. Instead, we label oils as follows:

EXTRA VIRGIN OLIVE OIL

This has less than 0.8 per cent acid and is the best quality oil. This is oil that has not been refined and has had no chemical treatment. Extra virgin olive oil tends to be more costly but imbues a dish with a richness and flavour characteristic of the oil itself. To dress dishes, look for local extra virgin olive oils, as imported oils may be many months old and even rancid. The harvest season is late autumn and, generally, these oils are left to settle and are bottled and released some time in the middle of the year.

As Spanish oils tend to be fruitier than Australian oils we try a lot of different local extra virgin olive oil every season, looking for that fruitiness. Recent droughts in Australia have affected yields and quality, resulting in some dank and overly grassy oils. Oils from cooler climates have tended to be better in recent years. Spanish varieties that are doing well here are *picqual* and *arbequina*. Try before you buy. Buy small amounts often and use up your good olive oil because it oxidizes and will go rancid over time.

PURE OLIVE OIL OR OLIVE OIL

Pure olive oil and olive oil have been refined in some manner and tend to be bland, but are suitable for cooking and frying. The most readily available products have been imported in tins and are quite cheap.

VIRGIN OLIVE OIL

Virgin olive oil has more acid and is of a lesser quality than extra virgin olive oil. We don't use this oil at MoVida.

OLIVES — ACEITUNAS

To me the sign of true hospitality is offering guests something to drink and something to nibble on when they walk in the door. It's an acknowledgment that they have travelled to be with you and may need a snack before they eat their meal.

This is why table olives are so important. They are tempting and sharp without being too filling. At MoVida, we don't serve olives that are restrained in their flavour; an olive should taste like an olive.

We buy some *arbequina* olives from Spain but just as many from an olive grove in Western Victoria. Ten years ago, a fire burned parts of the old grove to the ground. The surviving root stock shot up new branches and on them grew tiny sweet little olives that are unique to Southern Australia.

To sweeten our olives we take very large green olives (blond kalamatas in our case) from the brine and allow them to marinate in olive oil with orange and lemon zest, dried oregano leaves, fennel stalks and garlic cloves. We leave these in jars and 3 weeks later we have perfectly sweet olives.

There is also nothing better than opening a tin of anchovy-stuffed olives from Spain, draining off the brine and serving them with a glass of manzanilla sherry.

We still preserve a lot of our own olives. See page 57 for a recipe.

PASTA — PASTA

In Spain, pasta is not a staple food as it is in Italy but it has been a major part of the Spanish culinary landscape since the Middle Ages. Back then, the Kingdom of Aragon, which included modern Catalonia, annexed Sardinia, Sicily and Naples and pasta was brought from the Italian ports to Barcelona. An influx of Italian watchmakers to the city in the nineteenth century cemented the region's love affair with *canelones* and *fideos*. The word *canelones* is pretty easy to decipher and *canalones* are used in similar ways to cannelloni. *Fideos* — short, thin strands of pasta — are cooked in a similar way to paella. Spanish *fideos* can be bought at Spanish grocers but you can substitute with macaroni or spaghetti broken up by hand.

PORK — CERDO

During the fifteenth century the Spanish Inquisition was hellbent on making sure everyone was practising the right sort of religion. As such, converts to Christianity would hang pork sausages in front of their homes to prove they were not Jewish or Muslim and pork was used more and more. Paradoxically, there is an old Castilian joke that '*jamón* was more likely to get people to convert to Christianity than torture'.

Castile is the home of the suckling pig. The most celebrated establishment for pig is Meson Cándido, an old inn under the shadow of a Roman aqueduct. Nearby there is a statue of the owner towering above four roast piglets. He is armed with a plate raised in his hand, proving his claim that his pork is so tender you could chop it with a plate.

At MoVida we are lucky enough to have a steady supply of rare breed Berkshire pigs and 3-month-old suckling pigs and, as in Spain, we follow the culinary tradition of using the whole animal. I like to respect the animal and use everything except the oink! We offer a culinary tour of the pig, from the delicious loin, the succulent ribs, the wicked belly with crisp toffee-like skin to the rich dark blood sausage or *morcilla*. One of my favourite dishes is tripe, slow-cooked with pig's trotters, tomato, wine and herbs. We serve tripe at MoVida and I get to eat the pig's trotter — a super-gelatinous piece of porky heaven.

If you can afford it and have access to it, buy rare breed organic pork, now available through some organic butchers and farmers' markets across the country. At least, aim for free-range pig and forget the idea of lean pork, as there is no such thing as flavoursome lean pork. A pig without fat is not a pig. If you're worried about fat, don't cook pork — eat fish instead. Once again a good butcher will help you through the buying process. Tell them the dish you're making and they'll cut the meat to order. A little secret — always ask for female pig if you want sweet meat, as the males can be a bit on the nose.

POULTRY — AVES

CHICKEN — POLLO

Compare the life of the average back yard bird to a chicken from a factory farm. The back yard bird, on which many great Spanish dishes are based, has lived a life catching bugs, eating grass and running away from the family dog. It's had time to build up strong bones and a lot of flavour. A factory chicken is basically a short-lived ball of feathers that turns pellets into bland breast meat in just weeks.

That is why we only ever buy free-range chickens — they have more flavour. We're lucky to have a good supplier, who makes all the bird feed on site by crushing grains in an old hammer mill, and whose chickens roam free on lucerne (alfalfa) pasture during daylight hours. There are excellent free-range poultry growers in every state. The birds may cost more but the flavour is worth the price.

In Spain, they sell birds with the claws and head still on so you can make sure they were still fresh. That's not done in Australia. I always look for a good bird with firm flesh and a bit of colour in the skin — a sign of corn feeding. Big breasts on a chicken are not always what you want, as this can mean the bird grew too quickly.

PARTRIDGE — PERDIZ

Partridge is *the* game bird of Spain. Every autumn, hunters from the country bring their birds to the city where they find many cooks and chefs eagerly waiting. Its dense sweet flesh takes on flavours of other ingredients beautifully and the flavour only improves with age.

To my chagrin, partridge is not as popular here but I am lucky to have a small but dedicated clientele who now expect partridge and appreciate its sweet, silky round flesh and specifically ask for *perdiz en escabeche* or *perdiz guisada* (partridge with cabbage, see page 240).

Fortunately there are still a few farmers in Australia who produce partridge and you can buy them in the local city markets at speciality poultry and game suppliers. If you can't find partridge, try the recipe with other game birds instead — make sure that you adjust the cooking times accordingly.

QUAIL — CODORNICES

About the size of 2-week-old chickens, all these little birds are farm-raised in Australia and make a great dish. Sweeter, darker and slightly gamier than chicken, they cook on the barbecue in a matter of minutes. There is, however, no in-between when cooking quail. It's either a blast of fast heat and then served pink and juicy or cooked low and slow in casseroles and stews. Quail are available all year round in most inner city markets, good poultry shops and good Asian grocers.

RICE — ARROZ

Rice has been grown in Spain since the Moorish occupation. Rice is grown on river flats, former marshes and river deltas on the eastern seaboard and inland in Murcia, near the town of Calasparra, where two main varieties are grown: *bomba* and *Balilla x Sollana*. The main variety of Spanish rice exported to Australia is Calasparra *bomba*. It's hard to grow and expensive but very, very flavoursome. During cooking it absorbs a lot of water and swells to three times its original size, in width only. It is the perfect paella rice. Calasparra rice is sold in good food stores, markets, some good supermarkets and delicatessens.

SALT COD — BACALAO

Salt cod is very popular in Spain. The combination of having large stocks of cod off the Atlantic coast and a Roman Catholic Church proclaiming as many as three meat-free days a week meant the Spaniards became adept at cooking this dried fish. I really don't think of salt cod as being fish. It has been transformed so much by salting and drying that, in my mind, it has become an entirely different ingredient. It is earthy at the same time as being of the sea. It is preserved yet lively and although considered the food of the poor, it can also make a decadent meal. A large piece in a dish can be the star of the meal but smaller pieces blended through a dish become a deliciously smooth background flavour.

The smell of salt cod cooking always reminds me of Easter, when mum makes Roman salt cod. This is a juicy fillet of desalinated salt cod that has been dipped in egg batter and deep-fried until golden. It is sprinkled with a little salt and eaten with a very simple salad.

Dried salted cod fillets look like mummified bats. We trim off the 'wings' for stock and use the thick sweet flesh near the spine.

The recipes in this book require salt cod to be desalinated in the following manner.

TO DESALINATE

Brush off any visible salt crystals. Place the entire fillet or fillets in a very large stainless steel bowl and cover with cold water. Place the fish skin side up, as this allows the salt to flow down through the flesh. Keep in the refrigerator for 48 hours, changing the water every 12 hours.

SAUSAGES — SALCHICHAS

Every region of Spain has hundreds of different sausages and smallgoods, with each one having its own tradition and speciality. In some ways I'm sad that Australia hasn't embraced Spanish smallgoods in the same way it has Italian meats such as salami and mortadella. It gladdens me, however, that chorizo (spicy pork sausage) is fairly readily available. If you can, buy good chorizo as the recipes in this book call for it frequently and it imparts a unique flavour. *Morcilla* (Spanish blood pudding) is a little harder to source and can be replaced with black pudding.

CHORIZO

Chorizo refers to both the fresh pork sausage — flavoured with sweet paprika, chilli and garlic — and the same sausage that has undergone curing. Use the fresh sausage for cooking and the cured chorizo for tapas. When buying chorizo, make sure it is authentic, as some butchers add premixed powder to meat and call the resulting sausage 'chorizo'. Real, fresh chorizo will be plump and reddish, with pieces of meat and fat visible through the skin and will weigh around 150 g (5½ oz) per sausage. Cured chorizo should be very firm and may have a whitish floral bloom on the outside, which is perfectly harmless and is peeled off prior to serving. (A floral bloom is a coating of moulds, which adds flavour and is similar to the bloom on the outside of camembert cheese.)

MORCILLA — SPANISH BLOOD PUDDING

Morcilla are sausages made from blood, rice, onions and spices. They have a lovely velvety texture and can impart a subtle spicy flavour to a dish. They are harder to find than chorizo. If you can't readily find *morcilla* use black pudding instead, but be aware that using black pudding as a substitute may impart a nutmeg flavour instead of the cinnamon that is used in making *morcilla*. Large *morcilla* weigh around 500 g (1 lb 2 oz).

SEAFOOD AND FISH — MARISCO Y PESCADO

Seafood is an essential part of, not just Spanish cuisine, but Spanish culture. It is eaten everywhere, savoured and respected. Species of seafood caught in the Mediterranean Sea and Atlantic Ocean are different from the species found off Australian shores, so I have adapted the recipes we make at MoVida to suit the fish here.

We use a lot of bream, snapper, tuna and Spanish mackerel — a beautifully oily fish found in the coastal waters around Australia (except South Australia).

In the restaurant trade we are lucky to have daily deliveries of excellent seafood from around the country. In particular, shellfish from Tasmania, sardines from Western Australia and prawns (shrimp) from Queensland. Our fish are delivered whole and our oysters un-shucked because freshness is essential. Repeat, essential. I suggest you buy whole fish from a fishmonger and ask them to do the gutting and scaling. It makes a world of difference. Don't be frightened to cook fish on the bone. Bones impart a rich flavour and smooth texture to fish flesh and I have included some really pleasing recipes that allow fish to be cooked whole.

Again, find a retail fish professional you trust and deal with them specifically, discussing the dishes you're cooking and what you need.

SHERRY — JEREZ

Sherry is an anglicization of Jerez, the Andalusian town where Spanish sherry is made. It is a brilliant drink and very important in Spanish cooking. Because it is matured in oak casks under a layer of yeast — called *flor* (flower) in Spanish — it picks up a lot of flavour from the oak and a delicious yeastiness from the flor. When used in cooking, these flavours add a layer of complexity and help to structure the taste of the food.

The wonderful complexity and consistency of Spanish sherry is ensured by storing the lightly fortified wine in a stack of barrels known as a solera. As older wine is decanted from the bottom of the stack, it is refreshed at the top with younger wine — a labour-intensive process that dates back to the Romans.

You can use locally made commercial dry sherry but, thankfully, there are some good Australian sherries made in the old-fashioned solera system. Good bottle shops should have a range of these, as well as a few imported sherries from Spain. Dry or fino sherry is best for cooking.

SPICES — ESPECIAS

Spanish cooking uses a lot of spices, but they are not necessarily hot. The Moors imported seeds, bark and spices — such as nutmeg, pepper and cinnamon — from India and Indonesia. When the Moors were expelled from Spain, the Spanish had already developed a predilection for spice. Over the centuries the use of spice has been modified and married to other ingredients of the land. The idea is for a spice to work with another flavour and never draw attention to itself, waving its arms about like a swimmer in trouble.

During prep time the MoVida kitchen can smell like a spice bazaar as spices are roasted and ground. I strongly recommend that you gently roast whole spices on a baking tray in a warm oven for about 5 minutes to release the essential oils. Afterwards, grind them using a mortar and pestle or an electric spice grinder. Roast and grind only as much spice as you need and don't store freshly ground spice.

Even saffron needs a little heat to bring out its flavour. You'll notice that it's added early on in many dishes, in direct contact with a hot pan so the heat can bring out the flavour.

Pimentón (paprika) is the powder of dried red capsicum (pepper). It can be sweet, hot, smoked or bittersweet. Imported tins from Spain are readily available and have the most outrageous artwork — from pictures of newlyweds to the Virgin Mary on top of the world. We use a lot of different *pimentón* in our cooking. You can invest in a range of paprikas, but if you can only afford one, buy the sweet paprika. Mind you, the flavour of smoked paprika is unique. This is a powdered spice that can be used straight from the tin.

Apart from paprika, I always buy whole spices. Avoid the powdered bottled variety, as they just don't have the pungency or subtlety of freshly ground spices. With spices you get what you pay for. Supermarkets carry a good range of whole spices in plastic bags. Good food stores carry some very good quality, but costly, spices sold in tins. You can also buy high quality spices online.

VEGETABLES — VERDURAS

I love our city markets. The colour, the bustle, the noise and the stands filled with fresh fruit and vegetables remind me of living in Spain where people still shop daily at the market. There, freshness and quality are not just respected but almost a law. Any vendor transgressing with less than the best vegetables is quickly rebuked in a very public manner and may I say Spanish mamas have tongues sharper than razor clams.

Freshness and ripeness is essential for all the food we make at MoVida. We will never put a tomato dish on the menu unless the tomatoes are absolutely perfect. Good, fresh, ripe food tastes so much better and makes you feel alive. It's worth the effort of going to the market or local greengrocer and buying the best vegetables that are in season. Asparagus in winter? It's probably from Chile or Thailand and won't be nearly as good as really fresh local spring asparagus.

Unlike the Italians, the Spanish were never seduced by the ease of using tinned tomatoes or concentrates. To the Spanish, it has to be fresh tomatoes, or none at all if they are not up to standard.

For the recipes in this book, it is assumed that vegetables are of a medium size and have been washed and peeled before use, unless stated otherwise. For an easy method to peel and seed tomatoes, see below.

PEELING AND SEEDING TOMATOES

Quite often the recipes in this book call for peeled and seeded tomatoes. I find the following method the easiest. Score a cross in the base of each tomato. Place in a heatproof bowl and cover with boiling water. Leave for 30 seconds, then transfer to cold water and peel the skin away from the cross. Cut the tomatoes in half and scoop out the seeds.

VINEGAR —VINAGRE

Sherry vinegar is essential for many Spanish dishes. It provides acidity but also the nuttiness found in the base sherry from which it was made. Sherry vinegar is now available in many good delicatessens, department store food halls and good food stores. We use aged sherry vinegar to a lesser extent as well.

We also use red and white wine vinegars. Thankfully, more and more wineries are making their own vinegars. They introduce a certain bacteria to wine and then, basically, let the wine go off! The resulting vinegar is then aged in oak and in doing so picks up a lot more flavour. Handmade vinegars cost more but they offer a complexity not found in commercial vinegars.

Deglazing with vinegar will leave the flavour of the vinegar (particularly sherry vinegar) in a dish but will lose the sharpness, as the acid changes during the cooking process. Vinegar added later in cooking will give a much brighter sharpness.

Cheap, sharp, commercially made vinegars can be used for pickling but are better suited to cleaning!

KITCHEN EQUIPMENT

Cooking Spanish food from the recipes in this book does not require you to go out and buy foreign gadgets or special pans. But if you have a cookware fetish, please feel free to purchase the following three items: a *cazuela,* a *paellera* and a *perol*.

CAZUELA

The *cazuela* is a glazed terracotta stew pot or casserole dish available in various sizes in which a number of both great and humble dishes are made. The terracotta evenly distributes the heat, making it perfect for slow cooking. They are very cheap and quite beautiful in their own rustic way. When using a *cazuela* for the first time, or after a decent hiatus from kitchen action, make sure it has been soaked in water for at least 12 hours. Once their moisture content is restored, *cazuelas* can be used over low to medium heat, including direct flame. They are readily available from gourmet kitchenware stores, online and in some department stores.

PAELLERA

Paella is the famous rice dish cooked in a flat steel pan called a *paellera*. If you're buying one, first determine how many people you're generally going to cook for, as this will determine the size of the pan you will need to buy. Carbon steel *paelleras* need to be seasoned like a wok before use otherwise they will rust. Enamel *paelleras* have a rustic outdoorsy charm to them but will chip over time. Stainless steel pans are good but costly. Copper-lined pans from Portugal are sometimes available but need to be washed with acetone first to remove the special varnish.

PEROL

Later in this book we have included a recipe for *perol* (see page 210). This is a wet rice dish that is traditionally made in a *perol* pan. A *perol* pan is a pot with high sides and a rounded base. Because similar domestic saucepans are so suitable to making *perol*, we do not recommend going to the extra expense of buying a new pan just to make this dish.

SAUCES AND BASES

The food at MoVida is based around some key Spanish techniques that aren't generally used in the home kitchen or taught at cooking schools. These recipes for sauces and bases are used time and time again in Spanish kitchens across the globe, including our cramped kitchen in Hosier Lane. These are very easy techniques to master and are the foundations of Spanish food.

INGREDIENTS

at least 2 garlic cloves, or to taste

2 pinches of sea salt flakes

2 egg yolks

1 tablespoon dijon mustard

150 ml (5 fl oz) extra virgin olive oil

150 ml (5 fl oz) sunflower oil

2 tablespoons lemon juice

MAKES ABOUT 400 G (14 OZ)

ALIOLI

GARLIC MAYONNAISE

In Spain, traditional *alioli* is an emulsion of just olive oil, garlic and salt. Many people, unaccustomed to its powerful and vibrant intensity, feel it is slightly too strong. Instead, for the Australian palate, we make this light and creamy mayonnaise. It is best fresh but can be stored in a jar in the refrigerator for a couple of days.

METHOD

Put the garlic on a wooden chopping board, coarsely chop then sprinkle with the sea salt and crush to a smooth paste using the flat part of a knife. Place a bowl on a wet tea towel (dish towel) that has been folded in half, then in half again — this stops the bowl flying off the bench. Put the egg yolks in the bowl, add the mustard and garlic paste and gently blend together using an egg whisk.

Add the extra virgin olive oil and sunflower oil, a few drops at a time, whisking continuously. Each addition of oil needs to be emulsified into the egg mixture before you add any more. Look for a change in consistency — it should become gradually thicker. Keep whisking, slowly adding the rest of the oils until you end up with a thick mayonnaise.

Check for seasoning. Season with the lemon juice and, if necessary, extra sea salt by dissolving the salt into the lemon juice before adding to the mayonnaise. This will avoid white salt spots developing in the finished mayonnaise.

Finally, whisk in 1 tablespoon warm water. This helps to retain the emulsification. *Alioli* will keep in the refrigerator for 2–3 days.

INGREDIENTS

2 large handfuls flat-leaf (Italian) parsley, sprigged

4 garlic cloves

100 ml (3½ fl oz) extra virgin olive oil

MAKES 100 ML (3½ FL OZ)

AJO Y PEREJIL
GARLIC AND PARSLEY

We often use a little of this garlic and parsley marinade/dressing to bring a bright, fresh note to a dish. Fine, sharp and green, it can be used as a marinade or a post-cooking dressing to many meat, fish or poultry dishes. Try brushing some over a steak. It will keep in a jar in the refrigerator for a couple of days.

METHOD

Blend all the ingredients in a small food processor to a medium—fine purée.

MAHONESA
SPANISH MAYONNAISE

Mayonnaise is not just a dressing for vegetables, salads and seafood but is an integral ingredient in its own right.

To make a basic Spanish mayonnaise, follow the directions on page 38 for *alioli*, but omit the garlic and add the salt at the beginning with the mustard.

INGREDIENTS

2 red onions

60 ml (2 fl oz/¼ cup) extra virgin olive oil

4 bay leaves

2 garlic cloves, finely sliced

pinch of saffron threads

2 carrots, julienned

250 ml (9 fl oz/1 cup) white wine vinegar

250 ml (9 fl oz/1 cup) white wine

1 tablespoon black peppercorns

1 large handful flat-leaf (Italian) parsley, sprigged

MAKES ABOUT 500 ML

(17 FL OZ/2 CUPS)

ESCABECHE

AROMATIC MARINADE OF SHERRY VINEGAR AND SPICES

Escabeche is a marinade, cooking technique and Nature's preservative all in one. It is also one of the most delicious ways of preserving fish and partridge. The flavours of the spices and vegetables infuse into the vinegar and wine, which in turn permeate the flesh of the fish. Following is our favourite recipe for this classic style of cooking. It makes a mouth-wateringly sour dish and, because of the high acidity, protects the food from going off.

METHOD

Cut the onions into 5 mm (¼ inch) thick wedges. Heat the olive oil in a heavy-based frying pan over low heat. Add the onion, bay leaves, garlic and saffron. Cover and cook for 15 minutes, or until the onion is soft and translucent, stirring occasionally. Do not allow the onion to brown.

Add the carrot, cover and continue cooking for 15 minutes, or until the carrot begins to soften. Add the wine vinegar, wine, peppercorns, 250 ml (9 fl oz/1 cup) water and 1 teaspoon salt. Bring to the boil over high heat then reduce to a simmer and cook for 20 minutes, allowing the ingredients to infuse and the wine to cook out.

Remove from the heat and allow to cool. Stir through the parsley. Store, covered, in the refrigerator for up to 1 week.

INGREDIENTS

1.6 kg (3 lb 8 oz) whole chicken

7.5 cm (3 inch) piece *jamón* bone
  (*see Note*)

2 carrots, roughly chopped

2 onions, roughly chopped

1 small handful flat-leaf (Italian) parsley

1 garlic bulb

3 bay leaves

2 tablespoons black peppercorns

**MAKES ABOUT 2.5 LITRES
(88 FL OZ/10 CUPS)**

CALDO DE POLLO
CHICKEN STOCK

It's hard to get an old broiler-fryer these days, but an old chook that has seen a few days around the yard adds a great amount of flavour to a stock. Poulterers at city markets and old-fashioned butchers carry them, often frozen. In my mind, they give the stock the oomph — the essence of the chicken.

METHOD

Rinse the chicken, including the cavity, under cold running water to remove any blood or impurities. Put all the ingredients in a large stockpot or very large saucepan with 1 tablespoon salt and cover with 4 litres (140 fl oz/16 cups) cold water. Bring to the boil then reduce to a gentle simmer.

Continue simmering for 2 hours, skimming the surface for foam every 30 minutes. Strain. The stock is at its best when used immediately. However, it will keep in the refrigerator for another 2 days — cool slightly before covering and refrigerating. Once chilled the stock can be frozen in 1 litre (35 fl oz/4 cup) containers for up to 2 months, but note that the potency/flavour will diminish the longer it is stored.

Note: If you can't find a *jamón* bone, you can use a similar sized piece of *jamón* or prosciutto rind or *jamón* offcut.

INGREDIENTS

1 kg (2 lb 4 oz) white fish bones and heads

500 g (1 lb 2 oz) salt cod wings and bones, desalinated (*see page 27*)

2 brown onions, quartered

5 bay leaves

6 tomatoes

1 garlic bulb, halved

1 handful flat-leaf (Italian) parsley, leaves and stalks

2 tablespoons black peppercorns

MAKES ABOUT 2.5 LITRES (88 FL OZ/10 CUPS)

CALDO DE PESCADO
FISH STOCK

This fish stock is a rich, flavoursome liquid that forms the foundation of many dishes in this book and is a delicious dish in its own right. The idea of a fish stock is to cook it long enough to extract the goodness out of the fish without breaking down the delicate bones. We use snapper or red emperor but never oily fish such as mackerel or tuna. The tomato adds balance and depth of flavour while imbuing a pleasant pink tinge.

METHOD

Wash the fish bones under cold running water to remove any blood or impurities. Put all the ingredients in a large stockpot or very large saucepan and add 4 litres (140 fl oz/16 cups) cold water. Bring to the boil then reduce the heat and gently simmer, uncovered, for 1 hour, skimming away any foam that forms. Strain the stock, discarding the solids. Use immediately, or allow to cool slightly, then freeze in 1 litre (35 fl oz/4 cup) containers for up to 2 months. Note that the potency/flavour will diminish the longer it is stored.

INGREDIENTS

2 leeks, trimmed, washed and roughly
   chopped

1 garlic bulb, halved

6 bay leaves

1 handful flat-leaf (Italian) parsley, leaves and
   stalks, roughly chopped

2 carrots, roughly chopped

3 celery stalks, roughly chopped

**MAKES ABOUT 2.5 LITRES
(88 FL OZ/10 CUPS)**

CALDO DE VERDURAS
VEGETABLE STOCK

Vegetable stock is a lighter and less costly alternative to chicken or fish stock. It doesn't have the same flavour as the other stocks but adds a lovely earthy and fresh quality to a dish. If you're making vegetarian versions of any of the dishes, please feel free to use vegetable stock.

METHOD

Put the leek, garlic, bay leaves, parsley, carrot and celery in a stockpot. Cover with 4 litres (140 fl oz/16 cups) cold water, bring to the boil then reduce the heat and simmer for 1 hour. Regularly skim away any impurities floating to the top.

Strain the stock and discard the solids. Use immediately, or cool slightly before covering and refrigerating. The stock will keep in the refrigerator for 2 days. Once chilled the stock can be frozen in 1 litre (35 fl oz/4 cup) containers for up to 2 months. Note that the potency/flavour will diminish the longer it is stored.

MOJO
CANARY ISLANDS DRESSINGS

Don't be alarmed — *mojo* has nothing to do with voodoo or Austin Powers. *Mojo* simply means 'wet' and that is the unifying theme of the sauces from the Canary Islands on page 46. Very fluid and very lively, they may be made from mint, coriander, sweet peppers, nuts, green capsicum or any combination of these ingredients. They are always sharp with vinegar or citrus and can bring to life a dish of fish or cut through the richness of a plate of meat. *Mojo* sauces are so prolific that whole cookbooks have been devoted to them. In this book we only have space for my two favourites. The following *Mojo* sauces will keep in the refrigerator for 2–3 days.

INGREDIENTS

2 large handfuls flat-leaf (Italian) parsley, including stalks

3 garlic cloves

100 ml (3½ fl oz) white wine vinegar

150 ml (5 fl oz) extra virgin olive oil

4 tablespoons cumin seeds, roasted and ground (*see page 32*)

MAKES ABOUT 300 ML (10½ FL OZ)

MOJO VERDE
GREEN SAUCE

Remove and discard the ends of the parsley stalks and roughly chop the remaining stalks and leaves. Put the parsley and garlic in a food processor, blend and start the emulsification process by adding a couple of tablespoons each of vinegar and oil. Continue blending and slowly add the remaining vinegar and oil. Add the cumin. Season to taste with two pinches of salt.

MOJO PICÓN
RED CAPSICUM DRESSING

Hot, sweet, spicy and refreshingly sour, this is a fun, lively and sexy dressing. You've heard of ranch dressing — well this is *raunch* dressing. Traditionally, it's served in the Canary Islands with *papas arrugada*s (potatoes cooked in salt, see page 179).

METHOD

Preheat the oven to 180°C (350°F/Gas 4). Roast the capsicums for 40–45 minutes, until the skins blacken and blister. Cover with plastic wrap and allow to cool. Remove the skin, seeds and membrane from the capsicums. Put the flesh into a blender with the remaining ingredients, a pinch of salt and 100 ml (3½ oz) water. Purée on high until smooth.

INGREDIENTS

2 red capsicums (peppers)

3 garlic cloves

2 tablespoons sweet paprika

2 tablespoons cumin seeds, roasted and ground (*see page 32*)

1 teaspoon hot paprika

100 ml (3½ fl oz) sherry vinegar

100 ml (3½ fl oz) extra virgin olive oil

MAKES ABOUT 400 ML (14 FL OZ)

INGREDIENTS

100 g (3½ oz) blanched almonds, roasted (*see page 14*)

yolks from 6 hard-boiled eggs

pinch of saffron threads

pinch of fine sea salt

MAKES ABOUT 220 G (7¾ OZ)

PICADA DE ALMENDRAS

ALMOND PICADA

Picada, meaning 'to chop', is a Catalán technique of making a thick tasty sauce by simply chopping or pounding something firm — like nuts, pulses or bread — with something wet and tasty — like olive oil or eggs. Your best tool is a mortar and pestle but if you want to avoid kitchen biceps feel free to enlist the help of an electric blender.

This *picada* is used to thicken, flavour and enrich braised chicken or rabbit. It is added to sauces at the last minute and the sauce is then brought to the boil and allowed to rest until served. A *picada* adds layers of flavour to a dish — like peeking through a series of curtains, each time finding a more exciting and beautiful one.

METHOD

Pound the roasted almonds using a mortar and pestle until broken up like fine breadcrumbs. Add the egg yolks and pound until well mashed together. Gently toast the saffron in a non-stick frying pan until you can just detect the aroma coming from the pan. This should only take a minute or so. Put the saffron in a small dish and add 1 tablespoon water. Let the saffron steep in the water for 1 minute then add to the almond mix. Blend through and season with the sea salt. Almond *picada* will keep in the refrigerator for 2–3 days.

INGREDIENTS

80 ml (2½ fl oz/⅓ cup) extra virgin olive oil

4 garlic cloves, unpeeled

4 slices 2-day-old *pasta dura* or other firm crusty bread, about 1 cm (½ inch) thick

110 g (3¾ oz/½ cup) cooked chickpeas (*see page 16*)

2–3 tablespoons cooking water from chickpeas, plus extra (*see page 16*)

sea salt

MAKES ABOUT 450 G (1 LB)

PICADA DE PAN

BREAD PICADA

Heat the olive oil in a frying pan and gently fry the garlic cloves in their skins for 30 seconds. Add the bread slices and season while in the pan. Fry the bread slices for about 2 minutes each side, or until golden. Remove the bread and garlic from the pan and drain on paper towel. Allow to cool a little, then break the bread into 5 cm (2 inch) pieces. Peel the garlic cloves and discard the skins.

Pound the cooked garlic a little using a mortar and pestle (or in a food processor) then add the bread, piece by piece. Pound or blend until it forms medium- to large-sized breadcrumbs, about 2–5 mm (1/16–1/4 inch) in diameter. We call these *migas*.

Add a few of the chickpeas, the cooking water from the chickpeas and some sea salt to taste. Mix until the chickpeas begin to break up.

Continue adding the chickpeas, feeling free to add a little more cooking liquid, and making sure you don't overblend the mix. It should remain fairly coarse — the consistency of really rough-looking mashed potato or stuffing for a roast chicken. Bread *picada* will keep in the refrigerator for 2–3 days.

INGREDIENTS

125 ml (4 fl oz/½ cup) olive oil

2 white onions, finely diced

2 garlic cloves, thinly sliced

4 bay leaves

4 large red capsicums (peppers), seeded, membrane removed and finely diced

4 ripe tomatoes, peeled, seeded and diced (*see page 33*)

MAKES ABOUT 450 G (1 LB/2 CUPS)

(*see page 33*)

SOFRITO

SLOW-COOKED CAPSICUMS, TOMATOES AND ONIONS

You can almost hear this cooking technique when you say the Spanish word *sofrito* — or 'softly fry'. This is a technique that describes an immeasurable number of sauces that form the basis of many other dishes. I often explain *sofrito* to newcomers as a rich, spicy, sloppy stock (bouillon) cube. Generally, they all start with oil or rendered pig fat in which onion and other foods such as tomatoes, green capsicums, ham or sausage are gently cooked, but the one thing that ties them together is the cooking method — 'low and slow', low heat and slow cooking. I always take great pride and pleasure in making a rich *sofrito*.

METHOD

Heat the oil in a large heavy-based saucepan over low—medium heat. Add the onion, garlic and bay leaves, with a large pinch of salt to draw out the moisture and intensify the flavour. Cook for 8—10 minutes, or until the onion is soft and translucent.

Add the capsicum and cook for 30 minutes, stirring occasionally until well softened. Add the tomato and continue cooking for 1¼ hours, or until rich and jam-like, stirring occasionally to make sure it doesn't stick to the base of the pan. *Sofrito* will keep in the refrigerator for 2—3 days.

INGREDIENTS

3 red capsicums (peppers)

2 very ripe tomatoes

1 garlic bulb

80 ml (2½ fl oz/⅓ cup) olive oil

one 2 cm (¾ inch) thick slice 2-day-old
pasta dura or other firm crusty bread

150 g (5½ oz) hazelnuts, roasted (see page 19)

150 g (5½ oz) blanched almonds, roasted
(see page 14)

60 g (2¼ oz/¼ cup) sweet paprika

2 tablespoons good quality red wine vinegar

375 g (13 oz/1½ cups) sofrito (see page 51)

MAKES ABOUT 600 ML (21 FL OZ)

SALSA ROMESCO
ROMESCO SAUCE

This is an all-round sauce that can be used with meat, fish and vegetables. It has a lovely earthy red colour with a deep rich flavour that is sharpened with a little good red wine vinegar. Note that this recipe calls for roasted blanched almonds.

METHOD

Preheat the oven to 180°C (350°F/Gas 4). Roast the capsicums, tomatoes and garlic bulb for 10 minutes then remove the tomatoes and set aside to cool. Continue roasting the capsicums and garlic for 30–35 minutes, or until the skin of the capsicums blacken and blister. Cover the capsicums in plastic wrap and allow the capsicums and garlic to cool. When cool, peel the capsicums and tomatoes and put in a bowl, discarding any stalks, skins and seeds. Cut the end off the garlic bulb and squeeze the roasted garlic over the capsicums and tomatoes.

Heat the olive oil in a heavy-based frying pan over medium heat and fry the bread for about 3 minutes each side, or until golden. Drain on paper towel and set aside to cool. Grind the nuts and bread in a food processor to the consistency of coarse breadcrumbs. Add the paprika, red wine vinegar and sofrito and season to taste. Add the capsicums, tomatoes and garlic to the food processor and pulse several times until all the ingredients are well blended, but still coarse in texture. Salsa romesco will keep in the refrigerator for 2–3 days.

OLIVES

Every year, ever since I can remember, my dad has cured our table olives. In true Cordovan style he waits until the olive season is well under way and the price has dropped. He goes to market and comes back with eight 10-kilo boxes of green olives. We spend the rest of the weekend preparing the olives for curing.

Things have changed since the old days. Olive groves have been planted near my parents' home and I now have a son of my own. But the family tradition lives on. Sometimes we go and pick our own olives but we still spend time together crushing them with a hammer to allow the brine to get into the olive. There is a great reward in eating your own cured olives but I think the most important part of the process is the strength of the family bond that brings everyone together year after year.

INGREDIENTS

2 kg (4 lb 8 oz) fresh green olives

500 ml (17 fl oz/2 cups) white wine vinegar

1 small handful thyme, sprigged

50 g (1¾ oz) garlic cloves, chopped

2 lemons, cut into fine wedges

1 mature fennel stalk, cut into 6 cm (2½ inch) lengths (*see Note*)

extra virgin olive oil, to cover the olives

MAKES ABOUT 2 KG (4 LB 8 OZ)

ACEITUNAS ALIÑADAS
MARINATED OLIVES

This is one method that my family uses to prepare olives for the table. The constant soaking and changing of water removes the bitterness. Fennel stalks can be found in markets and, if we're feeling adventurous, on roadsides — we choose the thinner green stalks. We make this in a large bucket, cover it with a cloth and keep it in a cool place.

METHOD

Wash the olives, removing any stalks and leaves. Split the olives with a firm whack of a hammer, leaving the stones inside.

Put the olives in a large plastic bucket and cover them with plenty of water. Cover the bucket with a clean tea towel (dish towel) and keep in a cool place. Change the water every day, for 7 days.

After a week, discard the water then add the white vinegar, thyme, garlic, lemon wedges and fennel to the olives. Top up with fresh cold water. Allow to stand in a cool place for 3 weeks. (My dad stores them in his shed, covered with a cloth.)

After 3 weeks, remove the olives from the brine, sprinkle with salt and put the olives in sterilized jars (sterilize the jars by boiling them, including the lids). Cover with the olive oil.

Other flavourings can be added at this stage, depending on the size of the jars, such as 1 teaspoon fennel seeds, a few lemon wedges and a chilli or two. Seal the lids and store in a cool, dark place. Use as needed. The olives will keep, unopened, for several years.

Note: Mature fennel stalks can be found at growers' markets and specialist greengrocers.

TAPAS Y RACIONES

TAPAS Y RACIONES — UN FENÓMENO CULTURAL ESPAÑOL

TAPAS AND SHARED PLATES — A SPANISH CULTURAL PHENOMENON

In Spain, drinking and eating in public is not just an event for the young, it's a cultural phenomenon that encompasses almost the entire adult population.

The main meal of the day is usually eaten at home around 2 pm. People then go back to work around 4 pm and finish about 8 pm. After work they prefer a light meal — and this is prime *tapeo* time. It's then that the streets come alive with well-dressed groups of people, all intent on enjoying themselves with a beer or a glass of wine and sharing a few plates of something small. These little plates may include a small pyramid of tiny pale-orange prawns, deep-fried, served cold and eaten whole. There may be some wafer-thin slices of *jamón* or an earthenware plate with morsels of succulent lamb. These little plates are called tapas. Originally a Madrid tradition of offering discs or 'tops' of bread to keep flies out of wine glasses, the dishes became more elaborate and the tradition spread nationwide. Today, eating tapas is a global phenomenon — a long, slow, grazing process of little nibbles from lots of really, really good plates of food. Not just the fuel to keep old and young alike out to all hours enjoying the cool of the evening, tapas are also flavoursome little highlights that punctuate the night and create a fleeting area of focus around which everyone comes together.

The *tapeo* tradition manifests itself in every region of Spain in one way or another. In the Basque regions to the north, tapas are called *pintxos*. In the smoky bars of San Sebastian, small, beautifully crafted bites are lined up on plates for customers to choose. One of the classic dishes is *ajoarriero* (mule driver's cod — see page 122). It's a smooth blend of salt cod and potato confit cooked with *piquillo* peppers and egg and served on tiny baguettes.

Another is *jamón de bellota ibérico* (ham from acorn-fed pigs), hand sliced by artisinal experts — succulent and salty, smooth yet sharp. You can help yourself to as many as you want and pay as you leave, such is the faith in the local honour system.

When I'm back in Spain, one of my favourite dishes is razor clams. They are cream-coloured molluscs with shells like incredibly long fingernails, which are displayed raw in refrigerated cabinets at the bar. Grilled to order, they are served with the simplest of flavourings — olive oil and sea salt.

In Catalonia there is a proliferation of modern tapas bars, such as Comerç 24 and Santa María. Comerç 24 is housed in an old preserves and salting shop in the heart of the city. Critics say it's the place for beautiful people to come to admire each other among cutting-edge architecture while eating cutting-edge food. But every dish that goes out is a perfectly balanced and beautiful piece of work, which has a cultural basis extending back centuries. This is what modern Spanish food is about and this is the tradition we follow at MoVida.

To the north of Spain, the region of Asturias is a temperate haven from the scorching heat of the interior. The Asturians drink in *sidrerías* (cider bars). The cider here is made still, without bubbles, so the bartender pours the slightly sharp cider from a great height to invigorate it with little bubbles of air. Served with the cider are little dishes of seafood, flavoured with onions and paprika.

The real delight in tapas is the approach to eating. It's a walk in, stand or sit at the bar type of affair where drinks and a few plates of food are ordered and where, meanwhile, everyone still keeps on talking without changing gear. Everyone shares the moment, the food and the drink. They blend in seamlessly with the conversation, the flirting, the political discourse and the business talk. Unlike restaurant food, tapas don't intend to take a lead role; they are part of the supporting cast. Over the course of the evening people might go to a few different tapas bars. It's true that the bars with the dirtiest floors are often the best, with all the little napkins and toothpicks thrown directly onto the floor. The more toothpicks crunching underfoot, the better the tapas.

The dining scene here in Australia, however, is dominated by the entrée/main/dessert trifecta. Across the nation, diners generally order a three-course meal — and they keep each one pretty much to themselves. In Spain the reverse is true. The Spanish order many smaller dishes to share with each other — even in the more upmarket and pricier establishments. These are the *raciones* (shared dishes) from which everyone can taste the beautiful food. In many cases it's less about construction than the cooking process itself — yet again the belief of bringing tradition into the modern context.

At MoVida we're celebrating this Spanish format of eating, which we believe is appropriate to the Australian psyche — accessible, flexible and stylish. Our bar is really just a large communal table around which occurs the theatre of the night, where staff and patrons are both performers and the audience. The atmosphere of a great tapas bar can be described in two words — serious fun.

Following are a few stock standard recipes for tapas that are so popular they have crossed regional borders within Spain to be now found in almost every bar across the nation. In the chapters to follow you'll find many more tapas and shared plates, grouped together around a particular ingredient such as meat or fish. But let's start with a few mouthwatering classics. You should have some chilled quality beer, Spanish sherry or dry white wine on standby.

DESSE

CHURROS - RICH DF

FLAN - CREME CARAH

HOT GANACHE - HOT GAN

HELADOS - HOMEMADE

PINA COLADA - PINEAPPL

QUESO - CHEESE OF

INGREDIENTS

200 g (7 oz) almonds

2 teaspoons salt

ALMENDRAS SALADAS
SALTED ALMONDS

Every time I go home, mum has a big bowl of these crunchy nuts covered in a fine dusting of salt waiting for me. They are so easy to make, so good to eat and such a good way to introduce our style of eating, I could not resist including them in this book. We serve them in the bar too and every time we do, people always ask me how we make these moreish nutty morsels. After some lengthy negotiations, mum has finally relented and allowed her recipe to be made public for the first time. It may seem strange to recommend using a microwave but Spanish cooks love adopting new technology and this microwave method produces great almonds, every time.

METHOD

Toss together the almonds and salt in a ceramic bowl with 2 tablespoons water. Cook the almonds in two batches to ensure more even cooking. Cover the almonds with plastic wrap and microwave on high for approximately 2 minutes. Remove the plastic wrap and shake the bowl. Re-cover the bowl and microwave for a further minute. The almonds should be just starting to brown in the middle. If not, re-cover the bowl with plastic wrap and microwave for another minute. Allow to cool. Brush off any excess salt before serving.

INGREDIENTS

6 thick slices *pasta dura* or other firm
   crusty bread

2 garlic cloves, halved

extra virgin olive oil, to drizzle

6 very ripe tomatoes, halved

fine sea salt, to sprinkle

TAPAS 6

PAN CATALÁN

CATALONIAN TOMATO BREAD

For the Cataláns, making *pan catalán* (tomato bread) is a way of life. With a few simple strokes of the hand, the addition of a little garlic, oil, tomato and salt transforms crusty, crunchy bread into something sublime. My Aunt Carmen is from Catalonia. She cuts the ends off a loaf of bread, scoops away the inside and then rubs away with garlic and tomato. In restaurants they often use toasted bread and bring the tomato to the table, allowing the guests to do the squeezing and rubbing themselves. It is essential that only the ripest and sweetest tomatoes are used. In Catalonia this recipe is simply known as *pa amb tomaquet* (bread and tomato).

METHOD

Toast the bread until golden. Rub the garlic halves on one side of the toast slices. Drizzle with a little olive oil. Squeeze the tomato halves over the bread like a lemon then rub the pulp over the bread, discarding the skins. Sprinkle with a little sea salt.

Notes: Use nice thick slices of bread with a rough texture, as this absorbs the flavour.
   This dish is perfect layered with a slice of *jamón* or a few marinated anchovies.

INGREDIENTS

500 g (1 lb 2 oz) jar pickled Spanish white
 anchovies, drained
1 white salad onion, finely sliced
3 garlic cloves, finely sliced

1 handful flat-leaf (Italian) parsley
150 ml (5 fl oz) extra virgin olive oil
150 ml (5 fl oz) white wine vinegar

TAPAS 12

BOQUERONES EN VINAGRE
MARINATED WHITE ANCHOVIES

Sharp and salty but with a smooth, clean finish, these delicious little fish are perfect with a cold beer or crisp little fino sherry and will prepare the palate for more to come. True anchovies are seldom found in Australian fish markets. I haven't worked out if there just isn't the demand for them, or if they don't exist in our southern waters. Luckily for lovers of Spanish food we can now source good quality pickled Spanish white anchovies in Australia.

METHOD

Lay the anchovies flat in a glass or ceramic dish. (A metallic bowl could react with the acidic marinade.)

Put the sliced onion and garlic on top of the anchovies. Pick the parsley leaves off the stems and sprinkle the leaves over the onion. Vigorously mix together the oil and vinegar and pour over the anchovies. Cover and refrigerate overnight. Serve chilled.

INGREDIENTS

4 roma (plum) tomatoes, peeled, seeded and
  cut into 2 cm (¾ inch) chunks (*see page 33*)

1 teaspoon sweet smoked paprika

12 marinated white anchovies (*see page 70*)

1 handful flat-leaf (Italian) parsley

335 g (11¾ oz) tinned palm hearts, cut into
  2 cm (¾ inch) lengths (*see Note*)

125 g (4½ oz) tinned Spanish olives stuffed
  with anchovies

extra virgin olive oil, to drizzle

sea salt, to sprinkle

TAPAS 12

GILDAS

SKEWERED WHITE ANCHOVIES WITH PALM HEARTS

Also known as *banderillas*, this Basque *pintxos*-style tapa is two bites of appetite-sharpening, sweet, sour and salty heaven on a little stick. *Gildas* are traditionally made with pinkish, plump anchovies, little green pickled peppers and green olives, which is why they are called *gilda*, which is Catalán for lollipop. At MoVida we make ours from selected preserved ingredients from Spain. Make sure you have more olives than toothpicks, as half always end up being devoured as you make this recipe.

METHOD

Dust the tomato chunks with the paprika. Drain the anchovies, reserving the marinade.

Place five whole fresh parsley leaves and a few slivers of sliced onion from the anchovy marinade on an anchovy then loop the fish over to form a horseshoe shape. Skewer a palm heart onto one end of a toothpick. Follow with the anchovy, a piece of tomato and finish off with a stuffed olive. Repeat with the remaining anchovies, palm hearts, tomato and olives. Drizzle with extra virgin olive oil and sprinkle with sea salt.

Note: Palm hearts are the young shoots of various types of palm, grown in Brazil. They look like segments of leek, but have a sharp taste, like tinned water chestnuts. Tinned palm hearts are available from gourmet or speciality food stores and delicatessens.

INGREDIENTS

7.5 cm (3 inch) piece *jamón* bone
    (*see page 20*)
1.25 litres (44 fl oz/5 cups) milk
2–3 bay leaves
175 g (6 oz) butter
1 brown onion, finely diced
165 g (5¾ oz/1⅓ cups) plain
    (all-purpose) flour
85 g (3 oz/⅔ cup) cornflour (cornstarch)
6 hard-boiled eggs, white part only,
    finely chopped

200 g (7 oz) *jamón* (*see page 20*),
    finely diced
½ teaspoon freshly grated nutmeg
2 eggs, lightly beaten
200 g (7 oz) panko breadcrumbs
    (*see page 15*)
vegetable oil, for deep-frying
sea salt flakes, to sprinkle

TAPAS 28

CROQUETAS DE JAMÓN CON HUEVO
HAM AND EGG CROQUETTES

Croquettes have had 'dag food' stamped all over them since they leapt from the pages of 1970s cookbooks to the fast-food freezer shelves of Australia in the late 1990s. However, these golden fried morsels, when freshly made to a traditional recipe, blow the frozen stuff in boxes into cuisine oblivion. Our *croquetas* are always made fresh and served hot. Their crunchy breadcrumb exterior conceals a smooth velvety texture, which holds the rich flavour of meat or fish. At MoVida we make them with smoked eel, poached chicken or seasoned beef and pork. Prawn and egg are popular too. Croquettes can also be neatly transformed for vegetarians by using the buttery béchamel sauce with garlic chives or mushrooms. Once mastered, the thick béchamel becomes a base that can be played around with by the inquisitive cook.

METHOD

Infuse the flavour of *jamón* into the milk by heating the *jamón* bone, milk and bay leaves in a saucepan over medium–high heat until the milk begins to boil. Reduce to a simmer and cook for a few minutes. Remove from the heat and steep the bone and bay leaves in the milk until the liquid has cooled to lukewarm. It must not be too warm, or the following roux will become lumpy. Remove the bone and bay leaves.

To make the roux, melt the butter over low–medium heat in a heavy-based saucepan and gently sauté the onion for about 10 minutes until translucent. Don't allow the onion or the butter to brown.

Add the flour, a little at a time, until it has been absorbed by the butter, continuously mixing with a wooden spoon. Gradually mix in the cornflour — the roux should be smooth and silky but also a very thick paste, which resembles a lump of soft raw pastry. When the roux is made, stir in the *jamón*-infused milk, a little at a time, making sure that each addition of milk is completely incorporated before adding more. This will ensure smooth and creamy croquettes.

Continue to cook the mixture over low–medium heat, stirring constantly, until you obtain a thick paste, the consistency of which should be similar to thick, creamy, smooth mashed potato — this should take about 40 minutes. The flour taste should be completely cooked out. (Avoid scraping up any residual mixture from the bottom of the pan, as this may colour the sauce.) Remove from the heat and mix through the egg white, finely diced *jamón*, nutmeg and 1 teaspoon salt. Cool slightly, then cover and refrigerate overnight.

With floured hands, take 2 rounded tablespoons of mixture at a time and form into croquette shapes, approximately 3 cm (1¼ inches) wide and 7 cm (2¾ inches) long. Dip the croquettes in the beaten egg, allowing the excess to drip off, then roll in the breadcrumbs. Continue this process until you've turned all the mixture into croquettes — you should have about 28. Fill a large heavy-based saucepan one-third full of oil and heat to 180°C (350°F), or until a cube of bread dropped into the oil browns in 15 seconds. Deep-fry the croquettes in small batches for 2–3 minutes, or until golden brown. Drain on paper towel, sprinkle with sea salt flakes and serve hot.

CONSERVAS ALIMENTICAS HECHAS A MANO
ARTISINAL PRESERVED FOODS

One of the great aspects of Spanish cuisine is the quality of its artisinal preserved foods. Harvested at their ripest, vegetables such as wild asparagus and *piquillo* peppers are pickled and decoratively packed in glass. They are appreciated as much for their flavour as they are for their aesthetic quality. A similar ethos is applied to seafood such as anchovies, mussels, cockles, tuna and clams — although seafood is more often packed in tins.

It is a testament to the professionalism of the artisan when preserved foods can be served straight from the jar or tin with unabashed joy. I can see no point in being snobbish about food from a tin — but it does have to be good. When the raw product is great and the artisan respectful — not only to the food but also to the consumer — you're in for a treat. It's not unusual for a tapas bar owner in Spain to serve pickled vegetables or fish straight from the tin — via an attractive plate of course. I encourage you to do the same. After a visit to the market or a stockist of good preserved products from the Iberian peninsula, go home, open up a jar and taste exactly the same taste that is being experienced in tapas bars across Spain.

INGREDIENTS

125 g (4½ oz/1 cup) plain (all-purpose) flour

125 g (4½ oz/1 cup) self-raising flour

pinch of fine sea salt

125 ml (4 fl oz/½ cup) light olive oil

150 ml (5 fl oz) dry fino sherry

150 g (5½ oz) tinned Spanish tuna (such as
Vigilante tuna)

150 g (5½ oz) drained *piquillo* peppers

80 g (2¾ oz) *alioli* (*see page 38*)

pinch of fine sea salt, extra

1 egg, lightly beaten

olive oil, for deep-frying

sea salt flakes, to sprinkle

TAPAS 24

EMPANADILLAS

LITTLE SHERRY PASTRIES FILLED WITH TUNA

I think these *empanadillas* are an enigma. Let me explain why. When people first bite into the golden-fried pastry, they are often puzzled by its yeasty nuttiness and short, crispy texture. Notionally, something that has yeast in it — like bread — should be springy and have holes, and not be short and mouthwatering. The secret of this pastry lies in the use of light olive oil for shortness and good fino sherry for flavour. Sherry is matured under a *flor*, or floating cap of yeast, and it is this which imparts the sweet yeastiness to these amazing little pastries. The filling of moist tuna and *piquillo* peppers completes the picture. Once you master the pastry, however, you can invent your own fillings, such as spinach and anchovies, or tomato, *jamón* and capers. *Empanadillas* should be cooked as soon as they are prepared.

METHOD

Sift the flours and pinch of sea salt into a large bowl and make a well in the centre. Pour the oil and sherry into the well and mix together until a soft dough is formed. Briefly knead for a minute or so until it just comes together and is elastic. When ready, it should feel heavier and wetter than a normal dough or pastry. If it seems a little dry, add another splash of sherry. It is important not to overwork the pastry to keep it nice and short. Cover with plastic wrap and leave at room temperature for 30 minutes.

To make the filling, strain the tuna and peppers in a colander over a bowl and set aside for 30 minutes. Discard the liquid. Finely dice the peppers. Break the tuna apart with your hands into small pieces. Mix together the peppers and the tuna with the *alioli*, extra sea salt and some freshly cracked black pepper. Check for seasoning. Cover and refrigerate until ready to use.

Take half the dough and, using a rolling pin on a cool, lightly floured surface, roll out as thinly as possible without tearing. Cut into rounds using a 10 cm (4 inch) pastry cutter.

Put 1 well-heaped teaspoon of filling in the middle of each round, lightly brush one half of each disc with a little of the beaten egg then fold over the pastry to make a semicircle. Using a fork, crimp the edge of each *empanadilla* to secure the seal. Repeat with the remaining dough and filling (do not reroll the scraps as it makes the dough too elastic).

Fill a deep-fryer or large heavy-based saucepan one-third full of oil and heat to 180°C (350°F), or until a cube of bread dropped into the oil browns in 15 seconds. Fry the *empanadillas*, in batches, for 5 minutes, turning each one after a few minutes. Remove from the oil, drain on paper towel for 30 seconds then transfer to a serving plate. Sprinkle with sea salt flakes and serve immediately.

INGREDIENTS

24 *piquillo* peppers

one quantity *ajoarriero*, cooked and slightly
    chilled (*see page 122*)

150 g (5½ oz) plain (all-purpose) flour

2 eggs, lightly beaten

300 g (10½ oz) panko breadcrumbs
    (*see page 15*)

olive oil, for deep-frying

sea salt flakes, to sprinkle

TAPAS 24

PIMIENTOS DE PIQUILLO CON AJOARRIERO

DEEP-FRIED RED PIQUILLO PEPPERS STUFFED WITH SALT COD

Sitting in the jar like bright red layers of folded velvet, *piquillo* peppers are one of the most popular preserved vegetables in Spain. Skinned and seeded, they are a small red pouch waiting to be filled with morsels such as beef, pork, black pudding and, classically, salt cod. Once filled with salt cod you have the makings of the best finger food on the globe — colourful, rich, salty and packed with mouth-filling flavour. With these delicious little morsels you can win best party dish of the year. Trust me — I'm a chef.

METHOD

Drain the peppers on paper towel. Carefully spoon a little of the *ajoarriero* mix into each pepper. Take care not to split the sides and gently pack the mix as you go. Fill with enough mixture to form a smooth top that is even with the edges of the peppers. Dip the stuffed peppers in the flour then dip them in the beaten egg (allowing the excess egg to drip off) and roll them in the breadcrumbs.

Fill a large heavy-based saucepan one-third full of oil and heat to 180°C (350°F), or until a cube of bread dropped into the oil browns in 15 seconds. Deep-fry the peppers for 2–3 minutes, or until golden brown. Drain on crumpled paper towel then sprinkle with a little sea salt and serve hot.

SOPAS

SOPAS
SOUPS

Spanish soups range from the fast food of a busy people to the national dish, based on the humblest ingredients. With traditional origins, they are always a thoughtful and intentional re-creation of a familiar recipe, the weft of the fabric of Spanish life. Soups are made to celebrate religious festivals, the unity of a family dining together or the sheer pleasure of summer life. Dishes that garner so much national fervour (most Spaniards will never make a soup to a recipe from outside their own borders) must have something powerful at the core. Central to every soup are basic flavours that are layered upon each other to create a dish that entertains the palate and restores the body and soul.

AJO BLANCO
CHILLED ALMOND SOUP WITH GRAPE GRANITA

It has taken 3 years, but finally people now walk into MoVida during the summer time and ask for *ajo blanco*. Initially, customers were a little wary of a cool soup made of bread, almonds and garlic, served with a sweet grape granita. It started slowly. A few heat-exhausted customers stumbled in on a hot summer's day and Andy, our bar manager, served them a small glass of this refreshingly smooth white liquid, which cleared their palates and enlivened their bodies and spirits — they were sold. Word has got around and now it's an integral part of the summer menu.

METHOD

Put the blanched almonds in a bowl, cover with water and soak overnight in the refrigerator.

Pour the sugar into a saucepan with 310 ml (10¾ fl oz/1¼ cups) water, bring to the boil then simmer for 15–20 minutes, or until the mixture has reduced by one-third. Set aside to cool.

Wash the grapes and remove them from the stem. Cut the grapes in half and remove the seeds with the tip of a knife. Purée the grapes in a food processor then strain the liquid into a bowl through a fine sieve, pressing lightly on the pulp with the back of a spoon to extract as much juice as possible. Discard the pulp. You should have about 170 ml (5½ fl oz/⅔ cup) of juice. Mix the juice with 80 ml (2½ fl oz/⅓ cup) of the sugar syrup. (Keep the remaining syrup in a jar in the refrigerator for other uses, such as cocktails or *jarabe/*syrup in desserts.) Pour the grape and sugar syrup into a shallow cake tin.

INGREDIENTS

250 g (9 oz) blanched almonds

135 g (4¾ oz) caster (superfine) sugar

250 g (9 oz) muscatel grapes or any
  other sweet grapes

one 2 cm (¾ inch) thick slice 2-day-old

pasta dura or other firm crusty bread

1 garlic clove

900 ml (32 fl oz) chilled water

90 g (3¼ oz) *alioli* (*see page 38*)

2 tablespoons aged sherry vinegar

MEDIA RACIÓN 6

Freeze for 2½ hours, or until the mixture is starting to freeze around the edges. Scrape the frozen edges back into the mixture with a fork. Repeat every 30 minutes for about 3 hours, or until evenly sized ice crystals have formed. If you are preparing the granita ahead of time, store it in the freezer and scrape once again just before serving.

Cut the crusts from the bread and discard them. Cut the bread into 2 cm (¾ inch) cubes. Cover the bread with cold water and soak for at least 2 hours.

Drain the almonds and put them in a food processor. Squeeze the excess water out of the bread and add the bread to the food processor with the garlic. Add ½ teaspoon salt. Blend for 1 minute then, with the motor still running, add the chilled water, a little at a time, to create a thick 'almond milk'. Keep blending until it is as smooth as possible.

Strain the almond milk twice through a very fine sieve. Gently stir the solids to help the liquid through. Do not push them through, as this could introduce small pieces of almond that would give the soup a gritty feel.

To make the soup, pour the *alioli* into a bowl. Gently whisk in the almond milk, a little at a time, until it is all used and the mixture reaches a smooth, even consistency. Refrigerate for at least 1 hour.

Place a heaped tablespoon of granita in the bottom of six chilled bowls and pour the soup over the granita. Sprinkle over a little sherry vinegar and serve immediately.

INGREDIENTS

1 kg (2 lb 4 oz) vine-ripened, soft tomatoes,
  roughly chopped

1 garlic clove

250 g (9 oz) 2-day-old *pasta dura* or other
  firm crusty bread, crusts removed

100 ml (3½ fl oz) fruity extra virgin olive oil

200 ml (7 fl oz) chilled water

3 hard-boiled eggs, roughly chopped

80 g (2¾ oz) *jamón*, cut into thin strips
  (*see page 20*)

fruity extra virgin olive oil, extra, to serve,
  (optional)

MEDIA RACIÓN 6

SALMOREJO CORDOBÉS

CÓRDOBA'S THICK TOMATO AND BREAD SOUP

Andy, the bar manager, describes this classic cold soup as 'the beach cricket of Spain — it screams summer'. For me, it's a celebration of the tomato. Real tomatoes. Sweet, tangy tomatoes at their vine-ripened best. Home gardeners with a surplus of late summer tomatoes and a loaf of 2-day-old bread will find this a pleasing solution to their oversupply. However, a word of caution. Follow the ingredients and method meticulously as deviations may cause an imbalance of flavours. This is a soup from my family's home in Córdoba — another reason to treat this dish with great respect.

METHOD

Purée the tomatoes and garlic in a food processor for 1 minute, or until as smooth as possible. Strain the tomato mixture through a sieve, stirring and gently pressing on the solids to extract as much juice as possible. Discard the skin and seeds.

Break the bread up into golf ball-sized pieces and put in a large stainless steel bowl. Pour the strained tomato mixture and olive oil over the bread with 1 heaped teaspoon salt. (You'll need this amount of salt as it is a cold soup and anything served cold needs extra seasoning.)

Using your hands (your hands should be very clean), squish the tomato mixture into the bread, really working the liquid through. Leave to stand for 15 minutes, allowing the bread to soak up the liquid.

Purée the entire mixture again in a food processor, adding enough of the chilled water until smooth and velvety. The soup should be a salmon pink colour. Refrigerate until ready to serve. Serve the soup in bowls with the egg, *jamón*, and a drizzle of extra virgin olive oil if desired.

INGREDIENTS

1 kg (2 lb 4 oz) tomatoes, roughly chopped

2 Lebanese (short) cucumbers, peeled, seeded and chopped

1 red onion, roughly chopped

1 red capsicum (pepper), seeded, membrane removed and roughly chopped

1 green capsicum (pepper), seeded, membrane removed and roughly chopped

1 garlic clove, chopped

100 ml (3½ fl oz) extra virgin olive oil

60 ml (2 fl oz/¼ cup) aged sherry vinegar

about 300 ml (10½ fl oz) chilled water

MEDIA RACIÓN 6

GAZPACHO ANDALUZ
CHILLED SUMMER SOUP

There is a small but annoying trend to serve little 'gazpachos' as part of a menu, often as a small taster. Sadly, they are often just puréed vegetables made the day before and are thin, feeble and taste like the refrigerator in which they were stored — everything a gazpacho isn't. Gazpacho is a luscious but light, fresh and enlivening, smooth and enticing soup made from fresh ripe vegetables. Although chilled soups are not the norm in this part of the world, this is one of those dishes that you must make at least once before you die.

METHOD

Purée the tomatoes in a blender until a smooth liquid forms. Strain the liquid through a sieve and discard the skin and seeds.

Pour the liquid back into the blender and add the chopped vegetables and garlic. Blend for several minutes until smooth.

Add the oil and the vinegar and combine well. With the motor running, add enough of the chilled water to form a smooth liquid that has the consistency of thin cream. As vegetables can contain varying amounts of water, you will find you sometimes need to add more, or less, water. The soup needs to be smooth and rich. Finally, season with 1 teaspoon salt. You'll need this amount of salt as it is a cold soup and anything served cold needs extra seasoning. Serve chilled.

INGREDIENTS

2 tablespoons olive oil

4 garlic cloves, sliced into thin slivers

150 g (5½ oz) sliced *jamón* (*see page 20*), finely chopped

1.5 litres (52 fl oz/6 cups) chicken stock (*see page 42*)

120 g (4¼ oz) *fideos* pasta (*see page 23*)

sea salt flakes

6 hard-boiled eggs, finely diced

1 handful mint, chopped

MEDIA RACIÓN 6

SOPA DE PICADILLO
JAMÓN AND PASTA SOUP WITH MINT

This is a festive soup made, mostly in central Spain, around Christmas and New Year from leftovers. It's a very humble dish that may start off a grander meal. In some regions it may contain dried legumes or carrots but it's almost always finished with chopped *jamón* and egg. Mum still makes it every Christmas, but I think that the flavours of mint and garlic work so well together that it can be made in Australia any time.

METHOD

Heat the olive oil in a saucepan over low–medium heat and gently fry the garlic and *jamón* for 2 minutes. Allow the garlic to lightly brown then add the chicken stock.

Bring to the boil over high heat. Add the pasta, bring to the boil again then reduce to a simmer and cook until the pasta is soft. (This may take longer than indicated on the packet, as you are not cooking it on a rapid boil.) Season with sea salt flakes, if necessary.

Ladle the soup into bowls and garnish with the egg and mint.

INGREDIENTS

4 thick slices 2-day-old *pasta dura* or other
    firm crusty bread

3 garlic cloves, sliced into thin slivers

1 tablespoon extra virgin olive oil

pinch of saffron threads

1.5 litres (52 fl oz/6 cups) chicken stock
    (*see page 42*)

Spanish sweet paprika, to sprinkle

MEDIA RACIÓN 6

SOPA CASTELLANA
BREAD AND GARLIC SOUP WITH SAFFRON

If you're seriously into the good life then there are times in your life when you're going to come home late and need a snack — if you know what I mean. And if you're seriously into food then you're also going to have chicken stock in the freezer and the rest of the ingredients needed to make this restorative soup. This is the traditional post *tapeo* pick-me-up that can be enjoyed any time of the day.

Originally from Castile–La Mancha, it relies on locally grown saffron to give it its golden colour and earthy foundation. The garlic is fried until it imparts a sweet nutty taste and the bread gives the soup its starchy substance. It's so simple it can be made in about 10 minutes.

METHOD

Preheat the oven to 150°C (300°F/Gas 2). Dry the bread on a baking tray in the oven for 5–10 minutes. The bread should be firm but not coloured — it needs to be dried so it will absorb the flavours of the soup.

Meanwhile, heat the olive oil in a saucepan over medium heat and fry the garlic for 30–60 seconds, or until just golden (any darker and it will become bitter). As the garlic starts to sizzle add the saffron to release its aroma. As soon as the garlic is golden, stop the cooking process by slowly and carefully adding the chicken stock. Bring to the boil then reduce to a simmer for 2 minutes.

Break the bread into golf ball-sized pieces, add to the soup and simmer for 1 minute. Allow the bread to swell while simmering for a further minute. Season with salt, if necessary. Serve the soup in bowls with a sprinkle of paprika.

SOPA DE PESCADO DONOSTIARRA

TOMATO AND SEAFOOD SOUP THICKENED WITH BREAD

This was one of the first dishes we ever served, back in the old days when MoVida was at the Carron Tavern in West Melbourne. Some people have described it as a Basque bouillabaisse and although it has a lot in common with its French cousin, this is a thicker, more robust and colourful dish topped with seared scampi. Scampi give a deep flavour of the sea but can be substituted with prawns. If using prawns, try to find very large ones — remove the shell but keep the head and tail.

METHOD

Scrub the mussels with a stiff brush and pull out the hairy beards. Soak the clams in cold water for a couple of hours to remove the grit from inside the shells. Discard any broken mussels or clams, or open mussels or clams that do not close when tapped on the bench. Cut the scampi in half lengthways and rinse in the shell under cold running water. Remove the shell, leaving the head and tail on. Make a shallow cut with a small, very sharp knife along the length of each prawn back. Remove and discard the dark vein.

Heat 60 ml (2 fl oz/$^1/_4$ cup) of the oil in a large heavy-based saucepan over medium heat and cook the onion, leek, carrot and garlic for about 10 minutes, until they are slightly caramelized. Add the tomato to the vegetables and cook over low heat for 15 minutes, stirring occasionally.

Increase the heat to high and once bubbling quickly stir in the wine and brandy. Bring to the boil for 1 minute to allow the alcohol to cook off.

INGREDIENTS

400 g (14 oz) mussels

400 g (14 oz) baby clams (vongole)

6 scampi, or 6 very large prawns (shrimp)

6 prawns (shrimp)

125 ml (4 fl oz/½ cup) extra virgin olive oil

1 small white onion, diced

1 leek, trimmed, washed and diced

1 carrot, diced

2 garlic cloves, finely chopped

6 ripe tomatoes, peeled, seeded
and roughly chopped (*see page 33*)

150 ml (5 fl oz) dry white wine

150 ml (5 fl oz) brandy

1 litre (35 fl oz/4 cups) fish stock (*see page 43*)

two 5 cm (2 inch) thick slices 2-day-old *pasta
dura* or other firm crusty bread

2 garlic cloves, extra, finely sliced

600 g (1 lb 5 oz) blue eye fillets, cut into 100 g
(3½ oz) pieces

1 handful flat-leaf (Italian) parsley,
roughly chopped

1 handful fennel leaves, roughly chopped

RACIÓN 6

Add the fish stock and bring to the boil. Reduce the heat and simmer for 20 minutes, then remove from the heat and allow the soup to cool slightly.

Meanwhile, preheat the oven to 150°C (300°F/Gas 2). Tear the bread into irregular golf ball-sized pieces and dry in the oven for 5 minutes. The bread should be dried but not browned.

Roughly purée the soup in a blender or food processor and then strain through a coarse sieve, keeping the liquid and discarding the solids.

In a separate saucepan, heat 1½ tablespoons of the oil over medium–high heat and fry the extra garlic for 30–60 seconds, or until just lightly golden, then add the strained soup and bring to the boil. Reduce the heat and allow to simmer for 5 minutes.

Working quickly now, heat the remainder of the oil over very high heat in a large frying pan and fry the fish pieces, skin side down, seasoning with a little salt. After 1 minute turn the fish over and add the scampi and prawns. The scampi and prawns should take only 1 minute each side to cook. Remove the scampi and prawns once cooked and set aside. Reduce the heat. The fish should not be fully cooked through, as it needs to cook further in the soup.

Add the mussels and clams to the frying pan. Pour the soup over, bring to the boil, then reduce the heat and simmer, covered, for 6 minutes until the mussels and clams open. Discard any unopened mussels and clams. Add the bread and push into the liquid, allowing the bread to swell and soak up the soup. Season to taste. Arrange the fried scampi and prawns on top of the soup, sprinkle over the parsley and fennel and serve immediately.

PORRUSALDA

BASQUE POTATO AND LEEK IN SALT COD BROTH

Porrusalda is a dish from the north of Spain and as my family is from the south I grew up only hearing about this dish. I never tried it until I was working in the region. Vanessa and I were on a day trip and we stopped at a little mountain restaurant near Rioja where *porrusalda* was on the *menú de dia*. Rising from the sea of pale green soup was a pearly tile of white fish, surrounded by swirls of verdant green and deep red oils.

The version we serve is just as velvety and has the wonderful underlaying roundedness of the fish stock from page 43. It's really worth taking the time to whizz up the flavoured oils because they don't just add colour but also a little hit of concentrated flavour.

METHOD

Preheat the oven to 180°C (350°F/Gas 4). Roast the capsicum for 40–45 minutes until the skin blackens and blisters. Cover with plastic wrap and allow to cool. Remove the skin, seeds and membrane from the capsicum.

Reduce the oven to 150°C (300°F/Gas 2). Remove the 'wings' from the desalinated cod fillet and use for the fish stock.

Cut the remaining flesh into six equal portions. With your fingers, gently remove the flesh from the spine, being careful to keep the skin on as you go. Use the bones for the stock. Put the fillets in an ovenproof frying pan, just large enough to hold them, skin side up, and pour

INGREDIENTS

1 red capsicum (pepper)

800 g (1 lb 12 oz) piece of salt cod, 2–3 cm (¾–1¼ inch) thick, desalinated (*see page 27*)

1 litre (35 fl oz/4 cups) olive oil (*you may not need all the oil*)

2 garlic cloves

60 ml (2 fl oz/¼ cup) extra virgin olive oil

4 leeks, trimmed, washed, halved lengthways then cut into 5 mm (¼ inch) slices

3 garlic cloves, extra, sliced into fine slivers

3 large russet (idaho) or king edward potatoes, diced

1.5 litres (52 fl oz/6 cups) fish stock (*see page 43*)

1 thick slice 2-day-old *pasta dura* or other firm crusty bread

1 large handful flat-leaf (Italian) parsley

170 ml (5½ fl oz/⅔ cup) extra virgin olive oil, extra

1 tablespoon smoked Spanish sweet paprika

sea salt flakes, to sprinkle

MEDIA RACIÓN 6

over enough olive oil to cover the fish to just below the skin. Add the garlic cloves, cover with foil and bake in the oven for 30 minutes. When cooked the flesh will be pearly white, have a flaky texture and some of the fish juices will have leached into the oil. Set the fish aside, cover with foil and keep warm. Increase the oven to 180°C (350°F/Gas 4).

In a large saucepan, heat the extra virgin olive oil over medium heat, add the leek and garlic slivers and gently cook for 10 minutes, stirring occasionally. Once the leeks have softened add the potato and continue to cook for 5 minutes. Cover with the fish stock, bring to the boil then reduce the heat and simmer gently for 40 minutes.

While the soup is cooking, make the croutons. Roughly tear apart the bread, put the pieces on a baking tray and toast in the oven for 5 minutes.

To make the oils, wash and pick the leaves from the parsley, pat dry with paper towel then purée in a blender with 100 ml (3½ fl oz) of the extra oil for 1 minute, until a smooth consistency is achieved. Pour into a small container and rinse the blender. Repeat the process, this time adding the roasted capsicum, together with the paprika and the remaining extra oil.

To serve, drain the cod on paper towel. Place one fish fillet in each of six wide shallow bowls, then ladle the soup around each fillet. Drizzle the flavoured oils over the soup and sprinkle with croutons and some sea salt flakes.

INGREDIENTS

125 ml (4 fl oz/½ cup) olive oil

2 leeks, trimmed, washed, halved lengthways
then cut into 3 mm (⅛ inch) slices

2.5 kg (5 lb 8 oz) mussels

200 ml (7 fl oz) dry white wine

200 ml (7 fl oz) fish stock (*see page 43*)

4 large (250 g/9 oz each) floury potatoes,
boiled and cubed

100 g (3½ oz) *alioli* (*see page 38*)

fine sea salt

MEDIA RACIÓN 6

MEJILLONES AL GAZPACHUELO

FRESH MUSSELS WITH LEEK AND POTATO, ENRICHED WITH GARLIC MAYONNAISE

My cousin Rosa taught me this recipe when I was staying with her in Córdoba a few years ago. She is my father's sister's daughter, lives a stone's throw from the Guadalquivir River, and is not just a good cook but also a generous teacher. As we cooked, we talked about our shared love of molluscs and our different ways of cooking mussels. We both agreed that large and heavy mussels were good but there is something lovely about the small sweet ones. This dish is a simple mix of salty seafood and earthy vegetables, enriched with *alioli* and sharpened with a little white wine.

METHOD

Heat the olive oil in a saucepan over medium heat and cook the leeks for 10–15 minutes until soft. Set aside.

Scrub the mussels and pull out the hairy beards. Rinse well and drain. Discard any broken mussels, or open ones that don't close when tapped on the bench.

Put the mussels in a large saucepan over high heat with the wine and fish stock and shake the pan around a little to combine well. Cover, allow the liquid to come to the boil then cook for a few more minutes, frequently shaking the pan. Remove from the heat. Remove the open mussels and put in a bowl. Cover and cook for a further minute or so, in case any more mussels open. Discard any unopened mussels. Leave the cooking juices in the pan.

Remove the mussels from their shells and put in a bowl. Any juices left in the shell should also be added to the bowl. Carefully tip off all the accumulated mussel juices from the bowl into the pan. Cover the mussels with foil to keep warm. Discard the shells. Return the pan to high heat and add the potato and leek. Once the mixture starts to boil remove from the heat, allow to cool for 5 minutes then stir in the *alioli*. If the liquid is too hot the mayonnaise will separate and become oily.

Crush the potato and leek mixture with a potato masher until it is finely broken up but the potato still has a little texture. Season with a little fine sea salt, if necessary.

Arrange the mussels in a warmed serving dish and pour the soup over. Serve warm.

INGREDIENTS

400 g (14 oz) brown lentils

one 150 g (5½ oz) whole raw chorizo
(*see page 28*)

300 g (10½ oz) jap or kent pumpkin, roughly
chopped

1 brown onion

1 garlic bulb, unpeeled

10 roma (plum) tomatoes, peeled, seeded and
halved (*see page 33*)

1 tablespoon Spanish sweet paprika

1 red capsicum (pepper), seeded, membrane
removed and cut into 6 large pieces

1 green capsicum (pepper), seeded, membrane
removed and cut into 6 large pieces

two 150 g (5½ oz) *morcilla* or black pudding
(*see page 28*)

Spanish sherry vinegar, to serve

sea salt flakes, to sprinkle

MEDIA RACIÓN 6

SOPA DE LENTEJAS

LENTIL SOUP WITH CHORIZO AND SPANISH BLOOD PUDDING

On a wet winter's day, walking down the lane out the front of MoVida, with the graffiti and the wet cobbles, I feel like I could be in any big city in the world. But when I walk in the door and am embraced by the warmth of our dining room and kitchen and can smell the *sopa de lentejas*, I am back in Spain.

It's the smell of the family kitchen, the anticipation of the spicy morsel of sausage lazing on top of a thick, rich, earthy soup. This, to me, is the very essence of Spanish food. It relies on staple ingredients and the simplicity of the single pot. I love the way the chorizo is used like a bouquet garni and that the very essence of the vegetables is released into the soup and then the skins discarded. I know some balk at *morcilla* and I won't be offended if you make it without it, but perhaps, one day, just give it a try. With a loaf of crusty bread, this makes a hearty midwinter Sunday lunch.

METHOD

Pick over the lentils and remove any discoloured lentils or stones. Wash under cold running water. Put the lentils in a large saucepan and add 2.5 litres (88 fl oz/10 cups) water and all the other ingredients, except the *morcilla*, vinegar and sea salt. Bring to the boil then reduce the heat and simmer for 55 minutes, skimming off any impurities every 20 minutes. Add the *morcilla* and cook for a further 5 minutes. Season to taste.

To serve, remove the sausages and discard the capsicum, onion and garlic. Slice the sausages into 1 cm (½ inch) thick discs. Ladle the soup into a bowl and drizzle with a few drops of sherry vinegar. Place the sausage in the soup and sprinkle with sea salt.

CHICKPEA AND MEAT BROTH

This is one of the great one-pot dishes of the world. It's the Spanish equivalent of the Italian *bollito misto* or French cassoulet. It is a year-round national favourite in Spain but I reckon this fits best into the Australian autumn and winter. A friend with a vineyard in central Victoria cooks *cocido* during vintage because she can feed the pickers from one big pot and still have time to work the crusher.

That said, it is a three-course meal. First, there is an invigorating steaming broth enriched with noodles. This is followed by a dish of tasty boiled vegetables and chickpeas. Finally, there is a plate of chunks of beef, chicken, *jamón* and chorizo slathered in the same rich broth. The next day any leftover meat can be blended through béchamel sauce to make the classic croquette filling.

Mum still makes *cocido* once a week. It is not an impromptu dish because the chickpeas need soaking overnight. But once they are done it becomes one of the easiest dishes in the world to cook because it sits on top of the stove and slowly cooks away.

Don't forget to serve this with lots of crusty bread to mop up the delicious broth.

METHOD

Wash the chickpeas and remove any discoloured chickpeas or stones. Cover the chickpeas with warm water and soak overnight (see page 16).

Put the beef and pork belly pieces into a very large saucepan or stockpot. Add the *jamón*, *jamón* bone and 3 litres (105 fl oz/12 cups) water. Bring to the boil then reduce to a simmer and cook for 1 hour, making sure to remove any foam or fat that collects on top.

INGREDIENTS

600 g (1 lb 5 oz) dried chickpeas

400 g (14 oz) gravy beef, halved

300 g (10½ oz) pork belly, skin and top layer
  of fat removed, halved

150 g (5½ oz) piece *jamón* (*see page 20*)

7.5 cm (3 inch) piece *jamón* bone
  (*see page 20*)

two 150 g (5½ oz) raw chorizos (*see page 28*)

½ chicken (about 800 g/1 lb 12 oz on the
  bone), cut into 6 pieces

1 large brown onion, studded with
  6 whole cloves

1 floury potato

4 carrots, cut into large batons

½ savoy cabbage, roughly diced

150 g (5½ oz) *morcilla* (*see page 28*)

200 g (7 oz) *fideos* pasta (*see page 23*)

MEDIA RACIÓN 6

Drain the chickpeas. Before you add them to the soup, add 250 ml (9 fl oz/1 cup) cold water to the pan to cool the liquid a little. (This helps the chickpeas become tender.) Add the chickpeas, bring to the boil, then reduce the heat and simmer for 30 minutes. Add the chorizos, chicken pieces and onion, bring back to a simmer and cook for 30 minutes, continually skimming away any fat or foam.

Meanwhile, cut the potato in half. Put the cut side on the board and cut, as if cutting wedges, but don't cut all the way through, just snap off to reveal a jagged edge. (This causes more starch to be released, which will thicken the soup and cook the potato quicker.)

Add the potato, carrot and cabbage to the soup. Cook for 20 minutes. Add the *morcilla* and simmer for 5 minutes. Remove from the heat and take out and discard the *jamón* bone. The meat in the pot should be tender without being overcooked, and the chickpeas plump. Season the broth to taste (it shouldn't require too much salt as there is plenty in the *jamón* and *jamón* bone).

To serve, remove the meat from the broth, cut the larger pieces of meat and sausage into an adequate number of portions for the diners and put on a plate. It is important when serving the meat to present the beef together, the *jamón* together, sausages together, and so on, and arrange the meats in an attractive manner. Cover with foil and keep warm. Remove the vegetables and chickpeas and put on a plate or in a bowl, keeping the chickpeas together, the potatoes together, and so on, and arrange in an attractive manner. Cover with foil and keep warm.

Bring the broth to a boil and stir in the *fideos* pasta. Continue cooking until the pasta is soft — there is no such thing as *al dente* pasta in the Spanish kitchen. Ladle the soup and pasta into bowls then follow this by a dish of vegetables and then a dish of mixed meats.

TO MARKET, TO MARKET ...

When I was living in Spain, I went to the market every day. Shopping with my relatives was a revelation. It wasn't the bustle of the crowd, the colour and fragrance of the produce, nor the architecture of the old market buildings. For me, it was the true understanding that market shopping is not a means to an end but a pleasurable social outing; the act of living in the moment and soaking up the sensational colours, smells and the bustle. There's the scrutiny of selection, questioning the provenance of the produce, the friendly friction of the purchase and the social interaction, as friends, family and neighbours catch up and gossip. In Australia, what we may lack in tradition we make up for in cultural diversity. I go to my local Footscray market, which is a multicultural melting pot. I shop with the Indo-Chinese people. They share with me a culinary love of quail, goat, pork, shellfish, fish on the bone, citrus and other fruits. Food is a great leveller and, when I meet anyone from another culture, it is the start of a new conversation.

HUEVOS

HUEVOS
EGGS

Walk into any bar in Spain and there will be a tortilla sitting on the bar. Made fresh that day with the best eggs and a handful of local or seasonal products, it's a light pick-me-up that goes equally well with beer or a glass of light wine. Sliced to order and sprinkled with salt, the tortilla is the perfect snack food.

There are just as many recipes for the tortilla as there are for the French omelette, but unlike the omelette in which the filling is encased in folded egg, like an envelope, the tortilla's fillings are incorporated into the egg mixture and cooked in the pan.

Tortilla paisana, served at the seventeenth century *parador* (inn) in Ciudad Rodrigo, for example, is a mix of thinly sliced potatoes, onions, peas, red capsicums and strips of silky Serrano ham, folded through a mix of lightly beaten egg. Down in Granada, the most popular tortilla is *tortilla sacramonte*, a creamy yet spicy omelette made with offal — often sheep's brains. At MoVida we make several *tortilla de patatas* fresh every day and every now and then we put a juicy cod or rustic asparagus tortilla on the menu.

Our use of eggs is not, however, confined to tortilla. Every day we make the luxurious *ajoarriero* (mule driver's cod, see page 122) and very occasionally I'll put *huevos revueltos* (creamy scrambled eggs) on the menu.

You will see from the following recipes that eggs have a definite place on the Spanish menu — generally as a lighter meal or a supper, as the main meal is eaten in the middle of the day.

Wherever you are, I implore you to use the best free-range eggs you can find. Not only will you be rewarded by the warm feeling you get knowing that you're buying eggs from happy hens — they will also be the tastiest eggs on the market.

TORTILLA DE PATATAS
SPANISH POTATO OMELETTE

When Vanessa and I were working in a bar in the Pyrenees, the mother of the owner, Aurora, explained to us in her own inimitable manner that there was only one way to make a tortilla and that was *her* way. She started her *tortilla de patatas* by holding a potato in one hand and a stubby, yet cruelly sharp, knife in the other then, in a blur of motion, scored the potato one way then the other and, as she did, wafer thin slips of white potato flesh would fall into the pan. She passed the knife and a potato to us and watched as we hacked away, barely missing our thumbs. Once she'd left the kitchen we snuck out the old wooden chopping boards and thinly sliced the potatoes in a slightly safer way.

What she did instil in us was a respect for the ingredients. She would quickly confit (see Note) the potatoes in plenty of oil but not fry them. She made us cook the egg/potato mix over high heat but always gently — the idea was to never let the tortilla form a brown crust. She also taught us to always baste the thick round omelette with more beaten eggs as it cooked to make the edges smoother and fill in any *agujeros* (holes). This recipe takes lots of practice, so don't be put off if it doesn't work perfectly the first time.

METHOD

Cut the potatoes into paper-thin slices using a mandolin or a very sharp knife and then cut into 1 cm (½ inch) squares.

In a large heavy-based frying pan confit the potato, onion and garlic. To do this, cover them with the olive oil and heat over high heat until the oil just starts to warm then reduce the heat to low—medium and cook for 30–35 minutes. You should only be able to see very fine bubbles occasionally — it should not be rapidly bubbling. The idea is to soften the potatoes but not turn them into little chips. As the potato cooks, use the back of a large spoon to break them up into smaller pieces. After 30–35 minutes try a piece, it should be very soft to touch.

INGREDIENTS

1 kg (2 lb 4 oz) floury potatoes	8 eggs
1 brown onion, finely diced	sea salt flakes
1 garlic clove, very finely chopped	60 ml (2 fl oz/¼ cup) olive oil, extra
about 1 litre (35 fl oz/4 cups) olive oil	**TAPAS 12, MEDIA RACIÓN 6, RACIÓN 4**

When done, put the potato mixture in a chinois or fine sieve and drain the oil. The oil can be strained and used another three or four times to confit other dishes in this book.

Meanwhile, in a large bowl gently whisk the eggs until smooth and mix in 1 teaspoon salt. Reserve 185 ml (6 fl oz/¾ cup) of the egg mixture in a separate bowl. Add the potato mixture to the egg mix in the bowl and briefly mix. Season with sea salt flakes to taste. Heat the extra olive oil in a 28 cm (11¼ inch) non-stick frying pan over medium–high heat. Pour in the egg and potato mixture. As the mixture starts to thicken shake the pan in a circular motion — the edges should start to round. Using a wooden spatula, start shaping the mixture into a thick disc that is rounded at the edges like a fat Frisbee. After 1 minute cover the frying pan with a plate or round flat tray, and quickly flip the plate and pan so the tortilla is on the plate. Gently slide the tortilla back into the pan, uncooked side down, and reduce the heat to low–medium.

Smooth out any imperfections in the cooked surface of the tortilla by pouring over a little of the reserved beaten egg and smoothing it in with a wooden spoon. Cover and cook for 2 minutes. Flip the tortilla again and repeat the smoothing process with some of the remaining beaten egg on the freshly exposed side. Cover and cook for a further 2 minutes. Repeat the process then cover and cook for 2 minutes.

Flip the tortilla, pour on any remaining egg mix, smooth, cover, and cook for 1 minute. Flip and cook, covered, for a further minute.

When done the tortilla should not be completely firm and should have a little wobble in it when you gently shake the pan. Remove from the heat and keep in the pan in a warm place for 5 minutes. Slide onto a plate and cover with plastic wrap for 5 minutes. This allows the residual heat to set the remaining uncooked egg without the interior becoming rubbery. Serve at room temperature.

Note: Confit is a process of cooking in oil under 100°C (200°F). If it is hotter than that, the water in the food boils and evaporates as steam, which forms bubbles to escape.

INGREDIENTS

1 leek, trimmed, washed and finely sliced

1 white onion, finely diced

1 green capsicum (pepper), seeded, membrane removed and finely diced

100 ml (3½ fl oz) extra virgin olive oil

600 g (1 lb 5 oz) piece salt cod fillet, 2–3 cm (¾–1¼ inch) thick, desalinated (*see page 27*)

10 eggs

pinch of sea salt flakes

1 small handful flat-leaf (Italian) parsley, chopped

TAPAS 12, MEDIA RACIÓN 6, RACIÓN 4

TORTILLA DE BACALAO
SALT COD TORTILLA

This is a dish I reverse-engineered after eating it in a tapas bar in Bilbao. I was taken not just by its rich earthiness but also by its sweet juiciness. Egg and cod work so well together, as proven time and time again. As with any tortilla this is normally served at room temperature, but there is much to be said for slicing off a thick wedge as soon as the tortilla is cool enough to eat. Although it is made with salt cod, which remains quite salty despite the soaking, don't be afraid to sprinkle over a little extra salt — tortillas really require a lot of salt.

METHOD

Preheat the oven to 180°C (350°F/Gas 4).

In a 28 cm (11¼ inch) heavy-based frying pan with rounded edges, slowly cook all the vegetables together with 2 tablespoons of the extra virgin olive oil, covered, over low–medium heat for 10–15 minutes. The vegetables should be soft and the onion should be just golden.

Meanwhile, cook the salt cod by placing it on a baking tray, drizzling with a little olive oil, and baking in the oven for 10 minutes. When cooked, the flesh should be pearly white. Remove and allow the fish to cool enough to handle.

Break the eggs into a large bowl with the sea salt flakes and gently whisk together.

Using your fingers, break the cod apart, carefully removing any bones. Mix the cod with the vegetables and return the pan to medium heat. Cook for about 10 minutes, or until the juice from the cod reduces and evaporates and the vegetables start to brown. Increase the heat to high — the residual oil should be bubbling.

Reserve 150 ml (5 fl oz) of the beaten eggs. Add the remaining beaten eggs and the parsley to the cod and vegetables and mix through with a wooden spoon for 1 minute until the mixture begins to thicken. Cook over high heat for 30 seconds to allow a skin to form on the bottom. Reduce the heat to low and work the edges over to form nice round curves, while gently shaking the pan in a circular motion. When the edges begin to form, cook for

5 minutes. Then take a large plate and place over the top of the pan and flip the tortilla onto the plate. Return to the pan, uncooked side down. Increase the heat to medium. Cook for 2 minutes then repeat the flipping process and cook on the original side for 1 minute.

Smooth out any imperfections in the exposed surface by pouring over a little of the reserved beaten egg and smoothing it in with a wooden spoon. Cook for 2 minutes. Flip the tortilla again and repeat the smoothing process on the freshly exposed side, if required, by filling in any holes with some more of the reserved egg and smoothing with a wooden spoon. Cook for 2 minutes.

Remove from the heat and allow to cool a little then cover it with plastic wrap. Place near a hot oven or stovetop for 10 minutes to keep warm. The centre should feel soft but not runny. Serve at room temperature with a salad as a light supper or cut into wedges and serve as tapas.

INGREDIENTS

16 asparagus spears, woody
   ends trimmed

60 ml (2 fl oz/¼ cup) extra virgin olive oil

10 eggs

TAPAS 12, MEDIA RACIÓN 6, RACIÓN 4

TORTILLA DE ESPÁRRAGOS

ASPARAGUS TORTILLA

This is a classic little tortilla that makes the most of springtime asparagus. Local asparagus poke their heads up out of the soil from the beginning of spring and this is the time of year to cook with them. Asparagus are still in the market after Christmas in Australia, but by then they have really run out of puff and are getting a little loose and stringy.

If you're lucky enough to have wild asparagus growing in your area then you will be able to appreciate a leaner, earthier and stronger 'asparagus flavour'. For this tortilla it is better to use asparagus that are evenly sized and not too fat.

This is a smaller, lighter tortilla, to be enjoyed as a spring supper with bread and salad.

METHOD

Cut the asparagus into 2 cm (¾ inch) lengths. Heat the olive oil in a non-stick frying pan over low heat and gently sauté the asparagus for 5–10 minutes, or until the asparagus just starts to become tender.

Meanwhile, break the eggs into a bowl, add 1 teaspoon salt and whisk gently until the yolk and the white are combined.

Increase the heat to medium, pour the egg over the asparagus and mix through with a wooden spoon for 1 minute until it begins to thicken. Allow a skin to form on the bottom. Reduce the heat to low and work the edges over with a spatula to form nice round curves. When the edges begin to form, cook for 2 minutes. Take a large plate and place over the top of the pan and flip the tortilla onto the plate. Return the tortilla to the pan, uncooked side down. Increase the heat to medium. Cook for 2 minutes then repeat the process of flipping and cook on the original side for 1 minute.

Remove from the heat and allow to cool a little then cover with plastic wrap and place near a hot oven or stovetop for 10 minutes to keep warm. Serve at room temperature.

AJOARRIERO

MULE DRIVER'S COD

When Vanessa and I were working in Bodega de Pepe in Biescas, Aragón, we made *ajoarriero* every day. It's a blend of garlic, salt cod and potatoes made into a rich, rustic wet dish, which is served cold. We'd send it to the bartenders in a big terracotta *cazuela* and they would spoon it over freshly toasted crusty bread and serve it with a glass of *garnacha* (grenache) from Somontano.

The name *ajoarriero* literally means 'carrier's garlic', but is more widely known as 'mule driver's garlic', and is also the name of this recipe. It derives from a time when the wealth of Spain was transported across the mountains and valleys on the backs of donkeys. Wool, olives, cheese and clothing were moved from maker to buyer on mules, lead by equally obstinate mule drivers. At the end of a long day, while the animals fed on pasture, their masters would cook a meal made from garlic, salt cod and potatoes, thickened with a few locally garnered eggs.

At MoVida we stuff this mix into *piquillo* peppers and deep-fry them (see page 81), but you can serve this as tapas on a thin slice of toasted sourdough bread.

METHOD

Remove the skin from the salt cod and separate the flesh from the bones. Reserve the skin and bones for making stock (see page 43) and finely shred the salt cod flesh with your fingers.

Slice the potatoes into 2 mm (1/16 inch) thick slices using a mandolin or very sharp knife then cut into 1 cm (1/2 inch) squares. Put the shredded cod and potato squares in a large non-stick wok (see Notes) and cover with the olive oil.

Cook the cod and potato over high heat for 5–10 minutes, or until bubbles appear. Reduce the heat to low and confit for 25–30 minutes until cooked and tender (see Notes). When the potato becomes soft enough, use the back of a wooden spoon to crush the potato and fish together into small pieces.

INGREDIENTS

300 g (10½ oz) fleshy piece salt cod fillet,
  2–3 cm (¾–1¼ inch) thick, desalinated
  (*see page 27*)

2 floury potatoes

625 ml (21½ fl oz/2½ cups) olive oil

3 *piquillo* peppers

1 garlic clove

3 eggs

1 handful flat-leaf (Italian) parsley, chopped

TAPAJ 12, MEDIA RACIÓN 6

Drain the cod and potato mixture in a chinois or fine sieve and set aside for 20 minutes. The oil can be strained and used another three or four times to confit other dishes in this book.

Purée the peppers and garlic in a blender for 30 seconds. Crack the eggs into the blender and purée once more for 30 seconds to combine.

Return the cod and potato mixture to the wok, pour over the pepper and egg mixture, add the parsley and a pinch of salt and stir through. Cook over low heat using two wooden spoons, stirring and mashing the mixture. Beat the mix like you would beat a drum to break up the potatoes and make the mixture as smooth as possible. Continue cooking for 10–15 minutes until the mixture is thick and creamy. Season to taste.

Note that the dish will be served at room temperature, so it should taste a little bit saltier when warm. Allow to cool then refrigerate for up to 2 days until ready to use. Serve in a bowl with thinly sliced and toasted sourdough bread, allowing your guests to spread the *ajoarriero* over the toast themselves.

Notes: A normal spun steel wok will suffice but you may need to use a heat diffuser under it, as they tend to get too hot.

Confit is a process of cooking in oil under 100°C (200°F). If it is hotter than that, the water in the food boils and evaporates as steam, which forms bubbles to escape.

GOOD EGGS

From my station in the kitchen I can see every part of the restaurant and I watch my staff with pride. In the early days it was hard to get the right balance of staff to achieve an approximation of the atmosphere of a Spanish tapas bar within the heart of Melbourne. Initially the customers resisted, expecting fine dining. Eventually the front of house crew worked out how to get the customers to talk and become involved in the tapas experience. Eating at a tapas bar is never a passive experience and although Australians will probably never scream their orders like the Spanish do, our team has broken down those artificial barriers that dining rooms can create. The crew out the front perform an almost theatrical tightrope act, balancing hospitality and absurd fun and I think that's because they believe in everything we do — especially in the kitchen.

The kitchen can be a pressure cooker with seven people working side by side in the heat and throng. It's an act of trust and discipline. Marty and I have worked together since we were apprentices, James has been with me for 5 years since the first MoVida, and young Vietnamese-born Toan, the apprentice, started as a dishwasher.

They are looked after and they get to cook with the best produce I can find. The menu we put out every day is everybody's menu — an act of collaboration. I may be the chef and owner but it's everybody's restaurant. That said, I think any one of them — front of house or kitchen — would cut the mustard if they went to work in Spain.

INGREDIENTS

1 tablespoon extra virgin olive oil

450 g (1 lb) *morcilla* or black pudding,
 peeled and thickly sliced (*see page 28*)

10 eggs

1 small handful flat-leaf (Italian) parsley,
 finely chopped

TAPAS 18, MEDIA RACIÓN 6

REVUELTO DE MORCILLA

SCRAMBLED EGGS WITH SPANISH BLOOD PUDDING

Some restaurant menus in Spain have a whole section on *huevos revueltos* — rich and creamy scrambled eggs. This is a heart-stopping version — eggs and *morcilla* cooked together in the one beautiful cholesterol-defying dish. It is decadent and velvety but, ironically, is the food of the poor.

I think this makes one of the most extravagant breakfast foods, particularly when enjoyed with champagne or cava. I learned this particular version from my dad, who cooked it for us when mum was out visiting her sisters. He prepared this with his own hand-made *morcilla* — rich and redolent with garlic and cinnamon.

METHOD

Heat the olive oil in a frying pan over low—medium heat and gently sauté the *morcilla* for 5—10 minutes, breaking apart the sausage with a wooden spoon. The *morcilla* should have the texture of cooked minced (ground) meat.

Break the eggs into a bowl and gently beat them. Reduce the heat to low, add the egg to the pan and continue stirring gently. The idea is to create a very thin film of cooked egg then continuously fold this back into the uncooked mixture. Cook over low heat for about 5 minutes and don't be afraid of removing the pan from the heat every now and then.

Fold through half the parsley and season to taste with salt, if necessary. The dish is ready when the egg is still wet but most of the egg has cooked. Sprinkle over the remaining parsley before serving.

INGREDIENTS

300 g (10½ oz) mushrooms, such as
    portobello, shiitake, enoki

1 tablespoon olive oil

2 garlic cloves, chopped

1 tablespoon chopped thyme

fine sea salt

8 eggs

2 tablespoons finely chopped flat-leaf
    (Italian) parsley

sea salt flakes, to sprinkle

TAPAS 12, MEDIA RACIÓN 4

SCRAMBLED EGGS WITH MUSHROOMS

In the hills around Melbourne we are lucky enough to have wild morels growing. Sometimes, at the end of winter they make it into the city markets, selling for up to ten times the price of normal mushrooms.

I've based this dish on mushrooms that are available in the market all year round. You can use a base of 100 per cent portobello mushrooms, or you can mix in some shiitake or enoki mushrooms for a bit of fun. If you are fortunate to come across some morels please feel free to add them as well — you won't need many to get a really good flavour.

METHOD

Remove any dirt from the mushrooms, cut away the part of the stem that may have been in the earth and wipe down the caps with a damp cloth. Slice the larger mushrooms into irregular pieces.

In a large frying pan, heat the olive oil over medium heat and sauté the garlic for 30 seconds. Add the mushrooms and thyme and a pinch of fine sea salt. Cook for 10–15 minutes until cooked through and the cooking juices have reduced. Reduce the heat to low.

Gently beat the eggs in a large bowl with a pinch of fine sea salt. Add the egg to the pan and stir continuously — slowly and gently. The idea is to create a very thin film of cooked egg then continuously fold this back into the uncooked mixture. Cook over low heat for 6–8 minutes and don't be afraid of removing the pan from the heat every now and then.

The dish is ready when the egg is still wet but most of the egg has cooked. Season to taste with a little salt, if necessary. Sprinkle with the parsley and some sea salt flakes before serving.

PESCADO Y MARISCO

PESCADO Y MARISCO
FISH AND SEAFOOD

When our family arrived in Australia we literally devoured the landscape. My parents settled in Corio, a working class suburb of the industrial city of Geelong, an hour west of Melbourne. The family home is not far from the shores of Port Phillip Bay and is surrounded by the Barwon River catchment. (As I grew up I learned these were the traditional hunting grounds of the Wathaurung Aboriginal tribe.)

After a lifetime of living under the authoritarian rule of Franco, my father and mother celebrated their new-found freedom in Australia by catching and cooking every water creature they recognized. On weekends our family became hunters and gatherers and caught the same shellfish, crustaceans and fish that the traditional Aboriginal people caught in the waterholes, rivers and shores that surrounded my childhood home. I have memories of almost endless supplies of seafood that we caught ourselves.

To the north of my old home, in the Brisbane Ranges, it is still possible in a good year to net bucketfuls of yabbies (freshwater crayfish), which we cook in big pans over a hardwood fire. My family cooks yabbies — as long as your hand — in a tomato and olive oil base with garlic and mint. The contact of the shell adds so much flavour to the sauce and invigorates and enriches the dish. In the restaurant I always serve my prawns and langoustines in their shell, as this adds so much flavour.

When I serve our luxurious *almejas a la marinera* (clams in velvet pea and parsley sauce, see page 140) I am constantly reminded of those endless golden summers on the beach, swimming in the bay and helping dad dig for clams. Cooked with butter and peas, the sweet little clams fit into your mouth — shell and all — and are sucked clean of their rich sauce.

What I am most proud of is the fact that Australians, and the rest of the world, are finally becoming aware of the sweet taste of salt cod. Since the Middle Ages, these salted cod from the Atlantic Ocean have been traded across Europe. Follow the desalinating instructions closely on page 27 to enjoy the sweet, subtle and juicy flavour of salt cod.

We also use a lot of whole fish at MoVida because the flavour is in the skin and bones, but we cook it in a way that is easy to eat. The *sardinas en sal* (whole sardines baked in a salt crust, see page 151) is a perfect example of this — whole sardines baked in sea salt, where the skin comes away with the salt crust and the bones are removed in one fell swoop.

The big difference between my kitchen and a traditional Spanish kitchen is that I follow in the footsteps of the new generation of Spanish chefs, who trained in France and came back to Spain with a greater respect for Spanish produce. We all appreciate our great maritime tradition but realize that overcooking fish for hours doesn't bring out the best in the fish. Instead, we try to let the produce speak for itself. We use faster, hotter cooking times and take fish off the heat earlier, allowing the residual heat to cook the flesh to perfection.

INGREDIENTS

1 kg (2 lb 4 oz) Lebanese (short) cucumbers

about 300 ml (10½ fl oz) liquid glucose

fine sea salt

24 freshly shucked oysters

1 kg (2 lb 4 oz) rock salt (optional)

50 g (1¾ oz) jar salmon roe

fruity extra virgin olive oil, to drizzle (optional)

TAPAS 24

OSTRAS CON SORBETE DE PEPINOS
FRESH OYSTERS WITH CUCUMBER SORBET

A freshly shucked oyster is full of salty iodine-rich liquid that tastes of the sea. Learning to open oysters is a simple skill that will improve the quality of your life. A quick flick of a stubby knife prises the shells apart to reveal the freshest of oysters. This simple dish matches the vitality and saltiness of the oyster with a sweet, green and slightly astringent cucumber sorbet, which leaves the palate cleansed and ready for the next morsel. It uses liquid glucose, a type of simple sugar available at some supermarkets, good food stores and chemists. To make things easier, we have included a surplus of ingredients to make the sorbet, so don't be alarmed if you have some left over. This makes a surprisingly good dressing for sliced tomatoes or, with a little salt sprinkled on top, diced mango! But it keeps well in the freezer — the perfect excuse to buy more oysters.

METHOD

Top, tail and peel the cucumbers. Cut the cucumbers in half lengthways and gently scoop out the seeds with a teaspoon. Discard the seeds. Cut the cucumbers into rough chunks and purée in a blender for several minutes until completely smooth.

Measure the amount of cucumber purée. Add to the blender exactly half this amount of liquid glucose. Return the cucumber purée to the blender and blend for 1 minute. Season to taste with fine sea salt.

If you have an ice cream maker, make a sorbet following the manufacturer's instructions. If not, use the following method. Transfer to a shallow metal tray and freeze, whisking every couple of hours, until the sorbet is frozen and has a smooth texture. Freeze for 5 hours or overnight. Soften in the refrigerator for 30 minutes before serving.

To serve, place the oysters on a layer of finely crushed ice or rock salt on a large serving plate or tray. Put 1 teaspoon of sorbet on top of each oyster, sprinkle with ¼ teaspoon of salmon roe and drizzle with olive oil, if desired.

INGREDIENTS

24 fresh scallops, on the shell

1 tablespoon olive oil

1 white onion, finely diced

80 g (2¾ oz) *jamón*, finely diced (*see page 20*)

1 tablespoon Spanish sweet paprika

500 ml (17 fl oz/2 cups) *albariño* or other
dry white wine

fine sea salt

165 g (5¾ oz/2 cups) fresh white breadcrumbs

VIEIRAS CON VINO Y MIGAS DE PAN

SCALLOPS BAKED IN THEIR SHELLS WITH WHITE WINE AND BREADCRUMBS

It is said that the bones of Saint James were taken from the Holy Land to Spain during the Middle Ages and buried where the Cathedral of Santiago de Compostela stands today. Since then, people have made the pilgrimage to Santiago de Compostela from all over Europe, following the *Camino de Santiago* (Way of Saint James). Last year, nearly 20 000 people walked, hobbled or rode mountain bikes through the Galician countryside. In true Spanish style there is no one particular road or path. Some of the major routes, however, are marked with images of scallop shells, the sign of Saint James.

The scallop is still very important to the Galician economy and tons are grown in suspended baskets in the sea, but you don't have to walk to Spain to make these little scallops. The layer of golden breadcrumbs hides a just cooked scallop, surrounded by flecks of *jamón* and juicy white breadcrumbs that have soaked up the *albariño*, a dry white wine from the same countryside that the pilgrims walk through each year.

METHOD

Preheat the oven to 220°C (425°F/Gas 7). Clean the scallops and remove the tube, leaving the coral. Return to the shell. Place the scallops in a single layer on two baking trays.

Heat the olive oil in a frying pan over medium heat and cook the onion for 1 minute. Mix in the *jamón* and cook for 1 minute, or until the *jamón* just starts to change colour. Stir in the paprika and continue cooking for 1 minute then stir in the wine. Bring to the boil then reduce to a simmer and cook for about 12 minutes, or until its volume has reduced by half then remove from the heat.

Season each scallop with a small pinch of fine sea salt. Pour 1 tablespoon of the onion and *jamón* mixture over each scallop and sprinkle with 1 tablespoon of breadcrumbs. Bake in the oven for 5 minutes, or until the scallops are just cooked through and the breadcrumbs are lightly golden. Serve immediately.

INGREDIENTS

1.5 kg (3 lb 5 oz) clams (vongole)	455 ml (16 fl oz) fish stock (*see page 43*)
90 ml (3 fl oz) olive oil	225 g (8 oz) cooked peas
1 brown onion, very finely diced	2 handfuls flat-leaf (Italian) parsley, chopped
5 garlic cloves, finely chopped	80 g (2¾ oz) butter, chilled and cut into
150 ml (5 fl oz) *albariño* or other dry	small pieces
white wine	

MEDIA RACIÓN 6

ALMEJAS A LA MARINERA

CLAMS IN VELVET PEA AND PARSLEY SAUCE

Almejas a la marinera can translate as 'sailor's clams' but, for some reason, we didn't sell that many when we first described them that way on the menu. They are in fact juicy little clams sitting in a rich, smooth sauce of peas and a little butter, which is sharpened with a splash of dry white wine.

Almejas a la marinera can also be used as a sauce to pour over a large pan-fried fish. Cook the fish in a frying pan for a few minutes each side then bake in a 180°C (350°F/Gas 4) oven for 8–10 minutes. Finally pour this lovely sauce over the top. That said, *almejas a la marinera* is just as good on its own.

METHOD

Soak the clams in cold water for 2 hours to remove the grit from inside the shells, changing the water several times. Drain well.

Heat the oil in a large, deep-sided frying pan over low–medium heat and cook the onion and garlic for 10 minutes, or until soft and translucent. Increase the heat to high, add the clams and wine and toss in the pan for 1 minute. Bring to the boil then add the fish stock. Cover and return to the boil. Once boiling remove the lid and reduce the heat to a simmer.

Take out the clams that have opened and put in a bowl. Cover with foil and set aside. Continue simmering for a few minutes and remove the rest of the clams as they open. Remove and discard any clams that haven't opened within 6 minutes of boiling. Increase the heat to medium and continue cooking the stock for 2–3 minutes until it has reduced by half.

Add the peas and half the parsley, cover the pan and cook for 1 minute to heat through. Reduce the heat to low and add the butter, stirring continuously for a few minutes to emulsify and thicken the sauce. Once the butter has combined with the sauce, remove from the heat. Return the clams to the pan, cover and rest for 30 seconds, stirring a few times. Serve immediately, garnished with the remaining parsley.

INGREDIENTS

12 raw king prawns (shrimp)

2 tablespoons olive oil

100 ml (3½ fl oz) *ajo y perejil*
   (*see page 40*)

2 large pinches of sea salt flakes

2 lemons, halved

lemon wedges, to serve

TAPAS 12, MEDIA RACIÓN 4

GRILLED GARLIC PRAWNS

Statistics say that the Spanish eat an astonishing 37 kg (82 lb) of seafood every year. Judging by the number of prawn shells on tapas bar floors I reckon that figure is mainly made up of prawns. Walk into any tapas bar and there is the *cocinero* (cook) preparing them right in front of you. It's an intense experience — the combined smell of hot steel, scorched shell and briny sea, and finally a cloud of steam, when the *cocinero* roughly squeezes lemon over the grill to dress the prawns. The secret to *gambas a la plancha* is to make sure you get the grill really hot to soften the shell. Then the whole prawn is edible — including the head!

METHOD

Make a shallow cut with a very sharp small knife along the length of each prawn back. Remove and discard the dark vein, leaving on the head, tail and shell.

Put the prawns in a bowl and drizzle over the olive oil, *ajo y perejil* and then sprinkle with sea salt. Preheat a barbecue grill or cast-iron grill to high.

Cook the prawns on the barbecue for 2 minutes. Season by squeezing two lemon halves over the prawns, then turn them and cook for a further 2 minutes. Quickly squeeze the remaining lemon halves over the prawns and serve immediately with the lemon wedges.

INGREDIENTS

3 tentacles of a large octopus (about 1 kg/2 lb
    4 oz), frozen, thawed and drained

10 waxy potatoes (about 1 kg/2 lb 4 oz),
    such as kipfler (fingerling), unpeeled

sea salt flakes, to sprinkle

extra virgin olive oil, to drizzle

Spanish sweet paprika, to sprinkle

2 tablespoons finely chopped flat-leaf
    (Italian) parsley

MEDIA RACIÓN 6, RACIÓN 4

PULPO A LA GALLEGA

GALICIAN OCTOPUS

When I was a child, my dad would go fishing off the basalt shelves of Bass Strait. I remember him pulling his hand out of the water with a powerful octopus wrapped around his arm. Knowing how much it took to pull the creature off, it doesn't surprise me how strong and tough octopus can be. But I have a foolproof method for cooking octopus and it begins with using frozen tentacles, if you can find them. During freezing, the ice crystals break apart the cell walls and this makes the octopus more tender. The result in this recipe is little morsels of surprisingly sweet, warm octopus, and potato, dusted with Spanish paprika.

METHOD

To cook the octopus, bring a large saucepan of unsalted water to the boil. Meanwhile, wash the octopus under cold running water. When the water is rapidly boiling, plunge the octopus in the water for 15 seconds then remove. Allow the water to boil again then repeat four times, allowing the water to reach boiling point between each immersion.

On the last immersion, leave the octopus in the pan and reduce the heat to barely a simmer. Cook for 30–40 minutes, or until tender. The outside pink layer should still be intact. Remove the octopus from the pan and set aside to cool.

Increase the heat to high and bring the cooking water to the boil. Add the potatoes and cook for 30 minutes, or until tender. Remove from the pan and leave until cool enough to handle then peel.

Using a sharp knife slice the octopus tentacles into 1 cm (½ inch) discs. Slice the potatoes into similar sized pieces. Arrange the potato on four to six small serving plates. Cover the potato with the octopus. Sprinkle with sea salt flakes, drizzle with a little extra virgin olive oil, then sprinkle with the paprika and parsley. Serve immediately.

INGREDIENTS

12 raw king prawns (shrimp)

100 ml (3½ fl oz) olive oil

3 tablespoons finely chopped flat-leaf (Italian) parsley

2 garlic cloves, finely chopped

sea salt flakes

300 ml (10½ fl oz) cider, at room temperature

MEDIA RACIÓN 4

GAMBAS A LA SIDRA
PRAWNS COOKED IN APPLE CIDER

Gambas a la sidra come to the table bubbling and hissing in hellishly hot little terracotta dishes called *cazuelitas* (meaning little *cazuelas*, see page 34). *Cazuelitas* are cheap, rustic and available from good food stores and Spanish delicatessens. You can use a small cast-iron frying pan or pot instead. Whatever you use, it should be small, as a larger dish may stew the prawns too much. At MoVida, we make this dish using 16 cm (6¼ inch) diameter *cazuelitas*.

This recipe originates in the cool green climes of Asturia, northern Spain, prime apple growing and *sidra* (cider) making territory. Appley, smooth, yeasty and low in alcohol, Asturian ciders are as comparable to the cheap industrial Anglo-Saxon cider, as good champagne is to cask wine. Asturian cider can be hard to get but, thankfully, a handful of small cideries are still making good old-fashioned cider and the imported ciders from Normandy can be substituted as well.

METHOD

If using terracotta *cazuelitas*, soak four in cold water for at least 24 hours (the longer the better). Drain and dry before using.

Make a shallow cut with a very sharp small knife along the length of each prawn back. Remove and discard the dark vein and shell, leaving on the head and tail.

Place the *cazuelitas* over low–medium heat and heat until very hot, only about 30 seconds. If using a cast-iron pot, heat until a few drops of water added to the pot bubble and hiss. When hot, carefully add the olive oil, parsley and garlic, dividing equally among the four *cazuelitas*. Once the garlic has been sizzling for 10 seconds, add three prawns to each *cazuelita*.

Season the prawns with sea salt flakes and some freshly ground black pepper and cook for just under 2 minutes each side. They should be well sealed and be just turning pink. Add the cider, pouring in enough until it is just under the top of the prawns. Cook, turning as needed, for 5 minutes, or until the cider has reduced by one-third and the prawns are cooked. Season again.

Place the *cazuelitas* on a heatproof tray, board or plate and serve immediately, while the prawns are sizzling and the cider is bubbling.

INGREDIENTS

500 g (1 lb 2 oz) cuttlefish, body only
   (no wings or tentacles), cleaned (*see Note*)

1 tablespoon Spanish sweet paprika

1 tablespoon freshly ground cumin
   (*see page 32*)

60 ml (2 fl oz/¼ cup) extra virgin olive oil

300 g (10½ oz) broad (fava) beans, shelled

60 ml (2 fl oz/¼ cup) olive oil

1 tablespoon *ajo y perejil* (*see page 40*)

2 lemons, halved

6 vine-ripened tomatoes, skinned, seeded
   diced and drained (*see page 33*)

1 handful mint, roughly chopped

1 tablespoon aged sherry vinegar

sea salt flakes

MEDIA RACIÓN 4

CHOCOS CON HABAS
FRESH CUTTLEFISH WITH MINTY BROAD BEANS

There is a tension between tradition and invention, one pulling back and holding on to the past, the other pushing forward, adventuring into unexplored territory. At MoVida, when we explore new culinary ideas we pay deep respect to the past and this dish is the perfect example. In the traditional Andalusian version, the cuttlefish and beans are slowly braised in a wine sauce but we have given this dish a lighter touch. All respect to tradition, but seared cuttlefish has a flavour of its own and fresh broad beans have a light vitality to them that doesn't survive the traditional cooking method.

In fact, once you have tried this, you may like to adapt this recipe yourself and cook the spiced marinated cuttlefish on the barbecue to give it a smoky flavour. You'll join the long line of people throughout history who have appreciated the fact that cuttlefish and broad beans, despite their different backgrounds, were meant for each other.

METHOD

Cut the cuttlefish into 2.5 cm (1 inch) squares. Put in a large bowl with the paprika, cumin and extra virgin olive oil. Mix thoroughly, cover and leave in the refrigerator to marinate for at least 2 hours.

Blanch the broad beans in a large saucepan of boiling water for 1 minute. Remove the beans and refresh in chilled water. Take the outer skin off the beans by pinching the skin off one end and gently squeezing the inner beans out. Discard the skins and put the beans in a large bowl.

Heat half of the olive oil in a large frying pan over high heat. Sear the cuttlefish in three batches for 30–45 seconds each side, or until browned, adding more oil if needed. Return all the cuttlefish to the pan. Reduce the heat to medium and sprinkle with the *ajo y perejil*.

Squeeze the juice of one of the lemons into the pan. Allow to simmer slowly for about 4 minutes, or until the cuttlefish becomes opaque through to the centre and is tender to the bite (it should be firmer than calamari). Put the cooked cuttlefish on a warm plate covered with foil in a low oven.

Put the tomato in a bowl, then add the broad beans, the juice of the other lemon and mix through. Add the mint, sherry vinegar and the warm cuttlefish and toss. Season with some sea salt flakes and a pinch of black pepper to taste and toss again. Serve warm.

Note: Ask your fishmonger to clean the cuttlefish.

INGREDIENTS

eight 80 g (2¾ oz) sardines, gutted

8 small rosemary sprigs

1.25 kg (2 lb 12 oz) rock salt

4 egg whites

1 lemon, halved

TAPAS 8, MEDIA RACIÓN 4, RACIÓN 2

SARDINAS EN SAL

WHOLE SARDINES BAKED IN A SALT CRUST

From the oven emerges a spectacular golden crust of baked salt. Cracked open it reveals whole fish, steamed in their own evaporated juices. The taste is unlike fish cooked using any other method — sweet, rich and, surprisingly, not salty. Traditionally from the Mediterranean coast of Spain, this salt crust method is also used to cook sea bream or snapper, so translates perfectly to the Australian kitchen. It is best to keep the scales on the fish to protect the fish from the salt.

METHOD

Preheat the oven to 180°C (350°F/Gas 4).

Trim the fins from the fish with a pair of kitchen scissors and discard. Leave the tail on the fish. Rinse the inside of the fish clean and pat dry with paper towel. Lightly season the inside of each fish with salt and insert a rosemary sprig into the cavity of each fish.

In a bowl, mix the salt and egg whites together thoroughly. It will form a very thick, mortar-like slurry. On a baking tray, lay a thin bed of this mixture, enough to support the fish, with a small space between each fish. Place the fish on the bed of salt, leaving small gaps in between, so the salt mix can seal off each fish. Cover the fish completely with the remainder of the mix, leaving the tail and head protruding.

Bake for 15–20 minutes. The crust should be hard and brown. If it gives when pressed, it needs a little more cooking time.

Remove from the oven and break the crust on top with your fingers. When you remove the upper crust some of the skin and scales should come away with the crust. Before eating, remove any skin that sticks to the flesh (it slides off easily) and brush away any excess salt. Squeeze the lemon over the fish.

Serve the exposed fillet first by lifting the flesh away from the bone, tail end first. The tail, spine and bones can then be lifted off in one piece and discarded, revealing the other fillet underneath.

INGREDIENTS

500 g (1 lb 2 oz) piece of salt cod, 2–3 cm
  (³/₄–1¹/₄ inch) thick, desalinated (*see page 27*)

2 ripe tomatoes, peeled, seeded and diced
  (*see page 33*)

1 red capsicum (pepper), seeded, membrane
  removed and diced

¹/₂ green capsicum (pepper), seeded,
  membrane removed and diced

70 g (2¹/₂ oz) fruity olives, pitted (*see Note*)

1 red onion, finely sliced

1 small handful flat-leaf (Italian) parsley,
  chopped

juice of 2 lemons

juice of 1 orange

60 ml (2 fl oz/¹/₄ cup) red wine vinegar

1 tablespoon drained capers

100 ml (3¹/₂ fl oz) extra virgin olive oil

MEDIA RACIÓN 6, RACIÓN 4

BACALAO ESQUEIXADA

SALAD OF SHREDDED SALT COD WITH OLIVES, PARSLEY, TOMATO AND CITRUS

So common is this dish in Spain, that there are thousands of variations across the country. We based this version on a *bacalao esqueixada* that we ate in a restaurant on the Avenida Diagonal in Barcelona's business district — we had deliberately wandered away from the tourist dominated old part of town to dine among the working Barcelonans. It was part of a *menú de dia,* which started with cod salad. It is light and sharp, made with finely sliced capsicum, sharp little capers and fruity *arbequina* olives. For the record we continued our Barcelona lunch with some quail, slow cooked in wine, and finished with a little ripe melon for dessert.

METHOD

Remove the skin and all the bones from the cod and break the flesh apart into even shreds.

Mix together all the ingredients in a large bowl with 1 teaspoon salt and 1 teaspoon freshly cracked black pepper. Mix with your hands or a spoon, gently tossing the fish and vegetables through the dressing. Cover with plastic wrap and refrigerate for 1 hour. Serve chilled.

Note: You can use Spanish *arbequina* or manzanilla olives in this recipe. If you are not sure which olives are fruity, check with your local delicatessen.

INGREDIENTS

12 Slimy Mackerel fillets or other strong
    flavoured fish (about 100 g/3½ oz each)
seasoned plain (all-purpose) flour, to coat
200 ml (7 fl oz) olive oil
fine sea salt
2 litres (70 fl oz/8 cups) *escabeche*
    (*see page 41*)

1 small handful flat-leaf (Italian) parsley,
    finely chopped
125 ml (4 fl oz/½ cup) extra virgin olive oil

TAPAS 12, MEDIA RACIÓN 6, RACIÓN 4

CABALLA EN ESCABECHE

MACKEREL MARINATED IN SHERRY VINEGAR AND AROMATICS

If you've never had *escabeche* then a small act of faith may be necessary to believe me when I say this is one of the most wonderful ways of preparing fish. Whole fish, cutlets or fillets of lightly fried fish are steeped in a bath of spiced wine and vinegar. Fresh and invigorating, it is actually based on an ancient method of preserving fish, birds and game that goes back to Roman times. In fact, fish prepared in this way will keep wonderfully in the refrigerator for days.

I use mackerel, a highly underrated fish that is firmly textured, strongly flavoured and so, so, so good for you. You can use any other robustly flavoured fish. That said, a friend of mine, not in the restaurant trade, once had to use up 3 kg (6 lb 12 oz) of relatively bland gemfish, which had been defrosted. The *escabeche* perked up the tired fish and went on to make three or four spectacular appearances at summer barbecues over the course of the week.

METHOD

Lightly coat the fish in the flour. Heat the oil in a large frying pan over high heat. Pan-fry the fish for about 3 minutes each side until golden brown. Season each side with sea salt. The fish should flake easily but not be falling apart.

Remove the fish and allow to drain and cool on paper towel. Place the fish in a single layer in a large, non-metallic dish and pour the *escabeche* over the fish. Cover with plastic wrap and refrigerate overnight. The fish will keep covered in the refrigerator for several days.

To serve, remove the fish from the marinade, spoon over several tablespoons of the marinade and vegetables, sprinkle with the parsley and drizzle with the extra virgin olive oil.

REMOJÓN
GRILLED SALT COD SALAD WITH BLOOD ORANGES, PARSLEY AND SMOKED PAPRIKA

When I visit Adelaide, I am often struck by its similarity to Seville. Both are characterized by their stone buildings, meandering rivers, blinding intense light and searing hot summer days. These two could be sister cities if it wasn't for the fact that Adelaidians refresh themselves with an indigenous brew called Coopers Pale Ale, while the Sevillians sit down to a refreshing salad of oranges, endive, onion and salt cod called *remojón*.

INGREDIENTS

500 g (1 lb 2 oz) piece of salt cod 2–3 cm
  (³/₄ –1¹/₄ inch) thick, desalinated (*see page 27*)
125 ml (4 fl oz/¹/₂ cup) extra virgin olive oil
juice of 2 lemons
pinch of freshly ground cinnamon (*see page 32*)
1 teaspoon Spanish sweet smoked paprika
2 garlic cloves, finely sliced

1 kg (2 lb 4 oz) blood oranges, peeled and cut
  into 5 mm (¹/₄ inch) slices (*see Note*)
1 handful flat-leaf (Italian) parsley,
  roughly chopped
1 red onion, finely sliced
1 large bunch curly endive, leaves only

MEDIA RACIÓN 6, RACIÓN 4

Remojón means 'to soak' and refers to the desalinated salt cod used in the recipe. Once again, we've reinterpreted this dish at MoVida. In Seville, *remojón* is much heavier with much more olive oil. We've lightened up the dish and emphasized the freshness of the orange. Adelaide readers should try this dish with their excellent McLaren Vale olive oil and fresh Riverland oranges. Perhaps they could even tweak it a little and use some fish from the Spencer Gulf. It won't be *remojón*, but it would make a brilliant lunch when it's 40°C (104°F) in the shade.

METHOD

Preheat your grill (broiler) to medium.

Carefully remove any bones from the fish fillet but leave the skin on. Cut into equal-sized portions (six or four, depending on whether your serves are *media ración* or *ración*) and put in an ovenproof frying pan, skin side up. Drizzle with 60 ml (2 fl oz/¹/₄ cup) of the extra virgin olive oil and place under the grill for 15 minutes, or until the flesh is cooked to opaque and the skin becomes crispy. Allow the cod to cool enough to handle. Reserve any cooking juices.

Pull the cod apart into large flakes and put in a bowl. Cut the crispy skin into bite-sized pieces and add to the bowl. Pour in the reserved cooking juices.

Add the remaining extra virgin olive oil, lemon juice, spices and garlic. Gently mix through with very clean hands. Add the orange, parsley and onion and mix through. Season to taste, if necessary.

Make a bed of endive on a serving plate and lay the fish salad on top, carefully teasing out some of the larger flakes of fish, as they tend to hide among the other ingredients.

Note: If you can't find blood oranges, use regular oranges.

INGREDIENTS

1 kg (2 lb 4 oz) skinless skate or ray fillets, cut into 2.5 cm (1 inch) thick strips

plain (all-purpose) flour, to coat

fine sea salt

100 ml (3½ fl oz/¼ cup) olive oil

165 g (5¾ oz) butter, thinly sliced

60 g (2¼ oz) drained baby capers

165 g (5¾ oz) hazelnuts, roasted, peeled and very roughly chopped (*see page 19*)

1 large handful flat-leaf (Italian) parsley, chopped

juice of 2 lemons

1 lemon, cut into wedges, to serve

MEDIA RACIÓN 6, RACIÓN 4

RAYA CON AVELLANAS

SKATE WITH HAZELNUTS AND LEMON

The names we give fish determine their survival. Let me explain. We call shark 'flake' and as a result these fearsome predators of the deep are fast approaching annihilation off our coastal waters, because we are eating them faster than they can breed. If it were sold as shark no one would have ever eaten it. The reverse is true for the wonderful fish rather unflatteringly named 'flathead', making them sound more like a character from an Australian soap opera than a tasty fish. As a result, until very recently, they were a very cheap and highly underrated fish. So don't tell a soul when I say that skate and stingray are the last bargains from the sea. The flesh is firm and moist, high in omega-3 fatty acids, the fish are abundant and a quarter of the price of our supermarket favourites and are very, very easy to cook.

This skate recipe contrasts the richness of butter and hazelnuts with the sharp taste of capers and lemons.

METHOD

Preheat the oven to 180°C (350°F/Gas 4). Lightly coat the fish with flour and season with sea salt.

Heat the olive oil in a large ovenproof frying pan over medium–high heat until the oil just starts to sizzle when a pinch of flour is sprinkled over the pan. Fry the skate, in two batches, on all sides until golden all over. This should take about 30 seconds on each side. Season the fish with sea salt while cooking.

Put the pan in the oven for 8 minutes, or until the fish is cooked through. Transfer the fish onto a warmed plate, loosely cover with paper towel then foil and keep close to the hot oven or stovetop to keep warm.

Discard the oil in the pan and return the pan to the stovetop over medium–high heat. When hot, drop the butter into the pan. When the butter is thoroughly foaming, add the capers, hazelnuts and most of the parsley and fry for a few minutes. Add the lemon juice. The sauce should be foaming and bubbling but not too dark. Season to taste with salt.

Place the fish onto a warmed serving plate and pour over the sauce. Garnish with the remaining parsley and serve with lemon wedges.

INGREDIENTS

four 200 g (7 oz) red mullet, cleaned and
   scaled

125 g (4½ oz/1 cup) seasoned plain
   (all-purpose) flour

60 ml (2 fl oz/¼ cup) olive oil

fine sea salt

extra virgin olive oil, to drizzle

80 ml (2½ fl oz/⅓ cup) fino sherry

125 g (4½ oz) *sofrito* (*see page 51*)

125 g (4½ oz) *salsa romesco* (*see page 52*)

1 small handful flat-leaf (Italian) parsley,
   roughly chopped

150 ml (5 fl oz) fish stock (*see page 43*)

MEDIA RACIÓN 4

ROMESCO DE PEIX

FRIED RED MULLET WITH ROMESCO SAUCE

This is from Tarragona in Catalonia, where the *romesco* (ñora) pepper grows. Quite often it is made with monkfish, but we've adapted it to use red mullet, which have a good firm flesh and are very attractive when served whole. Red mullet aside, you can use any small whole fish, such as garfish or even large sardines.

METHOD

Preheat the oven to 150°C (300°F/Gas 2).

Rinse the fish under cold running water and pat dry with paper towel. Lightly coat the fish in the seasoned flour.

Heat the olive oil in a large frying pan over medium–high heat. Add the fish and cook for 2 minutes each side, gently shaking the pan every 10 seconds or so to prevent sticking. Season both sides of the fish with sea salt.

Remove the fish from the pan, place on a baking tray and drizzle with a little extra virgin olive oil. Bake for 8 minutes, or until the fish flakes easily when tested gently with a fork. Place the fish on a warm plate and cover with foil. Keep somewhere warm.

Discard the oil from the pan and return to high heat. Carefully add the sherry to the pan and stir vigorously to scrape up any cooked-on bits from the bottom of the pan. Mix through the *sofrito* and *salsa romesco* and reduce the heat to medium. Add the parsley and fish stock. Cook for 5–10 minutes until a thick sauce has formed. Season to taste.

To serve, spread the sauce evenly around four warmed serving plates using the back of a spoon. Place the fish on top and serve immediately.

PARGO AL FONDO

WHOLE SNAPPER BAKED ON POTATOES AND CAPSICUMS

Similar dishes, in which whole fish are cooked on a bed of potato and vegetables, can be found all over Spain. The bed of potato and vegetables is called *fondo*, meaning foundation.

Pargo al fondo typifies the pragmatic nature of the Spanish cook — cooking with one cooking vessel, thus using less fuel. Also using the *fondo* to absorb the cooking juices makes the potatoes tastier and leaves nothing to waste. In fact, the potatoes are my favourite part of the dish, as they take on every part of the intense flavour of the stock, wine and the richness of the fish. We use snapper but you can use any other whole fish of a similar size. Whole fish is tastier and better for you. When you cook whole fish the skin and bones break down to form gelatine, which is a very nourishing protein.

INGREDIENTS

four 500 g (1 lb 2 oz) whole snapper, cleaned
   and scaled

150 ml (5 fl oz) extra virgin olive oil

1.5 kg (3 lb 5 oz) brown onions, finely sliced

2 red capsicums (peppers), seeded, membrane
   removed and finely sliced

2 green capsicums (peppers), seeded,
   membrane removed and finely sliced

3 garlic cloves, finely chopped

7 bay leaves

fine sea salt

100 ml (3½ fl oz) *ajo y perejil* (*see page 40*)

olive oil, to drizzle

4 lemons, sliced

200 ml (7 fl oz) fish stock (*see page 43*)

4 waxy potatoes (such as nicola), sliced into
   5 mm (¼ inch) thick rounds

3 ripe tomatoes, peeled, seeded and chopped
   (*see page 33*)

100 ml (3½ fl oz) white wine

sea salt flakes, to sprinkle

RACIÓN 4

METHOD

Remove the fins, and the spines along the back of the fish with a pair of kitchen scissors and discard. Rinse the fish under cold running water and pat dry with paper towel.

To make the *fondo*, heat 80 ml (2½ fl oz/⅓ cup) of the extra virgin olive oil in a large frying pan over low–medium heat. Cook the onion, capsicum, garlic, three of the bay leaves and a pinch of salt for 15–20 minutes, covered, stirring occasionally. Preheat the oven to 180°C (350°F/Gas 4).

Put the fish in a large bowl with several pinches of sea salt and the *ajo y perejil* and rub all over the fish. Season the cavity of each fish with a little salt, a few slices of lemon and a bay leaf.

Drizzle a little olive oil over the base of a large baking tray. Lay about a quarter of the *fondo* in the tray. Pour the fish stock over the *fondo*, lay the potato on top then season. Lay the remaining *fondo* over the potato, sprinkle with the tomato and almost all the remaining lemon slices — reserve some to dress the fish — and season once more. Place the fish on top of the lemon slices and dress the fish with the reserved lemon slices. Drizzle the white wine and the remaining olive oil over the fish. Bake for 15–20 minutes, or until the fish flakes when tested gently with a fork.

Remove the fish, cover with foil and place near the oven or stovetop to keep warm. Cover the *fondo* with foil and return to the oven for 15 minutes, or until the potato is soft. Make a bed of *fondo* on four warm plates and place a snapper on top of each. Sprinkle with a small pinch of sea salt flakes and serve.

INGREDIENTS

600 ml (21 fl oz) olive oil

500 g (1 lb 2 oz) red onions, very finely sliced

large pinch of fine sea salt

1½ red capsicums (peppers), seeded, membrane removed and very finely sliced

1½ tablespoons Spanish sweet paprika

½ chilli, finely sliced

2 garlic cloves, cut into slivers

600 g (1 lb 5 oz) piece of salt cod, 2–3 cm (¾ –1¼ inch) thick, desalinated (*see page 27*)

1 small handful flat-leaf (Italian) parsley, roughly chopped

RACIÓN 4

BACALAO VIZCAÍNA

COD IN A SUPER RICH SAUCE OF PAPRIKA AND ONIONS

As the Spanish name suggests, this dish hails from Vizcaya, the capital of the Basque country and perhaps the salt cod capital of Spain, if not the world. There they make *bacalao vizcaína* with dried peppers, which are then soaked in water. As they are unavailable in Australia, we have adapted the dish using fresh local capsicum and sweet paprika. We also confit the salt cod in garlic-infused olive oil to enhance the moistness of the dish. The perfect way to cook and serve the cod is in a *cazuela* (see page 34). The rich colour of the terracotta seems to be a suitable match for the deep red and slightly spicy sauce, which holds the succulent morsels of moist fish.

METHOD

Soak a large *cazuela* in cold water for at least 24 hours (the longer the better). Drain and dry before using. Alternatively, use a large flameproof casserole dish.

To make the sauce, heat 100 ml (3¹/₂ fl oz) of the olive oil in a frying pan over low heat (if you are using a casserole dish, heat over low–medium heat). Add the onion and salt and cook, covered, for 15–20 minutes until soft and translucent, stirring occasionally. Add the capsicum, paprika and chilli and cook, covered, for 30 minutes. Add 170 ml (5¹/₂ fl oz/²/₃ cup) water and cook, covered, for 10 minutes, or until pulpy. Preheat the oven to 100°C (200°F/Gas ¹/₂).

Allow the sauce to cool for about 10 minutes, then pour into a food processor and blend for 30 seconds, or until roughly chopped. Pass through a coarse sieve, pushing the vegetable pulp with the back of a spoon until most of the vegetables have passed through. Discard any pieces of vegetables that are too large to pass through. Season to taste.

Heat the remaining olive oil in an ovenproof frying pan over high heat. Fry the garlic slivers for about 20 seconds, or until golden brown then remove from the heat and allow the oil to cool for 5–10 minutes.

Cut the cod into four portions. Do not remove the skin and bones. Carefully place the cod in the oil, skin side up. Cover with foil and bake for 15 minutes.

Remove the cod and drain on paper towel for 1 minute. Arrange the cod in the *cazuela* and pour over enough of the sauce to almost cover the cod. Bring to a simmer on the stovetop over low heat. Cook for 5–10 minutes, gently basting the fish and allowing the sauce to reduce a little. Garnish with parsley. Serve hot.

STORIES OF EASTER — A TIME TO EAT COD

Every year, 10 days after Easter, in my hometown of Córdoba, there is a 2-week festival along the banks of the Guadalquivir River. Hundreds of *casetas* (marquees) are set up and as you walk along they burst into music of all types, from flamenco guitar to dance music, and rock music streaming from the Communist Party *caseta*. The one thing they all have in common is food. Temporary kitchens are set up alongside bars. You are led by your nose around the city as the evening unfolds. People converge and young and old go out to *tapeo* (eat tapas) together. I can still remember the smells and the music from my childhood. When we moved to Australia, there was no celebration at Easter to look forward to, no music and no crowds. My parents even stopped going to church. The one thing we still did was to eat together. Mum made piles of *torrija* (fried bread pudding dusted with cinnamon and honey). She also made fried salt cod and potato fritters. They were so delicious and salty and exactly like the ones in Spain that I was able to ignore the flames of the Geelong refinery and pretend I was back with my aunts along the banks of the Guadalquivir.

INGREDIENTS

500 g (1 lb 2 oz) piece salt cod, 2–3 cm
($3/4$–1$1/4$ inch) thick, desalinated
(*see page 27*)

2 waxy potatoes (about 250–270 g/9–9$1/2$ oz),
unpeeled

3 anchovy fillets

60 ml (2 fl oz/$1/4$ cup) olive oil

1 brown onion, finely diced

2 garlic cloves, finely chopped

1 large handful flat-leaf (Italian) parsley,
sprigged and roughly chopped

80 ml (2$1/2$ fl oz/$1/3$ cup) pouring (whipping)
cream

6 eggs

plain (all-purpose) flour, to coat

oil, for deep-frying

sea salt flakes, to sprinkle

1 teaspoon sweet smoked paprika

TAPAS 24

BUÑUELOS DE BACALAO
SALT COD AND POTATO FRITTERS

This is a recipe we created at MoVida, based on the traditional Basque dish, which is now cooked throughout Spain. Because this is a deep-fried dish made of blended fish and potato, it is perfect for using up the less chunky parts of the cod, or the 'wings'. Break the flesh up with your fingers instead of chopping it so when you bite into the fritter you get little morsels of fish. *Buñuelos* should be light and soft. This comes from the liberal coating of beaten egg that puffs up when they are fried. For me, it is a culinary link back to our family in Spain during Easter.

METHOD

Remove the skin from the salt cod and separate the flesh from the bones. Reserve the skin and bones for making stock (see page 43) and finely shred the salt cod flesh with your fingers.

Boil the potatoes until tender. Drain and set aside to cool. Roughly chop the anchovies then crush them under the flat side of a knife until a paste is formed.

Heat the olive oil in a saucepan over medium heat. Cook the onion and garlic for 8–10 minutes, or until the onion is soft and translucent. Reduce the heat to low–medium, add the anchovies and parsley and cook for 1 minute. Add the salt cod and cook for 3 minutes, breaking it up into small pieces with a wooden spoon.

Using your hands, break up the potatoes into rough cubes. Add to the pan with the cream and cook for 10 minutes, crushing the potatoes thoroughly with the wooden spoon. The mixture should have the consistency of lumpy mash. Allow to cool for 10 minutes, then mix in two of the eggs, one at a time, mixing vigorously. Refrigerate the cod mixture for a few hours. This will help the fritters keep their shape.

Fill a deep-fryer or large heavy-based saucepan one-third full of oil and heat to 170°C (325°F), or until a cube of bread browns in 20 seconds.

Lightly beat the remaining eggs in a shallow bowl. Roll tablespoons of the cooled cod mixture into rough football (rugby) shapes, then dip into the flour, then into the beaten egg. The idea is to get a generous coating of egg clinging to the fritter. Deep-fry, in batches, for about 4 minutes, or until golden. Keep the cooked fritters in a warm oven while you cook the rest. Sprinkle with sea salt and dust with the paprika. Serve hot.

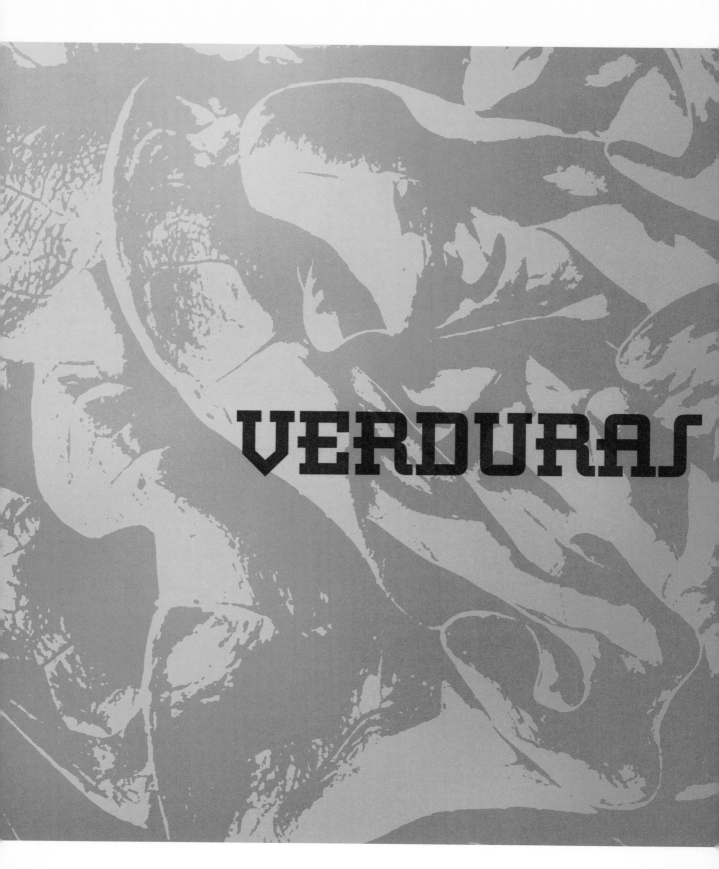

VERDURAS

VERDURAS
VEGETABLES

Perhaps the one thing that impressed me most when I went back to live in Spain was the shopping; particularly shopping for fresh produce. In Australia we have supermarkets with a seemingly never-ending bounty of produce throughout the seasons. In Spain, one of the first things I noticed was the culture of procuring food, which has its roots in an era when Spain was an agrarian society and, as such, reflects the seasons.

Before industrialization, which happened very late in Spain compared with other European countries, many people lived in small towns and villages and worked for the land-owning elite, often picking grapes or olives. *Campesinos* (peasants) would have their *huerto* or little garden in which they would grow many fruits and vegetables for their own kitchen. With such a direct link to food cultivation, the fresh food that arrived on the table was dictated by the seasons. For example, spring was the time for asparagus and autumn was the time for mushrooms. Some years were better than others. A handful of beans may have been flavoured with some cured pork and potatoes spiced up with a fresh herb sauce. The dishes were created from what was growing at the time and what was in the cupboard. Traditional vegetable dishes were cooked longer and the flavours allowed to intermingle 'the way God intended them'.

At MoVida we've taken the traditions of the agrarian-based kitchen but reduced the cooking times and lightened the seasonings. We still, however, believe in using vegetables when they are in season because, as any Spanish housewife will tell you, that is when they will be at their best.

INGREDIENTS

8 large carrots, trimmed and unpeeled

2 tablespoons fennel seeds, roasted and roughly chopped

1 tablespoon dried oregano

1 large handful mint, roughly chopped

juice of 1 lemon

60 ml (2 fl oz/¼ cup) aged sherry vinegar

100 ml (3½ fl oz) extra virgin olive oil

1 teaspoon *ajo y perejil* (*see page 40*)

fine sea salt

MEDIA RACIÓN 4

ZANAHORIAS ALIÑADAS

SPICED CARROT SALAD WITH FENNEL SEED, OREGANO AND MINT

I based this version on the *zanahorias aliñadas* we had in a little town near Ronda, southern Spain. This is a fresh, sharp salad that balances the sweetness of truly ripe carrots and sharpness of sherry vinegar with intermingling layers of spice and herbs. Carrots are at their sweetest after the frosts of winter, which is the perfect season to make this dish, as not only does it make an unassuming appetizer that gets the digestive juices flowing, it is also a cleansing foil for a rich dish like roast pork or braised rabbit.

METHOD

Put the carrots in a large saucepan, cover with cold water and add a pinch of salt. Bring to the boil then reduce the heat and simmer for about 25 minutes, or until they are almost cooked through.

Remove from the heat then drain. Cover the carrots and allow the residual heat to cook them through. When cool enough to handle, peel the carrots by slicing off the skin, lengthways, in five equal strips using a very sharp knife (peel this way so that the carrots have a pentagonal shape when sliced). Cut the carrots into 1 cm (½ inch) thick slices and put them in a bowl.

Combine with the remaining ingredients — except the sea salt — and ¼ teaspoon freshly cracked black pepper and gently mix. Season to taste with the sea salt. Allow to stand for 30 minutes. Serve at room temperature.

oil, for deep-frying

200 g (7 oz) *pimientos de Padrón*

sea salt flakes, to sprinkle

MEDIA RACIÓN 4

PIMIENTOS DE PADRÓN

FRIED PADRÓN PEPPERS

There is a Galician saying, *'Os pimientos de Padrón, uns pican e outros non'*, that roughly translates as 'some Padrón peppers are hot, some are not'. These little peppers look deceptively like diminutive green capsicums. They are deep-fried and served with a little salt, both of which intensify their herbal sweetness. One in ten, however, is blisteringly hot. With the chances of crunching into a hot Padrón so high, eating a plate of these is a bit like playing vegetable Russian roulette. Apart from the excitement of the gamble, the milder *Padróns* have a beautiful intense flavour and a lovely texture, which is between firm and fried. They can be found in major metropolitan markets.

METHOD

Fill a deep-fryer or large heavy-based saucepan one-third full of oil and heat to 180°C (350°F), or until a cube of bread dropped in the oil browns in 15 seconds.

Wipe the peppers clean with a damp cloth. Carefully drop them into the hot oil, in batches, and fry for a minute or so. When done, the smell of hot pepper should fill the air and you will hear a popping sound.

Remove the peppers from the oil and drain on paper towel. Serve on a warm plate and sprinkle over some sea salt flakes.

INGREDIENTS

20 g (¾ oz) butter

1 garlic clove, finely chopped

600 g (1 lb 5 oz) washed and picked English
   spinach leaves

300 g (10½ oz) cooked chickpeas (*see page 16*)

400 ml (14 fl oz) chickpea cooking liquid
   (*see page 16*)

125 g (4½ oz) bread *picada* (*see page 49*)

1½ teaspoons Spanish sweet paprika

1 teaspoon freshly ground cumin
   (*see page 32*)

2 tablespoons sherry vinegar

sea salt flakes, to sprinkle

MEDIA RACIÓN 6

ESPINACAS A LA ANDALUZA

SPINACH AND CHICKPEAS SLOWLY COOKED WITH SPICES AND SHERRY VINEGAR

I learned this dish from my Aunty Pepa in Andalusia. My mum has always made this rich spinach dish, but I suppose I didn't value her cooking until I went back to live in Spain and watched Aunty Pepa pound the cooked chickpeas and add some bread *picada* to thicken the cooking juices. This recipe is packed full of flavour and always makes me feel good after I have eaten it. Sometimes Aunty Pepa added salt cod or poached eggs to the bubbling sauce at the last minute. At MoVida we do a simpler version, which is one of our most popular dishes. We serve hundreds of portions per week, going through tens of kilos of chickpeas and scores of boxes of spinach.

METHOD

Melt the butter in a large frying pan over medium heat. Gently sauté the garlic for 1 minute then add the spinach. Using a pair of tongs, carefully turn the spinach over and over as it cooks until it has wilted down to about half its original volume. This should take about 2 minutes.

Increase the heat to high then add the chickpeas and the chickpea cooking liquid. Using the back of a spoon, crush some of the chickpeas into the spinach to bring out a little of the earthy flavour.

After 5–10 minutes, mix in the bread *picada*, letting it soak up the liquid in the pan. Add the paprika, cumin and a generous pinch of salt and mix well. Season to taste.

Reduce the heat to low and cook for 5 minutes. Add the sherry vinegar and cook for another 5 minutes, allowing the sauce to thicken to a creamy consistency. Sprinkle with sea salt flakes and serve hot.

INGREDIENTS

1 kg (2 lb 4 oz) small kipfler (fingerling) potatoes, unpeeled

20 g (¾ oz) fine sea salt

300 ml (10½ fl oz) *mojo picón* (*see page 46*)

MEDIA RACIÓN 6

PAPAS ARRUGADAS
CANARY ISLANDS SALTED POTATOES

The Canary Islanders are passionate about their *mojo*. Their intense sauces are a vibrant expression of the herbs and produce grown on the islands. *Papas arrugadas* are salty, wrinkled potatoes that also serve as the vessels for scooping the sauce out of the bowl and into your mouth. If you can, find small kipfler potatoes, as these are the best. Their skins shrivel and their rich earthy flavour intensifies upon cooking. This is great barbecue food and brilliant for college parties where you need to cook a lot of food on a budget.

METHOD

Wash and gently scrub the potatoes. Put them in a saucepan, cover them with cold water and add a pinch of salt. Bring to the boil over high heat, then reduce to a gentle simmer and cook for 45 minutes, or until tender.

Drain the potatoes and transfer them to a large frying pan over low–medium heat. Sprinkle with the sea salt. Toss the pan occasionally and cook for approximately 15 minutes. The potatoes will dry and the skin will shrivel up.

To serve, put the potatoes in a bowl and pour the *mojo picón* into another smaller bowl. The idea is to dip the salted potatoes into the *mojo*.

INGREDIENTS

60 ml (2 fl oz/¼ cup) olive oil

500 g (1 lb 2 oz) small portobello mushrooms

80 g (2¾ oz) butter

1 tablespoon chopped thyme leaves

2 tablespoons *ajo y perejil* (*see page 40*)

2 tablespoons sherry vinegar

sea salt flakes

MEDIA RACIÓN 3

SETAS CON VINAGRE DE JEREZ

MUSHROOMS WITH GARLIC AND SHERRY VINEGAR

This is our singularly most popular dish at MoVida. It's an any-time-of-the-day vegetarian recipe that goes perfectly well with beer or red wine. It's surprisingly lively, offers contrasting textures and can be served by itself, as a side to meat dishes or as part of a lazy Sunday morning breakfast.

METHOD

Preheat the oven to 240°C (475°F/Gas 8).

Heat the olive oil over high heat in a large heavy-based, ovenproof frying pan. When the oil is very hot, add the mushrooms, skin side down, and cook, without turning, for 5 minutes. Season with salt. The caps should be well browned and the gills glistening.

Cut the butter into small pieces and add to the pan with the thyme leaves and *ajo y perejil*. Toss the mushrooms around the pan, coating them in the butter.

Put the pan in the oven and roast the mushrooms for 4 minutes. Remove from the oven, toss the mushrooms then return the pan to the oven for 4 minutes. Return the pan to the stovetop and cook briefly over high heat until browned. (This process of roasting and frying ensures that the butter, herbs and garlic cook into the mushrooms, thus enriching the flavour.)

Add the sherry vinegar, season with sea salt flakes and some freshly cracked black pepper and cook for 1 minute to reduce the vinegar. When serving, tilt the pan to allow the oil to drain to one side so as not to serve the mushrooms with too much oil.

INGREDIENTS

4 large nicola potatoes (about 750 g/1 lb 10 oz), unpeeled

2 carrots, unpeeled

4 eggs

1 white salad onion, finely diced

1 teaspoon salt

9 *piquillo* peppers *(see Note)*

100 g (3½ oz) cooked peas

300 g (10½ oz) *alioli*, plus a little extra to serve *(see page 38)*

500 g (1 lb 2 oz) crabmeat, freshly cooked or tinned (drained, if tinned)

150 g (5½ oz) pepper-stuffed olives

MEDIA RACIÓN 8

ENSALADILLA RUSA CON CANGREJO

RUSSIAN SALAD OF POTATO, PEAS, FRESH CRAB, PIQUILLO PEPPER AND MAYONNAISE

Russian salad is served everywhere in Spain, although there was a brief period during our dark fascist past when Franco ordered it to be called *ensaladilla nacional* — a bit like the Americans calling French fries 'freedom fries'. Potatoes form the starchy base of this dish but in reality it is all about the piquant salty highlights of peppers, olives, garlic mayonnaise and luxurious crab. The other interesting thing to note is just how pragmatic its preparation really is. Based on home cooking, it reflects a simpler past when the Spaniards were less affluent and everything was cooked in the one pot.

METHOD

If necessary, clean the potatoes. Put them with the carrots and eggs in a large saucepan of cold water over high heat and bring to the boil. After 3 minutes on the boil remove the eggs. Boil the potatoes and carrots for a further 35 minutes, or until cooked. Test with a skewer — they should be tender but not too soft. Drain the vegetables and set aside until cool enough to handle. Peel the potatoes and carrots, and shell the eggs.

Dice the potato into 1 cm (½ inch) cubes. Don't be too neat as the rough bits help to absorb the flavour and will break off into the *alioli* to make a nice starchy sauce. Dice the carrot into similar but neater cubes. Put the carrot and potato into a bowl and immediately add the onion, to allow the residual heat of the potato and carrot to soften the onion.

Season the vegetables so they soak up the salt before the *alioli* is added. Roughly chop eight of the *piquillo* peppers and add to the bowl. Add the peas.

Add the *alioli* and stir through the vegetables, working gently to make a sauce without turning the whole thing into mash. Gently mix in most of the crabmeat, reserving some for

decoration. Slice the olives, reserving a few slices for garnish, and mix the rest into the sauce. Roughly chop the egg whites from three of the eggs and slice the egg white of the fourth egg. (Reserve the yolks for another dish: put the yolks in a small bowl, cover with plastic wrap and store in the refrigerator — they should keep for 3 days.) Add the chopped egg white to the mixture.

Now is a good chance to practice your culinary decorative arts, circa 1972. Put the salad into a serving bowl and smooth over the top with the back of a spoon. Dollop a little extra *alioli* on top and spread it around to create a thin layer.

Slice the remaining *piquillo* pepper. Decorate the salad with the sliced egg white, *piquillo* pepper slices and the reserved olives and crabmeat.

Note: *Piquillo* peppers (*pimientos del piquillo*) are literally 'little peppers' originating from Navarra. They are usually hickory smoked then peeled by hand and packed in a jar with their cooking juices.

INGREDIENTS

600 g (1 lb 5 oz) broad (fava) beans, shelled

100 g (3½ oz) Iberian *jamón*, with fat
  (*see page 20*)

60 ml (2 fl oz/¼ cup) extra virgin olive oil

1 brown onion, finely diced

2 garlic cloves, finely chopped

2 tablespoons finely chopped mint

sea salt flakes

MEDIA RACIÓN 4

HABAS CON JAMÓN

BRAISED BROAD BEANS WITH HAM AND MINT

This is a modern version of a traditional dish that slow cooks *jamón* and fresh broad beans, with the outer skin of the beans left on. I've lightened the dish a little for the modern palate by skinning the broad beans first. A friend of mine who grows his own broad beans picks them very early and uses the sweet beans whole. Buy *jamón* with a good layer of fat, as this renders down to make a rich dressing. You can omit it for health reasons but you will sacrifice the flavour.

METHOD

Blanch the beans by dropping them into a large saucepan of boiling water for 1 minute. Remove the beans and refresh in chilled water. Remove the outer skins by pinching the skin off one end and gently squeezing out the inner beans. Discard the skins. Put the beans in a bowl and cover with a tea towel (dish towel).

Remove the outer layer of fat from the *jamón* and finely chop. Finely chop the lean *jamón*. (Keep the *jamón* fat and the lean *jamón* separate.) Gently heat the *jamón* fat and the extra virgin olive oil in a sauce-pan over low–medium heat for 1 minute, stirring occasionally. Do not fry the fat, as this will change its flavour.

Add the onion and garlic and cook for 5–10 minutes, or until soft and translucent. Reduce the heat to low, add the lean *jamón* and warm through. Add the broad beans, cover and gently cook for 5 minutes.

Remove from the heat and fold through the mint. Season to taste with sea salt, if necessary. Serve warm.

ESCALIVADA

CHARGRILLED LEEK AND PEPPER SALAD WITH ROMESCO SAUCE

During the ninth-century siege of Barcelona, Wilfred the Hairy, Count of Barcelona, lay dying. As a mark of respect, his comrade, King Charles the Bald of Aragon, ran his hand across Wilfred's wound and dragged his blood-drenched fingers across Wilfred's golden shield. From that moment, this image became the flag of the Kingdom of Aragon and later that of the Province of Catalán. Or so the story goes …

Escalivada, a purely vegetarian dish, celebrates this bloody myth with long red strips of roasted capsicum and golden pieces of roasted leek and eggplant. *Escalivada* means 'charred' and it is traditionally cooked in a wood-fired oven. Dressed with the rich garlicky cooking juices, it is served at room temperature. James, my sous chef, maintains that this is his favourite dish. He espouses the reward in laying out the vegetables and takes pride in sending out such a beautiful, but simple, dish.

INGREDIENTS

3 leeks, trimmed, washed and halved
   lengthways

2 large eggplant (aubergine), about 500 g
   (1 lb 2 oz) each

3 red capsicums (peppers)

2 garlic bulbs

olive oil, to drizzle

fine sea salt, to sprinkle

sea salt flakes, to sprinkle

1 tablespoon extra virgin olive oil

200 ml (7 fl oz) *salsa romesco* (*see page 52*)

MEDIA RACIÓN 6

METHOD

Preheat the oven to 250°C (500°F/Gas 9).

   Arrange the vegetables in a large roasting tin with a little space around them, putting the garlic bulbs in the centre of the tin. (If all the vegetables don't fit into one you may like to make up two tins and cook them separately.) Drizzle the vegetables with olive oil, sprinkle with the fine sea salt and cook for 35 minutes, turning every 15 minutes or so, until the skins are blackened and the vegetables are very tender. The idea is to get as much colour and smoky flavour without burning the flesh.

   Once cooked, remove the tin from the oven and cover tightly with plastic wrap. Set aside until the vegetables are cool enough to handle.

   Remove the outer layers of the leek and discard. Cut the rest of the leek, lengthways, into 1 cm (½ inch) strips. Carefully remove and discard the skin of the eggplant. Strip off the flesh into 1 cm (½ inch) wide strips following the length of the eggplant. Cut the end off each garlic bulb, about 1 cm (½ inch) from the point then carefully squeeze out the garlic — try to keep the clove shape. Peel and discard the skin from the capsicums. Remove and discard the stalk, seeds and membrane and cut the flesh into 1 cm (½ inch) wide strips. Reserve 1 tablespoon of the cooking juices from the tin.

   Place the vegetables in neat alternating strips on a serving plate. Place the garlic on the side of the dish. Sprinkle with sea salt flakes. Make a dressing by mixing the extra virgin olive oil with the reserved cooking juices and pour over the vegetables. Finally, top with small mounds of *romesco* sauce.

INGREDIENTS

10 red capsicums (peppers)

2 large brown onions, unpeeled

2 garlic bulbs

olive oil, to drizzle

8 tomatoes, peeled, seeded and cut into wedges (*see page 33*)

1 handful flat-leaf (Italian) parsley, chopped

100 ml (3½ fl oz) extra virgin olive oil

150 ml (5 fl oz) sherry vinegar

1 tablespoon freshly ground cumin (*see page 32*)

several pinches of sea salt flakes

MEDIA RACIÓN 8

ASADILLO

ROASTED CAPSICUM AND TOMATO SALAD WITH CUMIN AND SHERRY VINEGAR

Asadillo has been with MoVida since the first day we opened in the old pub in West Melbourne. It is a bright refreshing salad of velvety red roasted capsicum, served with softened tomatoes and a spicy cumin dressing. It can either be served warm shortly after the capsicums have been roasted, or stored in the refrigerator for a few days, where the flavours will further develop.

METHOD

Preheat the oven to 200°C (400°F/Gas 6).

Put the capsicums, onions and garlic in a large roasting tin, sprinkle with salt and drizzle with olive oil. Roast the vegetables for 50 minutes. The capsicums are ready when they are soft and a little browned. Remove the capsicums and garlic, put in a bowl and pour over the cooking juices. Return the onions to the oven and cook for a further 30 minutes, or until very soft.

When the capsicums are just cool enough to handle, remove and reserve the skins, seeds and cooking juices together in a bowl. Break up the capsicum flesh into broad strips and put in a separate bowl. Cut off the tops of the garlic bulbs and squeeze out the now paste-like interior into the bowl with the capsicum flesh. Add the tomato to the bowl and mix through, letting the residual warmth from the capsicum soften the tomato just a little.

When the onions are ready, remove them from the oven and set aside until cool enough to handle. Remove and discard the skin. Cut the onions into rough wedges and mix through the capsicum and tomato mixture.

Strain 100 ml (3½ fl oz) of the reserved cooking juices (discarding the solids and the rest of the juice) and add to the salad with the remaining ingredients. Mix thoroughly.

Serve immediately or refrigerate. If refrigerating, allow the salad to reach room temperature before serving.

INGREDIENTS

60 ml (2 fl oz/¼ cup) extra virgin olive oil

1 brown onion, cut into large wedges

fine sea salt, to sprinkle

3 bay leaves

1 red capsicum (pepper), seeded, membrane removed and cut into 1 cm (½ inch) thick slices

1 green capsicum (pepper), seeded, membrane removed and cut into 1 cm (½ inch) thick slices

½ garlic bulb, skin on but broken into cloves

1 kg (2 lb 4 oz) waxy potatoes, such as nicola or kipfler (fingerling), cut into 5–8 mm (¼–⅜ inch) thick slices

750 ml (26 fl oz/3 cups) olive oil (you may not need all the oil)

1½ tablespoons *ajo y perejil* (*see page 40*)

MEDIA RACIÓN 4

PATATAS A LO POBRE

SLOW-COOKED POTATOES WITH ONION AND CAPSICUM

It is said that *patatas a lo pobre* take as long to cook as the time it takes for a farm wife to put the pot on the stove and walk the kilometre or so to the fields to tell the men that dinner is ready and then walk back. Based on peasant cooking, *patatas a lo pobre* — poor men's potatoes — has a rich flavour with the earthiness of the potatoes, freshened with the capsicums and the fruitiness of olive oil. It is very rustic and filling so you don't need to serve much. The key to this dish is to make sure all the ingredients are roughly the same size when they go into the pot so everything cooks evenly.

METHOD

Heat the extra virgin olive oil in a large saucepan over high heat. Add the onion and sprinkle with fine sea salt. Add the bay leaves and stir. Reduce the heat to low–medium, cover and cook for 5 minutes.

Once the onion is soft, add the capsicum and garlic and cover. Cook for 20 minutes, or until soft, stirring occasionally. Add the potato and enough olive oil to cover the vegetables and increase the heat to high. The idea is to confit (see Note on page 115) the vegetables gently at just below boiling point. When small bubbles appear reduce the heat to low–medium. Cook gently for about 1 hour, or until tender.

Gently lift out the vegetables with a slotted spoon. The oil can be strained and used another three or four times to confit other dishes in this book.

While the vegetables are cooking preheat the oven to 220°C (475°F/Gas 8). Spread out the vegetables on a large baking tray and season with a little sea salt and the *ajo y perejil*. Cook in the oven for 30 minutes until the edges of the potatoes are a little crispy.

WHAT IS MOVIDA?

There's a guy with a spray can finishing off another piece of graffiti art on the wall opposite the restaurant. To some, it's a scourge. To me, looking out from the kitchen, across the bar and dining room, it's the ever-changing backdrop for what we do here at our little place in the city of Melbourne. We like it. It keeps away the culinary 'tyre kickers' and helps to define who we are. We're not 'Get 'em in, feed 'em three courses and get 'em out — Next!' We're a bar and restaurant that serves tapas and good wine. It's a pretty simple concept. We've taken the essence of the Spanish tapas dining experience, which is in turn based on centuries of traditional family cooking, and translated it into a context that suits modern Melbourne.

ARROZ

ARROZ
RICE

There's a preconception that Spanish rice is festival food, the grain to use in a Costa del Sol paella, which goes hand in hand with the stereotype of sand, sun and sangría. You can have as many prawns and lobsters in your paella as you want, but unless the rice is cooked properly, it is not a proper paella.

Rice, and Spanish rice in particular, are simple grains that require nurturing throughout the cooking process. The rice should absorb the flavours of the other ingredients without being overwhelmed by them. To put it basically — you need to be able to taste the rice.

The paella we make at MoVida is traditional, made to order using Calasparra rice. We also cook the rice in a way that allows each grain to retain a toothsome integrity and which also creates a wonderfully crispy base.

Traditionally, a paella is cooked over a bed of coals, which ensures even cooking all over. Most home cooks, unless they have a large burner, will need to move the paella around on the stovetop during cooking to simulate this even cooking. Rice needs to be cooked in increments, adjusting heat, stirring and seasoning. It's not something that you can set and forget.

Don't be alarmed when you make a paella to find a crispy, darkened crust cooked on the bottom, known as the *socorat*. This crust is an essential part of great paella. The crust adds a smoky quality to the dish, and can be eaten as well. It may sound a little strange getting an instruction to slightly burn the bottom, but remember your first experience with *al dente* pasta — the idea of slightly undercooking the pasta didn't sound that appetizing but once you became familiar with it and tasted the result, it all made sense.

Perhaps, before we go on, we should learn one little Spanish word — *reposar*. It means to let rest or repose. And that's what we let our rice dishes do before serving them. Allow them time to relax, for the rice to finish cooking and the flavours to mingle and unfold. Perhaps a lesson that we could learn from those humble little grains.

INGREDIENTS

1.5 kg (3 lb 5 oz) farmed white rabbit

6 garlic cloves, unpeeled

3 rosemary sprigs

about 1.5 litres (52 fl oz/6 cups) olive oil

200 g (7 oz) mussels

12 raw king prawns (shrimp)

60 ml (2 fl oz/¼ cup) extra virgin olive oil

pinch of saffron threads

1 tablespoon thyme leaves, chopped

1 teaspoon chopped rosemary

2 garlic cloves, extra, finely chopped

400 g (14 oz) Calasparra rice

250 g (9 oz/1 cup) *sofrito* *(see page 51)*

125 ml (4 fl oz/½ cup) dry white wine

1.25 litres (44 fl oz/5 cups) hot fish stock
   (see page 43)

600 g (1 lb 5 oz) periwinkles or snails, rinsed
   (optional) *(see Note)*

200 g (7 oz) firm-fleshed fish such as marlin,
   swordfish or tuna, cut into 2.5 cm (1 inch)
   pieces

100 g (3½ oz) cleaned squid, cut into 5 mm
   (¼ inch) strips

185 g (6½ oz/1 cup) green beans, broad (fava)
   beans or peas (optional)

2 tablespoons chopped flat-leaf (Italian)
   parsley, to garnish

2 lemons, halved

RACIÓN 4-6

PAELLA DEL MOVIDA
MOVIDA PAELLA

Traditional paella is an outdoor dish. It is customary in Spain for men, rather than women, to make paella. (We can imagine a Gender Studies essay topic as: 'The Spanish paella and the Australian barbecue: compare and discuss the male role in each'.)

I have great memories of outdoor paellas cooked in Spain over a dying fire on the edge of the forest. We used rice from a sack, a few onions and tomatoes, with the addition of some wildlife gleaned from the hills, such as wild snails and pieces of freshly shot rabbit.

For this version we have replaced the snails with periwinkles and are cooking on a stovetop in the kitchen. But I know a lot of adventurous cooks who will make their own bed of coals. A word of warning — make sure the paella is perfectly flat and level on the coals, otherwise the liquid will run to one side and cook only one half of the paella, leaving the other side high and dry.

METHOD

Preheat the oven to 140°C (275°F/Gas 1).

Cut the rabbit into 12 pieces — cut the hind legs into two pieces, leave the front legs of the rabbit whole and leave the saddles attached at the backbone, but cut in a cross section into six pieces.

Confit the rabbit by laying the pieces flat in a deep roasting tin, which is just large enough to comfortably fit the rabbit pieces in a single layer. Lay the garlic cloves and rosemary sprigs on top. Cover with the olive oil. You may need more or less oil, depending on your roasting tin. Bake slowly for 2½–3 hours. Cooking time will depend on the rabbit (farmed rabbit will cook faster than wild rabbit). The rabbit is done when the flesh comes away easily from the bone. Remove the rabbit from the oil and drain on paper towel.

Scrub the mussels and pull out the hairy beards. Rinse well and drain. Discard any broken mussels, or open ones that don't close when tapped on the bench. Cover with a damp cloth and refrigerate until ready to use. Make a shallow cut with a very sharp small knife along the length of each prawn back. Remove and discard the dark vein and shell, leaving on the head and tail.

To make the paella, heat the extra virgin olive oil in a 34 cm (13½ inch) paella pan or large, deep, heavy-based frying pan over medium heat. Add the saffron, thyme, rosemary and chopped garlic, and stir for 1 minute to release the flavour from the herbs and spices. Add the rice and season with two pinches of salt. Stir thoroughly to coat the rice and cook for a few minutes until the rice is slightly translucent around the edges. Add the *sofrito* and stir it through the rice. Cook for a minute or so to allow the flavours to meld. Add the wine and stir it through for a brief moment. Next add the hot fish stock and stir through. Increase the heat to medium–high and bring to the boil.

From this point onwards, do not stir the paella, as the *socorat* (crust) needs to form on the bottom of the pan. If the flame or element doesn't cover the base of the pan, move the pan around during cooking to allow the paella to cook evenly.

Once the paella is boiling add the rabbit, placing the pieces evenly around the pan. After 3 minutes add the periwinkles, if using, in between the pieces of rabbit. After another 5 minutes place the fish pieces and squid on top of the rice.

By now the rice will have expanded a little so reduce the heat to medium. Continue to move the pan around during cooking to allow the paella to cook evenly.

When the majority of the stock has been absorbed and small holes appear between the rice (this will take about 10 minutes), place the prawns on top and allow the escaping steam to gently cook them. Cook for 5 minutes, or until the prawns are just pink then turn to cook the other side. Add the broad beans or peas, if using. After 5 minutes, remove from the heat and cover the pan with foil so that any remaining stock is absorbed and the rice separates a little.

Meanwhile, quickly cook the mussels by bringing 100 ml (3½ fl oz) water to the boil in a shallow saucepan. Add the mussels, cover and bring the water back to the boil. Cook for 3–4 minutes. Remove from the heat and discard any unopened mussels. Drain well and place on top of the paella. Garnish with the chopped parsley and serve with lemon wedges.

Note: Periwinkles, conical, spiral-shelled molluscs, are available fresh from Asian markets or good fishmongers.

INGREDIENTS

60 ml (2 fl oz/¼ cup) olive oil

1 brown onion, finely diced

6 garlic cloves, finely chopped

200 g (7 oz) shiitake mushrooms, sliced

200 g (7 oz) enoki mushrooms, trimmed

200 g (7 oz) oyster mushrooms, sliced

200 g (7 oz) portobello mushrooms, sliced

2 tablespoons thyme leaves, chopped

several pinches of fine sea salt

6 tomatoes, peeled, seeded and finely chopped *(see page 33)*

400 g (14 oz) Calasparra rice

1.25 litres (44 fl oz/5 cups) hot vegetable stock *(see page 45)*

1 handful flat-leaf (Italian) parsley, chopped

RACIÓN 4–6

ARROZ CON SETAS
WILD MUSHROOM RICE

I look forward to driving to the country after the first rains of autumn. The wet soil, still warm from summer, bursts into life. Moss swells and returns to its verdant green colour, the air is sweet with the smell of wet earth and, under trees and in open fields, thousands of mushrooms erupt from the earth — pine mushrooms, slippery jacks and flavoursome field mushrooms.

This recipe was originally made with pork but we have removed the meat because good mushrooms have an earthy sweetness of their own. At home, I use wild mushrooms but for this recipe we have included mushrooms available from the market. Feel free to substitute with wild mushrooms that you know are safe to eat.

METHOD

Soak a 30 cm (12 inch) *cazuela* (see page 34) in cold water for at least 24 hours (the longer the better). Drain and dry before using. Heat the *cazuela* over low heat for 5 minutes. Add the olive oil, onion and half of the chopped garlic and cook for 10–15 minutes until the onion is lightly golden.

Add the mushrooms and thyme and fine sea salt. Mix through, cover, increase the heat to medium and continue cooking for 5–10 minutes until the mushrooms have softened and wilted and reduced to about one-quarter of their original volume. Add the tomato, gently mix through and cook for 5 minutes to soften.

Add the rice and stir it through the vegetables. Cook for 2 minutes, or until the rice just starts to become translucent. Pour in 1 litre (35 fl oz/4 cups) of the hot vegetable stock and stir for 10 seconds, or until well mixed and then bring to the boil.

From this point onwards, do not stir the rice, as a the *socorat* (crust) needs to form on the bottom of the *cazuela*. If the flame or element doesn't cover the base of the *cazuela*, move the *cazuela* around during cooking to allow the rice to cook evenly.

Meanwhile, make a little *picada* by grinding the remaining chopped garlic with the parsley, using a mortar and pestle. Alternatively, chop them together until very fine.

After the rice has been boiling for 10 minutes mix the *picada* through the rice. Season to taste with salt, if necessary. Reduce the heat to low—medium and cook gently for another 10 minutes until the rice is cooked. Remove from the heat, cover with a clean tea towel (dish towel) and allow to rest for 10 minutes until all the liquid has been absorbed and the grains have separated a little. Serve the rice warm.

ARROZ CON PULPO
OCTOPUS PAELLA

This is the essence of simplicity and contrast. The sweetness of the octopus flesh is a foil for the earthiness of the rice. The lovely rich, soft gelatinous texture of the octopus is also a counterpoint for the rice's starchiness.

This is the antithesis of over-accessorised paella, which is loaded with chorizo and shellfish. It's just octopus, rice, garlic, *sofrito* and paprika. Because of its textural qualities, this dish is also well worth cooking simply to explore wine matching possibilities. Friends of mine tried this with *albariño*, arneis, Australian chenin blanc and a little Pouilly Fume. They couldn't make up their minds, so met again a week later to try again.

INGREDIENTS

1 kg (2 lb 4 oz) octopus tentacles (about 2 or 3 tentacles), frozen, thawed and drained (see *Note*)

60 ml (2 fl oz/¼ cup) olive oil

2 garlic cloves, finely chopped

250 g (9 oz/1 cup) *sofrito* (*see page 51*)

400 g (14 oz) Calasparra rice

1 handful flat-leaf (Italian) parsley, chopped

1 tablespoon Spanish sweet paprika

sea salt flakes, to sprinkle

RACIÓN 4–6

METHOD

To cook the octopus, bring a large saucepan of unsalted water to the boil. Meanwhile, rinse the octopus under cold running water. When the water is rapidly boiling, plunge the octopus in for 15 seconds then remove. Allow the water to boil again then repeat the process four times, allowing the water to reach the boil again between each plunge. After the last plunge reduce the heat and leave the octopus on a very low, slow simmer for 30–40 minutes. The octopus should be tender and the outside pink layer still intact. Carefully remove the octopus from the water, allow to cool, drain and cut into 1 cm (½ inch) slices. Reserve approximately 1 litre (35 fl oz/4 cups) of the octopus stock over low heat, as it will be used to make the paella.

Heat the olive oil in a 34 cm (13½ inch) paella pan or large, deep, heavy-based frying pan over medium heat. Sauté the garlic for 30 seconds then add the *sofrito* and cook for a further minute. Reduce the heat to low–medium.

Add the rice and mix to coat the rice with the sauce. Cook for 2 minutes, or until the rice just starts to become translucent. Gradually stir in the reserved octopus stock and increase the heat to medium. From this point onwards, do not stir the paella, as a the *socorat* (crust) needs to form on the bottom of the pan. If the flame or element doesn't cover the base of the pan, move the pan around during cooking to allow the paella to cook evenly. Cook for 10 minutes, or until the rice has swollen just a little. Reduce the heat to low–medium and arrange the octopus slices around the top of the paella. Sprinkle with the parsley and paprika.

Cook for a further 10 minutes then increase the heat to high for 1 minute to form a crust on the bottom of the pan. Remove from the heat, cover with a clean tea towel (dish towel) and allow to rest. Sprinkle with sea salt flakes and serve warm.

Note: During freezing, the ice crystals break apart the cell walls and this makes the octopus more tender.

INGREDIENTS

500 g (1 lb 2 oz) baby clams (vongole)

125 ml (4 fl oz/½ cup) olive oil

4 scampi, halved lengthways and cleaned

4 raw king prawns (shrimp)

sea salt flakes

250 g (9 oz) marlin or swordfish, cut into
2.5 cm (1 inch) cubes

150 g (5½ oz) cuttlefish, cleaned and cut into
2.5 cm (1 inch) squares

300 g (10½ oz) *sofrito* (*see page 51*)

1.5 litres (52 fl oz/6 cups) hot fish stock
(*see page 43*)

250 g (9 oz) Calasparra rice

30 g (1 oz) blanched almonds, roasted
(*see page 14*)

pinch of saffron threads

1 small handful flat-leaf (Italian) parsley,
roughly chopped

RACIÓN 4

ARROZ CALDOSO

WET RICE WITH SEAFOOD AND SAFFRON

Paella may be the world famous Spanish rice dish but it is not generally cooked in the family kitchen. It is cooked out in the open or ordered in a restaurant. Spanish homes are not large as a rule and domestic kitchens don't have the burner size to attempt a proper paella. Instead they cook slightly soupier dishes — simply called *arroz*. I found myself explaining this particular version to the staff one day and was scratching my head trying to find an Australian comparison. 'It's fast to make and it's comfort food', I explained. 'It's a family favourite, the Aussie version would be ...' I was struggling for words. 'Bangers and mash!', shouted Andy from the bar. He gets it right everytime.

In this recipe, the flavour of saffron and the addition of prawn shells makes a lovely rich dish that is both fulfilling to eat and rewarding to share. Dig in.

METHOD

Soak the clams in cold water for 2 hours to remove the grit from inside the shells, changing the water several times. Drain well. Make a shallow cut with a very sharp small knife along the length of each prawn back. Remove and discard the dark vein, leaving the head, shell and tail intact.

Heat 60 ml (2 fl oz/¼ cup) of the olive oil in a *perol* (see page 34) or large heavy-based saucepan over high heat. Add the scampi, shell side down, and cook for about 3 minutes. Turn the scampi over then add the prawns. Season with freshly ground black pepper and sea salt flakes. After 2 minutes, remove the scampi, set aside and turn the prawns over. Season again and cook the prawns for 2 minutes. Remove and set aside.

Add the marlin to the *perol* and cook each side for about 45 seconds, or until sealed. Lightly season each side as you cook. Once all the sides are sealed, remove and set aside with the other seafood. Add the cuttlefish to the *perol* and cook for 45–60 seconds, or until sealed. Lightly season and cook the other side. Remove and set aside.

Drain the oil and wipe the *perol* clean with paper towel. Heat the remaining oil in the *perol* over medium heat. Add the *sofrito* and cook for 1 minute, stirring continuously.

Increase the heat to high and add about 250 ml (9 fl oz/1 cup) of hot stock. Allow it to come to the boil for 5 minutes to reduce the liquid and intensify the flavour. Repeat with another 250 ml (9 fl oz/1 cup) of hot stock then add the remaining stock. Bring to the boil then reduce the heat to medium and bring to a simmer. Sprinkle the rice over the stock and stir in.

Meanwhile, make a little *picada* by pounding the almonds and the saffron together using a mortar and pestle until the almonds are quite fine. Add a little of the hot stock from the *perol* to the mortar and stir in well to release the flavour of the saffron. Add the *picada* to the simmering *perol* and mix in well. Once the rice has been simmering for 5 minutes, add the cuttlefish and marlin and stir in. Season to taste with salt, if necessary. After 5 more minutes add the clams and stir through.

Continue simmering for 10 minutes until the rice is just cooked but still with a little resistance to the tooth. Stir in the parsley then add the prawns and scampi. Season to taste. Bring back to simmering point then serve immediately.

Bring the *perol* to the table and allow people to serve themselves.

INGREDIENTS

125 ml (4 fl oz/½ cup) olive oil

500 g (1 lb 2 oz) cuttlefish or calamari, cleaned and cut into 2.5 cm (1 inch) squares

1 brown onion, finely diced

2 garlic cloves, finely chopped

1 heaped teaspoon cuttlefish ink

5 tomatoes, peeled, seeded and diced (*see page 33*)

200 ml (7 fl oz) dry white wine

400 g (14 oz) Calasparra rice

1.25 litres (44 fl oz/5 cups) hot fish stock (*see page 43*)

RACIÓN 4-6

ARROZ NEGRO
CUTTLEFISH PAELLA WITH INK AND WHITE WINE

I have an image burned into my brain of the hellish sight of scores of gas burners cooking scores of paella in Restaurante de Arroz — a special paella house in Alicante. There, paella are made to order but instead of making the *sofrito* from scratch they have hundreds of paella pans filled with ready-made *sofrito* lined up like pizza bases in a pizza restaurant. It was here that we had an *arroz negro*. It's a rich dish of cuttlefish in black rice, which has been flavoured and coloured by the cuttlefish ink. Cuttlefish ink is available from fishmongers and speciality food stores.

METHOD

Heat 60 ml (2 fl oz/¼ cup) of the oil in a paella pan or large, deep, heavy-based saucepan over high heat. Seal the cuttlefish, in batches, by cooking it for about 1 minute each side. Season each side while cooking. Remove and cover with foil. Discard the oil.

In the same paella pan heat the remaining oil over medium heat. Add the onion and garlic and sauté for a few minutes, then reduce the heat to low–medium and cook for 5 minutes until the onion is soft and translucent. Add the cuttlefish ink and mix well. Add the tomato and cook for 5 minutes to soften slightly then add the white wine. Continue cooking for about 15 minutes, until the mixture has reduced to a thick paste. Increase the heat to medium and add the rice, stirring well to coat it in the paste. Cook for 2 minutes, stirring continuously, until the rice just starts to become translucent.

Pour in the hot fish stock and mix well. Increase the heat to high, bring to the boil then reduce the heat to medium. If the flame or element doesn't cover the base of the pan, move the pan around during cooking to ensure an even cooking. Place the cuttlefish on top of the rice and cook for 10 minutes.

By now the rice will have expanded a little so reduce the heat to low–medium. Cook for 10 minutes. Just before removing from the stove, increase the heat to high and cook for 1 minute to help form the *socorat* (crust) on the bottom of the pan. Remove from the heat and cover with a clean tea towel (dish towel) for 10 minutes before serving warm.

ARROZ DE PEROL
WET RICE WITH CHICKEN

It's not just paella that is the man's domain. In Spain, many rice dishes are cooked by men. When we were visiting my Aunt Carmen in Córdoba, she took us up to the hills with her boyfriend, Isidro. It's fascinating to watch the ritual that the casual male cook makes of cooking. I suppose it's half to do with putting on a show and half remembering what comes next. Isidro made a little fire and let it burn down, adjusting the wood and eventually the coals. He carefully browned the rabbit pieces, slowly made the *sofrito* in the *perol* and, with understated flair, half dropped, half flung the rice into the *perol* (see page 34) like a peasant farmer scattering seed. Waiting for a meal to cook in the open air only intensifies hunger and this rich, vibrant, creamy *perol* with chunks of browned meat and flashes of green beans was one of the best I've ever eaten. *Perols* can be purchased from Spanish shops but a large round-sided pot is a perfect substitute.

INGREDIENTS

1.6 kg (3 lb 8 oz) chicken or rabbit, cut into 12 pieces *(see Note)*

fine sea salt

80 ml (2½ fl oz/⅓ cup) olive oil

1 brown onion, finely diced

1 red capsicum (pepper), seeded, membrane removed and finely diced

1 green capsicum (pepper), seeded, membrane removed and finely diced

4 tomatoes, peeled, seeded and finely chopped *(see page 33)*

1.5 litres (52 fl oz/6 cups) hot chicken stock *(see page 42)*

300 g (10½ oz) Calasparra rice

pinch of saffron threads

½ teaspoon Spanish sweet paprika

½ teaspoon thyme

½ teaspoon black peppercorns

4 garlic cloves

200 g (7 oz) green flat beans, cut into 3 cm (1¼ inch) lengths

RACIÓN 4-6

METHOD

Thoroughly season the chicken with fine sea salt and freshly ground black pepper.

Heat the olive oil in a *perol* or large, round-sided pot over high heat. Add the chicken pieces, reduce the heat to medium and cook for 4 minutes each side, or until browned. Remove and cover.

Add the onion and capsicum and sauté for 5–10 minutes, stirring frequently, until the onion has softened. Add the tomato, stir through and cook for 15 minutes, or until pulpy, stirring occasionally. Return the chicken to the *perol* and pour in the hot stock. Increase the heat to high, bring to the boil then reduce the heat and simmer for 40 minutes until the stock has reduced by about a third. Add the rice and stir through. Continue cooking for 5 minutes.

Meanwhile, crush the saffron threads with the paprika, thyme, peppercorns and garlic using a mortar and pestle until the peppercorns are well crushed. Add a few tablespoons of hot stock from the *perol* and mix well. Add the spice mix to the rice and stir through.

Add the beans to the *perol* and continue to cook for 15–20 minutes, or until the rice is just tender and the chicken well cooked. Season to taste with salt. Remove from the heat and serve immediately.

Note: If using rabbit, see page 198 for cutting instructions and increase cooking time accordingly.

Nº 559718 G
ARROZ "CALASPARRA"
DENOMINACION DE ORIGEN
Cooperativa del Campo
VIRGEN DE LA ESPERANZA
1 Kilo
PARRA (Murcia

CALASPARRA
DENOMINACION
1 Kilo
CALASPARRA (Mur
Cooperativa
"VIRGEN DE LA
CALASPARRA

ARTISINAL TABLEWARE

To think about a plate of food in a restaurant involves deep consideration for the customer. Perfecting the recipe is a major part of the process but serving wonderful food on bad crockery is disrespectful to the food, the kitchen and the customer.

From day one, we wanted to embrace the rustic simplicity of Spanish earthenware in the Australian context. I became friends with a local Melbourne ceramicist, who is also a very good landscaper. His understanding of form, of the way people use the space around them, and sympathetic consciousness of the palette of the Australian landscape allowed him to develop our stoneware plates, pitchers and bowls. They are the understated, beautiful and practical base of the hundreds of different dishes we make at MoVida.

ARROZ A BANDA
PAELLA WITH FISH IN TWO ACTS

While some dishes are based on regional produce and others on seasonal bounty, I believe this dish has its roots in the Spanish national characteristic of impatience. *Arroz a banda* is a way of making the fish stock for the paella and having beautifully poached fish ready to eat while the paella is cooking.

Ask your fishmonger to clean, scale and remove the fins from the fish. We use whole cleaned fish but large rockling and monkfish fillets can be used where available.

METHOD

Rinse the fish and pat dry with paper towel. Season the inside of each whole fish with a little salt.

Heat half of the oil in a large heavy-based saucepan over medium heat and cook the onion, tomato and half of the garlic for about 15 minutes, or until the onion is soft and translucent, stirring occasionally. Place the whole fish and fish fillet on the onion and tomato and add the stock, making sure most of the fish is covered. Add more water if necessary to cover them. Season the stock with a little salt and add the bay leaves.

When the stock begins to boil, reduce to a gentle simmer (it should be barely simmering, if at all). Gently poach the fish for 20 minutes, or until the fish is cooked through then remove, cover with foil and keep warm.

INGREDIENTJ

600 g (1 lb 5 oz) cleaned whole snapper

400 g (14 oz) cleaned whole red mullet

500 g (1 lb 2 oz) skinless firm white fish fillet,
    such as skate

60 ml (2 fl oz/¼ cup) olive oil

2 brown onions, diced

8 tomatoes, peeled, seeded and diced
    (*see page 33*)

8 garlic cloves, sliced

1.25 litres (44 fl oz/5 cups) fish stock
    (*see page 43*)

3 bay leaves

1 tablespoon Spanish sweet paprika

300 g (10½ oz) *sofrito* (*see page 51*)

500 g (1 lb 2 oz) Calasparra rice

pinch of saffron threads

1 handful flat-leaf (Italian) parsley

fine sea salt

1 handful flat-leaf (Italian) parsley, extra,
    roughly chopped

200 g (7 oz) *alioli* (*see page 38*)

RACIÓN 6

In a paella pan or large, deep frying pan, fry the remaining garlic in the rest of the olive oil over medium heat until the garlic is golden brown. Remove the garlic with a slotted spoon. Add the paprika and *sofrito* and fry for 1 minute.

Add the rice, stirring to coat well with the *sofrito*. Cook for 2 minutes until the rice just starts to become translucent. Strain 1.5 litres (52 fl oz/6 cups) of the fish stock over the rice. Stir through, bring to the boil over high heat then reduce to a simmer. If the flame or element doesn't cover the base of the pan move the pan around during cooking to ensure that the paella cooks evenly.

Meanwhile, make a little *picada* by pounding the saffron, fried garlic and parsley using a mortar and pestle until it forms a rough paste and add immediately to the simmering paella. Stir through.

Cook on low–medium for 20 minutes, without stirring, until most of the stock has been absorbed. In the last minute, increase the heat to high to help form a *socorat* (crust) on the bottom of the pan. Cover with a clean tea towel (dish towel) and allow to rest for 10 minutes.

Carefully transfer the fish to a baking dish, cover and reheat in a 200°C (400°F/Gas 6) oven for 3–5 minutes or until hot. Serve the fish on a warm serving plate and refresh by spooning over any cooking juices that may have settled while being kept warm. Dress with a little fine sea salt and the extra parsley.

Serve the fish with the *alioli* while the rice is resting. Then serve the rice.

AVES

AVES
POULTRY

There is a misconception that poultry is a bland, safe food that will not offend anyone. This is only partially true. Most chicken comes from factory farms and is white, lean meat that generally needs a sauce to make it tasty. But as long as there are enough people around who know what good birds taste like, there will be a big enough market for the handful of quality growers — such as organic, rare breed and free-range farmers — who make the effort to raise flavoursome poultry. True, the chickens they produce are more expensive but, traditionally, chicken was never cheap. It's only the rise of factory farming that has lowered the price.

The reason I rail against poor-quality poultry is because I grew up only knowing what real birds taste like. Our back yard was incredibly productive. After dad's hens had laid their last egg it was off with their heads. The girls had a few good years in them, which meant we grew up eating chicken that had been around a bit, eaten some good food and kitchen scraps and had had a chance to spread their wings. They had firm flesh and strong hard bones. They required slow cooking in a pot or in the oven to melt the connective tissue into lip-smacking gelatine. Slow cooking also allows the rich sauces to penetrate the muscles, which develops the flavour and moistens the flesh.

Dad also had a small dovecote out the back, so mum would baste young, tender squab in garlic, oil and fresh herbs then dad cooked them over the dying embers of the barbecue. They were light, sweet, tender and slightly milky. These and the little braces of quail he brought back from hunting expeditions in the hills around our home are the bedrock of my culinary memories.

I now understand why mum and dad worked so hard to grow and hunt their own birds. It wasn't just an economic decision; the flavour of their hand-reared birds was the flavour of the food our relatives were eating back in Spain. To them, the taste of real chicken was the taste of home.

1 litre (35 fl oz/4 cups) *escabeche* (*see page 41*)

3 boneless, skinless chicken breasts

TAPAS 8, MEDIA RACIÓN 6, RACIÓN 3

POLLO EN ESCABECHE

COLD CHICKEN BREAST POACHED IN AN AROMATIC VINAIGRETTE

Pollo en escabeche is the classic Spanish way of preparing and preserving birds. It makes such a wonderfully refreshing light lunch in summer, a great little tapas plate and even a sandwich filling. It comes from a time before the forces of evil invented all those 'E' numbered chemicals, which are now pumped into packaged food. In the days before artificial chemicals, preservatives came from the village where you lived, where the wine that had been made into vinegar contained enough acid to inhibit bacterial growth. The combination of that vinegar with salt made a very good preserving liquid. All sorts of birds were cooked in *escabeche* and stored for later use. This recipe is much lighter, and more focused on flavouring than preserving. You can experiment a little if you wish and try the *escabeche* to poach quail, turkey or the very traditional *faisán escabeche* (pickled pheasant). You will simply need to adjust the cooking time.

METHOD

Bring the *escabeche* to the boil in a large saucepan over high heat. Add the chicken breasts and when the liquid returns to the boil, immediately reduce to a simmer. Cook for 12 minutes, or until firm to the touch and cooked all the way through.

Remove the chicken from the pan and set aside until cool enough to handle. Slice thinly across the grain into 3 mm (1/8 inch) slices. Arrange on a serving plate, drizzle over some of the *escabeche*, including some of the carrot and onion.

INGREDIENTS

6 quails

2 lemons

several pinches of fine sea salt

1 bunch thyme, chopped

4 garlic cloves, sliced

MEDIA RACIÓN 6, RACIÓN 3

CORDONIZ A LA BARBACOA

BARBECUED QUAIL MARINATED IN LEMON AND THYME

I can never barbecue a quail without being reminded of the day dad took mum and me on the back of the scooter to eat in the mountains above Córdoba. Wedged between my parents, none of us wearing helmets, we climbed the hills until dad found a suitable place. I remember making the fire with mum and dad, then cleaning the birds and placing them on a greenwood skewer, which was balanced between two forked branches sunk either side of the fire. Dad sat by the fire with a glass of wine and twiddled the stick, rotating the quail a little each time. He dressed the quail with just a little salt. The skin was crispy and the flesh fell away from the bones.

METHOD

Spatchcock the birds by cutting along either side of the backbone with kitchen scissors. Remove the backbone and discard (or save for stock in another dish). Put the birds on a clean board, breast side up. Spread them open then flatten them by pressing down hard with the palm of your hand.

Put the quails in a bowl and squeeze over the juice of one lemon. Add the salt, thyme and garlic. Mix, thoroughly covering the quails with the marinade. Cover tightly with plastic wrap and marinate in the refrigerator for 3 hours.

Heat a chargrill, barbecue grill or grill (broiler) to high. Put the quails on the grill, breast side down, and reduce the heat to medium. Squeeze half a lemon over the quails and sprinkle with salt. Cook for 3 minutes then turn the quails, squeeze over the remaining lemon half then sprinkle with salt and cook for a further 3 minutes. Let rest for 2 minutes before serving.

POLLO AL CHILINDRÓN

PYRENEES CHICKEN WITH PAPRIKA, TOMATO AND CAPSICUMS

Aurora, mother of the owner of the bar, Bodega de Pepe, in which Vanessa and I worked, taught us how to cook this wonderful sauce, which is made from dried peppers. I remember the day she showed us this dish so well, because just prior to cooking she had taken us on an impromptu tour around town. As we wandered the narrow streets she very quietly and solemnly pointed out Civil War battle sites. On one side of the street were the Monarchists and on the other were the Republicans. She said that in the middle — *'la sangre corría por las calles'* — the streets ran with blood. The Spanish Civil War was such a time of social upheaval with family turning on family and village turning on village, that I think we are lucky that the Spanish culture remained intact. War destroys societies. Food brings people together, whether preparing, eating or talking about it.

We went back to the kitchen and Aurora carefully showed us how to cook the *pimientos choriceros* and reduce the sauce. As these peppers are so difficult to come by we have adapted the recipe to use red capsicums. Once you know how to cook the sauce you can use it for any lean poultry, game birds, rabbit and, in the next chapter, lamb. It makes a beautiful looking dish of dark chicken and deep red sauce. Bring it to the table and share it with your family.

METHOD

In a large bowl, season the chicken pieces with the thyme, a few good pinches of fine sea salt and ½ teaspoon freshly ground black pepper. Cover and refrigerate until ready to use.

To make the *chilindrón* sauce, heat 60 ml (2 fl oz/¼ cup) of the olive oil over medium–high heat in a large heavy-based saucepan. Sauté the onion, bay leaves and garlic for about 5 minutes until the onion is soft. Reduce the heat to low–medium.

INGREDIENTS

1.6 kg (3 lb 8 oz) chicken, cut into 12 pieces

2 tablespoons thyme leaves, roughly chopped

fine sea salt

185 ml (6 fl oz/¾ cup) olive oil

2 brown onions, finely diced

4 bay leaves

4 garlic cloves, finely chopped

4 red capsicums (peppers), seeded, membrane
   removed and finely diced

6 large tomatoes, peeled and chopped
   (*see page 33*)

500 ml (17 fl oz/2 cups) dry white wine or
   fino sherry

3 tablespoons Spanish sweet paprika

MEDIA RACIÓN 6, RACIÓN 4

Add the capsicum, cover and cook for 40 minutes, stirring occasionally, until the capsicum is soft. Add the tomato, stir, cover and cook for 30 minutes, stirring occasionally.

Add the white wine and continue to cook for 10 minutes. Add about 1 litre (35 fl oz/4 cups) hot water and increase the heat to high. Once the water is boiling, reduce the heat to low, add the paprika and continue cooking the sauce gently for a further 30 minutes. The mixture should still be quite liquid at this stage.

Meanwhile, preheat the oven to 200°C (400°F/Gas 6).

Heat the remaining olive oil in a large heavy-based frying pan over high heat and add six pieces of chicken. After 30 seconds reduce the heat to medium. Season the chicken with a pinch of salt. After 4 minutes turn the chicken over and season the other side. Cook for a further 4 minutes until lightly browned. Remove the chicken from the pan and set aside. Repeat with the remaining chicken pieces.

Once all the chicken has been browned put it in a large roasting tin, leaving a little space between each piece. Cover the chicken with enough *chilindrón* sauce to come up to just the top of the chicken.

Gently cook in the oven for 1–1½ hours. As it is cooking the sauce will evaporate, creating a dark crusty top on the chicken. The chicken is ready when the thigh flesh comes away easily from the bone. Serve immediately.

PAN DE POLLO

CHICKEN BALLOTINE STUFFED WITH CHICKEN MOUSSE, JAMON AND GREEN OLIVES

Pan de pollo is possibly the most entertaining dish in this book. It is a wonderful cold cylinder of tender chicken, encasing a rich centre of soft *jamón* and olive-infused terrine. It can be the centre of attention on a buffet table, or you can slice it up and add it to a tapas plate. It is also very simple to make. If you can't bone a whole chicken, ask your butcher to do it for you. Tell them you want the bones removed but the skin left on in one whole piece. A friend of a friend encourages special service from her butcher by bringing him little treats she has made from his meat. Although there could be something else going on there, I would encourage you to have a good *professional* relationship with your butcher so they'll go the extra yards to look after you.

METHOD

Put the bread in a bowl, cover with the milk and set aside for 20 minutes.

Meanwhile, remove the skin from the chicken thighs. Hand chop the skin into small pieces and then coarsely mince it in a food processor or mincer along with the thighs.

Make the stuffing by squeezing out all the milk from the bread and discarding the milk. Break the bread into small pieces in a large bowl. Add the minced chicken, olives, *jamón*, nutmeg, cloves, eggs, parsley, sea salt and 1 tablespoon freshly cracked black pepper. Mix well with clean hands, squeezing the stuffing mixture through your hands and continually folding for several minutes.

INGREDIENTS

150 g (5½ oz) 2-day-old *pasta dura*, or other firm
  crusty bread, crusts removed

375 ml (13 fl oz/1½ cups) milk

800 g (1 lb 12 oz) chicken thigh fillets,
  with skin

250 g (9 oz) Gordal or other green olives, pitted

100 g (3½ oz) finely sliced *jamón* (*see page 20*)

1 teaspoon freshly grated nutmeg

3 whole cloves, heads only, crushed

2 eggs

1 handful flat-leaf (Italian) parsley, roughly
  chopped

1 tablespoon fine sea salt

1.6 kg (3 lb 8 oz) chicken, flat boned
  (*see Note*)

1 onion, roughly chopped

1 garlic bulb, halved

1 carrot, roughly chopped

2 bay leaves

MEDIA RACIÓN 12, RACIÓN 6

To make the ballotine, lay the boned chicken, skin side down, on a clean bench. Lay some plastic wrap over the chicken and, with a meat hammer, gently even out the flesh to form the bird into an approximate 25 x 25 cm (10 x 10 inch) square. Remove the plastic wrap and season the chicken with a little salt and pepper.

Spoon the stuffing down the centre of the chicken and neaten it into a cylinder shape. Lift up the sides of the chicken around the stuffing and mould into an even-shaped cylinder, doing your best to cover all the stuffing.

Tightly wrap the *pan de pollo* in several layers of foil. Using kitchen string, truss the ballotine with even loops to hold it in shape while cooking. Put in a large saucepan or stockpot and add enough salted water to cover the chicken. Add the onion, garlic, carrot and bay leaves. Bring to simmering point over medium heat but do not boil. Reduce the heat to low and gently simmer for 90 minutes. Allow to cool in the stock for 20 minutes then remove. Remove the foil, wrap the *pan de pollo* in plastic wrap and put in the refrigerator overnight.

To serve, cut into 1 cm (½ inch) thick slices and serve with salad, crusty bread, gherkins and *piquillo* peppers.

Note: Ask your butcher to flat bone the chicken for you.

INGREDIENTS

1.6 kg (3 lb 8 oz) chicken, cut into 12 pieces

fine sea salt

150 ml (5 fl oz) *ajo y perejil* (*see page 40*)

185 ml (6 fl oz/³⁄₄ cup) olive oil

3 brown onions, finely diced

2 tablespoons chopped thyme

4 bay leaves

3 garlic cloves, finely chopped

500 ml (17 fl oz/2 cups) fino sherry

1 litre (35 fl oz/4 cups) hot chicken stock
  (*see page 42*)

MEDIA RACIÓN 6, RACIÓN 4

POLLO AL AJILLO

GARLIC MARINATED CHICKEN COOKED IN A SHERRY AND ONION SAUCE

When I left home and started cooking professionally, I'd get on the phone to mum and ask her how to make certain dishes. *Pollo al ajillo* was one of them. It's a beautiful rich braise of chicken, slow cooked in garlic, onions and sherry. Mum would tell me to season and marinate the chicken well, to fry it until golden brown and to gently cook the onions. Whenever I made it, it would never work out exactly the same because she had a particular wine glass that she used to measure the sherry, and used a particular type of onion grown by a neighbour. I had to stand over her shoulder and watch her cook to learn how to make it taste like hers. But mine was never exactly the same. It was then that I realized no two cooks ever prepare a dish exactly the same way; there are small nuances and techniques that make a dish taste ever so slightly different. But trust me when I tell you that every person who cooks this wonderfully robust *pollo al ajillo* has been pleased and satisfied. Perfect for rabbit too!

METHOD

Put the chicken pieces in a large bowl and season well all over with fine sea salt. Pour over the *ajo y perejil* and rub it into the chicken until well covered. Cover with plastic wrap and refrigerate for 2–3 hours.

Heat 125 ml (4 fl oz/¼ cup) of the olive oil in a large, heavy-based frying pan over medium–high heat. Sear the chicken for about 5 minutes on each side until well browned. Remove the chicken from the pan, put on a plate then cover with foil and set aside.

Discard the oil, scrape the pan clean and add the remaining oil. Gently sauté the onion, thyme, bay leaves and garlic over low–medium heat for about 20 minutes until the onion starts to brown.

Increase the heat to high and return the chicken to the pan. When the pan is sizzling, add the sherry and scrape the bottom of the pan with a wooden spoon. Be careful when adding the sherry as it may flame. Allow the sherry to bubble for 1 minute then add the stock and bring to the boil. Reduce the heat to low and cover the pan. Simmer gently for about 1 hour until the chicken is very tender and almost ready to fall off the bone. (If you are using rabbit you will need to extend the cooking time by 30–60 minutes, depending on the size, age and condition of the rabbit. You will also need to add more stock during cooking.)

The sauce should now have reduced enough to coat the back of a spoon. If not, continue simmering until the sauce has reduced further, or extend it with a little water as necessary. Season to taste and serve immediately.

THE LANEWAYS OF MELBOURNE

It is possible to walk from one end of Melbourne to the other using the city's interconnected network of tiny cobbled laneways. They were once the access lanes to the businesses whose impressive facades front the wide thoroughfares of Melbourne. I sometimes see them as the dingy little back stages to the showy main streets. Our laneways are ad hoc and slightly secretive with a sense of adventure, darkness and transgression.

A mate of mine's grandma can still remember seeing painted ladies reclining on chaise longues in shop front windows, 75 years ago. Today you're more likely to find graffiti and stencil artists vying for wall space, creating amazing open air galleries of cutting edge art next to the funky little bars, galleries, studios, cafes and quirky retail spaces. Because rents are lower in the laneways of Melbourne, they have allowed younger people without massive capital to open small businesses. They are our very own little incubators of culture that have injected so much energy and diversity into Melbourne. The laneways of Melbourne are alive with the feeling that something new and exciting is always about to happen.

INGREDIENTS

1.6 kg (3 lb 8 oz) chicken, cut into 12 pieces

seasoned plain (all-purpose) flour, to coat

185 ml (6 fl oz/¾ cup) olive oil

4 brown onions, finely diced

4 bay leaves

5 garlic cloves, sliced

2 pinches of saffron threads

750 ml (26 fl oz/3 cups) Spanish fino sherry

250 ml (9 fl oz/1 cup) dry white wine

6 juniper berries

about 700 ml (24 fl oz) chicken stock
 (*see page 42*)

1 quantity almond *picada* (*see page 48*)

1 large handful flat-leaf (Italian) parsley,
 roughly chopped

MEDIA RACIÓN 6, RACIÓN 4

POLLO EN PEPITORÍA

SAFFRON BRAISED CHICKEN THICKENED WITH ALMONDS AND EGG YOLK

The 'slow foodies' among you will appreciate this interesting little experiment. I got this recipe from my Aunt Andrea in Madrid. She always cooks this golden chicken dish the same way her family has for generations, by browning off nuggety pieces of Spanish chicken and then making a little *picada* out of pounded egg and almonds to thicken the sauce. It tastes so rustic and down to earth that I secretly call it Farmhouse Chicken. When I tested this dish for the book, I didn't have one of my usual free-range chickens, so I had to get one of the kitchen team to pick up one from a supermarket. The result was good but the poultry flavour was missing. When made with a good free-range bird, however, the egg and saffron really intensify the flavour of the chicken and create a meal that tastes as close to old-fashioned farmyard chicken as you can get.

METHOD

Lightly coat the chicken pieces with the seasoned flour. Heat 125 ml (4 fl oz/½ cup) of the olive oil in a large heavy-based saucepan over high heat and add six pieces of chicken. After 30 seconds reduce the heat to medium and season with a pinch of salt. After 4 minutes, turn the chicken over, season the other side and cook for a further 4 minutes until lightly browned. Remove from the pan and repeat the process with the remaining chicken pieces.

Discard the oil, scrape the pan clean, and heat the remaining oil in the pan over medium heat. Add the onion, bay leaves and garlic and sauté for about 10 minutes until the onion is soft and beginning to brown. Add the saffron and cook, stirring, for 1 minute. Add the sherry and wine and scrape the bottom of the pan with a wooden spoon. Allow to boil for a few minutes then reduce to a simmer and cook for 10 minutes.

Add the chicken and juniper berries and cover with enough of the stock to just cover the chicken pieces. Increase the heat to high, bring to the boil then reduce to a slow simmer. Cover and cook for 1 hour. After 30 minutes check for seasoning and add salt if necessary.

When ready, the meat should be beginning to separate and come away from the bone. Just before serving, stir through the *picada* and simmer for 1 minute to thicken the sauce. Sprinkle with the parsley and serve.

QUAIL BRAISED WITH POMEGRANATE

Years ago, with the idea of MoVida still forming in my head, Vanessa and I spent several weeks in Valencia researching ideas and recipes. We wandered into this great antiquarian bookshop. When I saw the cooking section my heart raced. There were old books and some that were out of print. One book that caught my eye was a book about food from the Balearic Islands. To me the Balearics are another culture; there they eat all manner of different foods such as *sobrasada* (a soft pork sausage) and a dish of melt-in-the-mouth quail, cooked in a rich dark sauce enlivened with fresh pomegranate juice. I spent around 50 000 *pesetas* on books and walked out the door, arms loaded, into the blinding sun wondering how I was going to get my books home.

METHOD

Trim the neck and any loose skin off the quail. Season the inside of each bird with a little fine sea salt and some freshly ground black pepper. With kitchen string, truss the wings and legs to the body. Heat half of the oil in a large flameproof casserole dish over medium–high heat and seal the quails on all sides, seasoning each side. Remove the quails from the casserole.

Discard the oil and scrape the pan clean. Add the remaining oil and sauté the onion, carrot, garlic and herbs over low–medium heat for 20–30 minutes until the onion has caramelized. Add the tomato and cook for 5 minutes. Preheat the oven to 180°C (350°F/Gas 4).

INGREDIENTS

6 quails

fine sea salt

125 ml (4 fl oz/½ cup) olive oil

2 brown onions, finely chopped

4 carrots, finely diced

3 garlic cloves, finely chopped

2 bay leaves

1 tablespoon thyme leaves, chopped

3 ripe tomatoes, peeled, seeded and chopped

  (see page 33)

300 ml (10½ fl oz) white wine

about 1 litre (35 fl oz/4 cups) chicken stock

  (see page 42)

2 pomegranates

500 g (1 lb 2 oz) floury potatoes

oil, for deep-frying

MEDIA RACIÓN 6, RACIÓN 3

Increase the heat to high, add the wine and scrape the bottom of the dish with a wooden spoon. Put the quails in the dish and add enough chicken stock to come to about two-thirds of the way over the quails. Bring the stock to the boil.

Remove the dish from the stove, cover with the lid and cook in the oven for 40 minutes. Remove the lid and cook for a further 20 minutes.

Meanwhile, remove the seeds of the pomegranates with a spoon over a sieve above a bowl. Reserve the seeds and 80 ml (2½ fl oz/⅓ cup) of juice. Set aside. Cut the potatoes into matchstick-sized strips using a mandolin or very sharp knife. Soak in cold water to remove some of the starch and set aside.

Remove the casserole from the oven and transfer the quails to a plate. Cover to keep warm. Put the casserole back on the stove over medium–high heat. Add the pomegranate seeds and juice and cook for 10–15 minutes, or until the sauce has reduced and thickened slightly. Keep warm.

While the sauce is reducing, deep-fry the potatoes. Fill a deep-fryer or large heavy-based saucepan one-third full of oil and heat to 175°C (345°F), or until a cube of bread dropped into the oil browns in 20 seconds. Drain the potato and pat dry with paper towel. Deep-fry the potato in batches for 3–5 minutes until golden brown. Drain on paper towel then sprinkle with a little salt.

Serve one quail per person (or two quails if serving is *ración* size) on a warm plate. Spoon several tablespoons of sauce over the quails and serve with the vegetables and potatoes to one side.

PERDIZ GUISADA
PARTRIDGE WITH CABBAGE

Most of my Anglo mates have only heard about this bird through the Christmas song about leaping lords, gold rings and a partridge in a pear tree. In Spain, they are the most prized of all birds, probably due to the strong cultural influence of hunting. In Australia, we are lucky to have a small, but dedicated, number of farmers who are patient enough to raise these tasty birds. Unlike other poultry they have a season that lasts from the end of summer to the middle of winter. Out of this period they are sometimes available frozen. If you can't find partridge then use guinea fowl or pheasant. They are a decent-sized bird and make a good main meal, especially when the cold weather starts — the perfect excuse to pull out the cast-iron enamel ovenware.

METHOD

Trim the birds by trimming off the neck and the wings to the first joint.

Make the marinade by mixing together the herbs, carrot, onion, extra virgin olive oil, garlic, sherry vinegar and 1 teaspoon freshly ground black pepper in a non-metallic container large enough to hold the partridges. Put the partridges, breast side down, in the marinade. Baste them with the marinade a few times and put some of the marinade in the cavities of the birds. Cover with plastic wrap and refrigerate overnight.

INGREDIENTS

4 whole partridge (about 500 g/1 lb 2 oz each)

4 thyme sprigs, chopped

1 rosemary sprig, leaves only, roughly chopped

1 handful flat-leaf (Italian) parsley, chopped

1 carrot, finely diced

1 brown onion, finely diced

80 ml (2½ fl oz/⅓ cup) extra virgin olive oil

2 garlic cloves, chopped

80 ml (2½ fl oz/⅓ cup) aged sherry vinegar

60 ml (2 fl oz/¼ cup) olive oil

½ brown onion, extra, finely diced

¼ green cabbage, cut into 2 cm
  (¾ inch) squares

500 ml (17 fl oz/2 cups) white wine

RACIÓN 4

Preheat the oven to 180°C (350°F/Gas 4).

Heat the olive oil in a large flameproof casserole dish over medium heat and sauté the extra onion for 10–12 minutes until golden brown. Stir in the cabbage. Tip out the marinade from the cavities of the partridges and place the birds on top of the cabbage, breast side down. Strain the marinating liquid into the dish. Add the white wine and enough water to almost cover the birds — about three-quarters of the way up. Bring to the boil over high heat.

Cover with the lid and cook in the oven for 40 minutes. Remove the lid, turn the birds, breast side up, and cook for a further 20 minutes to brown the birds a little. At this stage the liquid should have reduced to halfway up the birds. When cooked, the leg meat should be soft and come away from the bone.

Remove the partridges from the dish, cover with foil and set aside near the oven or stovetop to keep warm. Return the casserole dish to the stovetop over high heat and cook for 10–15 minutes, or until the cooking juices have reduced by one-third and thickened slightly. Season to taste.

Make a bed of cabbage on four warmed serving plates and place a whole bird on top. Spoon over the sauce and serve.

CARNES

CARNES
MEAT

If there is one flavour that stands out from my time cooking in Spain it is the taste of Aragonese lamb. Every week Xabi, the driver from the local butcher shop, would drop off six nuggety milk-fed lambs to the kitchen at Bodega Pepe. No matter how we cooked it, the lamb was always brilliant — sweet, lean and slightly herbal to taste. I always revelled in making the ever popular lamb *chilindrón*, just so I could taste the succulent pieces of lamb forequarter cooked on the bone in rich red sauce — so much so that sometimes Vanessa thought there wouldn't be enough left for the customers. Lamb is always on the menu at MoVida and some of the lamb we get here is as good as the lamb I used to get in Aragon.

As good as Spanish lamb is, it is pork that is king. It is the ubiquitous meat that pervades every meal, with a few slices even slipped into vegetable dishes. From the Iberian pigs that roam the oak forests of Extremadura to the stock standard white pigs, there has never been a move to make Spanish pork lean, as is the case in Anglo-Saxon countries. Spanish pork is laced with flavoursome, sweet fat and, as a result, Spanish pork dishes always have a wonderful richness. If you are lucky enough to have access to free-range or rare breed pork, please use this, as it offers a very satisfying quality similar to the pork from which these dishes originated.

With all meats, in all traditions, there is a saying that goes 'closer to the bone, sweeter is the meat' and that is true in Spanish cooking. Much of the connective tissue can be found here and long slow braises release that beautiful flavour. All the beef comes into the restaurant on the bone and is cooked on the bone, such as the delicious *chuletón* (Spanish rib eye, see page 264).

In Spanish cooking, nothing gets wasted from the animal and we proudly continue this tradition. My two favourite recipes are included in this chapter — *Callos a la madrileña* (ox tripe with a spicy chorizo and chickpea sauce, see page 266) and *lengua estofada* (twice-cooked ox tongue with sherry, carrot and parsley, see page 268).

I implore you to establish a good relationship with a great local butcher who can help you get the best cuts for the meat dishes you're going to cook.

INGREDIENTS

1 kg (2 lb 4 oz) lamb leg meat, boned and sinew
   removed, cut into 1.5 cm (5/8 inch) cubes
2 tablespoons freshly ground cumin
   (*see page 32*)
1 tablespoon Spanish sweet smoked paprika
1 teaspoon freshly grated nutmeg
1 teaspoon ground turmeric
1/2 teaspoon cayenne pepper
1 teaspoon fine sea salt

1 small handful curly parsley, chopped
2 garlic cloves, finely chopped
125 ml (4 fl oz/1/2 cup) fino sherry
60 ml (2 fl oz/1/4 cup) olive oil
60 ml (2 fl oz/1/4 cup) fino sherry, extra
1/2 teaspoon cayenne pepper, extra
1 teaspoon Spanish sweet smoked paprika, extra
1/2 lemon

TAPAS 12, MEDIA RACIÓN 6, RACIÓN 4

PINCHITOS MORUNOS
CHARGRILLED MOORISH LAMB SKEWERS

These lamb skewers have been marinated in a mix of crisp sherry, herbs and some of the spices introduced to Spain during the Moorish occupation. The fino sherry cuts through the fattiness of the lamb and the spices accentuate the smokiness of the chargrilling.

Chargrilling adds a flavour unsurpassed by any cooking done with gas or electricity. The food takes on the smoky flavour of the wood. To chargrill, make a decent-sized fire of hardwood then let the fire die down and cook the meat over the coals. Cooking over heat beads gives a similar even heat but a different flavour. These *pinchitos* are excellent when eaten straight from the grill but my dad considers them better when eaten an hour later.

METHOD

Put the lamb in the bowl and mix in the spices, salt, parsley, garlic, sherry and olive oil. Mix well. Cover, refrigerate and allow to marinate overnight, turning two or three times.

Thread the marinated lamb onto twelve 30 cm (12 inch) metal skewers. Spread the meat along the skewers and don't bunch it up too tightly. If there are some longer pieces then thread them lengthways. This allows the meat to cook evenly.

Make a basting liquid by mixing the extra sherry, cayenne pepper and paprika. Insert a fork into the skin of the half lemon to make a fruity basting brush. Preheat your barbecue grill to medium.

Place the skewers on the barbecue and grill for 15–20 minutes, turning and basting with the basting liquid and the half lemon several times each side. Remove from the heat and allow to rest for 5 minutes before serving.

INGREDIENTS

1.5 kg (3 lb 5 oz) lamb forequarter, cut into 5 cm (2 inch) squares

1 tablespoon thyme leaves, chopped

100 ml (3½ fl oz) olive oil

4 garlic cloves, chopped

2 brown onions, finely diced

4 bay leaves

5 red capsicums (peppers), seeded, membrane removed and finely chopped

6 large tomatoes, peeled, seeded and chopped (*see page 33*)

500 ml (17 fl oz/2 cups) dry white wine

2 tablespoons Spanish sweet paprika

1 tablespoon chopped flat-leaf (Italian) parsley

MEDIA RACIÓN 6, RACIÓN 4

CORDERO AL CHILINDRÓN

PYRENEES LAMB WITH WHITE WINE AND PAPRIKA SAUCE

If you are lucky enough to have a Spanish or even Italian butcher, the request to chop up a whole forequarter of lamb will come as no surprise. They know that forequarter is the tastiest part of the animal and that given a good chance to slow cook in an oven it will release its rich, succulent cooking juices. If you get a dumbfounded look from your butcher ask for 1.5 kg (3 lb 5 oz) of forequarter pieces such as chop, shoulder and shank and ask them to use their band saw to cut it into chunky morsel-sized pieces. If the butcher has lamb neck you can ask for one of these to be cut up. This is such a rustic dish that it really doesn't matter.

METHOD

Trim the lamb of any excess fat. Season with the thyme leaves, 1 teaspoon salt and ½ teaspoon freshly ground black pepper.

To make the *chilindrón* sauce, heat 60 ml (2 fl oz/¼ cup) of the olive oil in a large heavy-based saucepan over medium–high heat and sauté the garlic, onion and bay leaves for about 5 minutes until soft. Reduce the heat to low–medium. Add the capsicum, cover and cook, stirring occasionally, for another 30 minutes, or until well softened. Stir in the tomato, cover and cook for another 30 minutes, stirring occasionally. Add the white wine and continue to cook for 10 minutes. Add about 1 litre (35 fl oz/4 cups) hot water and increase the heat to high. Once the water is boiling add the paprika, reduce the heat to low and continue cooking the sauce gently for 30 minutes. Preheat the oven to 160°C (315°F/Gas 2–3).

Put the lamb pieces in a roasting tin. Pour in enough sauce to cover to just the top of the meat. (Any leftover sauce can be frozen and used to cook chicken or lamb.) Cook in the oven for about 2½ hours. As the lamb cooks, some of the sauce will evaporate, allowing the top of the meat to brown. When cooked, the meat should come away easily from the bone.

To serve, place the meat on a warm serving plate, spoon over some of the sauce and sprinkle with the chopped parsley.

INGREDIENTS

500 g (1 lb 2 oz) pork scotch (pork rib eye)

1 teaspoon thyme leaves, chopped

120 g (4¼ oz) *jamón*, cut into 5 mm (¼ inch) thick strips (*see page 20*)

200 g (7 oz) *Mahón* or *Manchego* cheese, cut into long strips, 5 mm (¼ inch) thick

seasoned flour, to coat

2 eggs, lightly beaten

300 g (10½ oz) panko breadcrumbs (*see page 15*), seasoned

sunflower oil, for deep-frying

sea salt flakes, to sprinkle

TAPAS 16, MEDIA RACIÓN 8, RACIÓN 4

FLAMENQUÍN

ROLLED PORK LOIN WITH JAMÓN AND SHEEP'S CHEESE

It is unlikely that these well-salted, cigar-shaped sticks of deep-fried pork loin stuffed with *jamón* and *Mahón* cheese will ever be awarded a Heart Foundation tick of approval. But then again stranger things have happened.

Flamenquín are very typical Cordovan tapas. They are so popular that they are sold pre-made. Just as butchers here in Australia are awarded 'best sausage' or bakers 'best pie', there is an annual ceremony in Córdoba for the best *flamenquín*. Some Córdobans take this as seriously as we do the Alan Border medal! *Flamenquín* need a little attention to perfect, but when you do it will be a eureka moment that will change the way you entertain at parties.

METHOD

Preheat the oven to 180°C (350°F/Gas 4). Trim any fat and sinew from the pork loin then cut into eight even fillets. Place the pork fillets, one at a time, between two sheets of plastic wrap. Flatten out the fillet with a meat mallet, fashioning it into a rough rectangular shape about 4 x 10 cm (1½ x 4 inches) and 3 mm (⅛ inch) thick.

Remove the plastic wrap from the fillets and sprinkle each with salt and a little thyme. Divide the strips of *jamón* and cheese equally among the fillets, laying the *jamón* and cheese in a single layer, alternately side by side, along the length of the middle of each fillet.

Roll the pork around the *jamón* and cheese to form a cigar-like shape. Smooth any edges and press them down.

Gently coat the *flamenquín* in the seasoned flour. Dip into the beaten egg then roll in the breadcrumbs. Heat the oil in a deep-fryer or heavy-based saucepan to 160°C (315°F), or until a cube of bread dropped into the oil browns in 30–35 seconds. Fry in batches for 4 minutes, or until golden brown. Put the *flamenquín* on a baking tray and bake for 5 minutes to make sure the pork is cooked through. Sprinkle with sea salt flakes and serve immediately. For a tapas size serving, cut the *flamenquín* in half.

INGREDIENTS

400 g (14 oz) dried figs

100 g (3½ oz) prunes, pitted

1.25 kg (2 lb 12 oz) boneless pork loin,
  skin and fat removed

2 teaspoons fine sea salt

60 ml (2 fl oz/¼ cup) extra virgin olive oil

1 tablespoon Spanish sweet paprika

sea salt flakes, to sprinkle

extra virgin olive oil, extra, to drizzle

MEDIA RACIÓN 6

LOMO

PORK LOIN STUFFED WITH FIGS AND PRUNES

We were wandering between tapas bars in the old part of Seville when we came across a classic bar, decorated with mosaic tiles showing scenes of old city life from 100 years ago. Despite the walls, floor and furnishings suffering from a century of constant use the place was infused with life. There was a good mixed crowd at the bar, some lively bar staff, and in the kitchen was a team who presented old traditions with a new twist. Dried fruit and pork are naturally compatible, so we were really impressed to see a plate of cold roast pork sent out that had been stuffed with prunes and figs. The richness of the pork was balanced by the sweetness and natural acidity of the fruit. This is our own version we make at MoVida. Please note that the quality of dried fruit is as important as the pork, so always source dried fruit that is both succulent and moist.

METHOD

Preheat the oven to 200°C (400°F/Gas 6). In a food processor blend together the dried fruit on pulse for several minutes, or until it forms a rough ball with a coarse texture. Put in a bowl and work together with a spoon for several minutes to break up the fruit.

Create a pocket for the fruit inside the pork loin by inserting a long, thin sharp knife in one end of the loin and making a slit. Repeat from the other end. Rotate the knife around to open up the pocket a little. You should be able to fit two fingers inside the pocket. Roll the fruit into a cylinder the length of the pork loin and cut in half. Slowly insert the fruit into the pocket — one half of the mix from each end. Once all the fruit is inside the loin close each end of the hole with toothpicks. If you are adept with string you can tie the loin up to help keep its shape while cooking, but this is not essential.

Combine the sea salt, extra virgin olive oil and paprika in a large bowl. Put the pork in the bowl and thoroughly coat with the spiced oil. Put the pork on a wire rack in a roasting tin and roast in the oven for 1 hour 20 minutes, or until cooked through. Allow to cool to room temperature before serving.

To serve, slice thinly, sprinkle with sea salt flakes and drizzle with a little extra virgin olive oil. This dish is perfect with a green salad or *asadillo* (see page 188).

INGREDIENTS

185 g (6½ oz) quince paste, at room temperature

120 g (4¼ oz/1 cup) *alioli* (*see page 38*)

2 kg (4 lb 8 oz) pork belly, on the bone with skin

60 ml (2 fl oz/¼ cup) olive oil

2 tablespoons fine sea salt

2 brown onions, roughly chopped

3 large carrots, roughly chopped

1 tablespoon chopped thyme leaves

6 bay leaves

4 garlic cloves, unpeeled

375 ml (13 fl oz/1½ cups) white wine

375 ml (13 fl oz/1½ cups) sherry vinegar

MEDIA RACIÓN 12. RACIÓN 6

CERDO ASADO

ROAST PORK BELLY WITH QUINCE ALIOLI

This is a roast with salty, brittle crackling covering layers of sweet, succulent pork. The meat is cooked on a bed of vegetables and vinegar and the acid seems to balance out the richness of the fat. It is served with a quince *alioli* that, although luxurious in itself, has enough fruit acid to help cut through the pork. Don't be alarmed by the richness of this dish. In the Spanish style of dining, the food is shared by many so you're not going to serve up a great slab of pork belly; instead, you'll be offering a little slice of sweet flesh topped with a ribbon of glazed skin.

METHOD

Preheat the oven to 220°C (425°F/Gas 7). Cut the quince paste into small pieces and mix with the *alioli* using a mortar and pestle or small blender for 1 minute, or until smooth. Refrigerate until ready to use.

Using a Stanley knife, lightly score the skin of the pork belly by making even, shallow 3 mm (⅛ inch) cuts in the skin, 1 cm (½ inch) apart. Rub the olive oil and then the salt into all sides of the pork belly. Place the pork in a 30 x 40 cm (12 x 16 inch) roasting tin, skin side up. Roast in the oven for 45 minutes, or until crackling starts to form. Reduce the oven to 180°C (350°F/Gas 4).

Remove the pork from the tin and set aside. Add the vegetables, herbs, garlic, wine, sherry vinegar and 375 ml (13 fl oz/1½ cups) water to the roasting tin and stir to combine. Return the pork to the tin, sitting it on top of the vegetable mixture, skin side up. Cover with foil and cook for a further 2 hours until the meat becomes tender.

Increase the heat to 220°C (425°F/Gas 7), remove the foil from the meat and roast for a further 15–20 minutes to crisp up the crackling. Remove from the oven and set aside until cool enough to handle. Carefully remove the bones and discard. Discard the vegetable base. Cut the pork belly into 2 cm (¾ inch) thick slices with a sharp serrated knife and serve slices of pork and crackling on a warmed plate with the quince *alioli*.

INGREDIENTS

500 g (1 lb 2 oz) 2-day-old *pasta dura* or other
    firm crusty bread, crusts removed

2 navel oranges

200 g (7 oz) cooked pork belly, crackling
    removed (*see page 252*)

two 150 g (5½ oz) raw chorizos (*see page 28*)

125 ml (4 fl oz/½ cup) extra virgin olive oil

6 garlic cloves, unpeeled

1 tablespoon Spanish sweet paprika

MEDIA RACIÓN 6, RACIÓN 4

MIGAS
PORK BELLY WITH CHORIZO AND BREADCRUMBS

In Spain, making *migas* (breadcrumbs) is a job that is still done by hand. The result is beautifully formed little crumbs of random shape and nature, a metaphor I have always thought, for the chaotic nature of Spanish life. Grandad Juan made this version of *migas* when we first came to Australia. It may seem odd to have a dish of pork belly called *migas* but it is named after the breadcrumbs, which are fried until golden brown and soak up the cooking juices.

METHOD

Tear the bread into chunks then process in a food processor or blender in two batches until rough crumbs are formed. Sift the breadcrumbs to lose any of the finer crumbs. Dissolve a small pinch of salt in 80 ml (2½ fl oz/⅓ cup) water. Put the breadcrumbs in a plastic container and sprinkle with the water. Mix well. Cover with the lid and refrigerate overnight.

Next day carefully remove the peel and pith from the oranges and cut into 3 mm (⅛ inch) thick slices. Arrange on a serving plate. Cut the pork into 1 cm (½ inch) thick rectangular strips and cut the chorizos into 1 cm (½ inch) thick slices.

Heat 100 ml (3½ fl oz) extra virgin olive oil in a *perol* (see page 34) or wok over high heat and fry the chorizo for 4 minutes, stirring constantly. Reduce the heat to medium–high then add the pork and fry for a further minute or two. Remove the meat from the *perol* and put onto a clean plate but keep all the fat in the *perol*. Cook the garlic in the fat for a few minutes until the skins are golden and the cloves have softened. Remove the garlic from the *perol* and reserve.

Add the remaining oil to the *perol*, increase the heat to high and add the breadcrumbs. Cook, stirring continuously, for 1–2 minutes, or until the breadcrumbs start to turn golden.

Add the pork and chorizo and stir. Season if required and sprinkle in the paprika. Keep tossing the pan to move the breadcrumbs. Cook on high for another 5–8 minutes until the breadcrumbs soak up the oil and continue to turn golden. The breadcrumbs should be nicely browned when done and a little chewy. Remove from the heat and serve the *migas* together with the oranges. Garnish with the reserved garlic.

INGREDIENTS

2 kg (4 lb 8 oz) pork rib racks, breastbone
 removed

several pinches of fine sea salt

4 garlic cloves, crushed

100 ml (3½ fl oz) extra virgin olive oil

juice of 2 lemons

1 tablespoon Spanish smoked paprika

2 tablespoons honey

250 ml (9 fl oz/1 cup) Pedro Ximénez sherry or
 other sweet sherry

125 ml (2 fl oz/½ cup) dry white wine

4 tablespoons dijon mustard

1 handful flat-leaf (Italian) parsley, chopped

125 ml (4 fl oz/½ cup) sherry vinegar

TAPAS 20, MEDIA RACIÓN 6, RACIÓN 4

COSTILLAS DE CERDO AL HORNO
BRAISED PORK RIB RACKS

Meaty, sticky, smoky and sweet — these braised pork ribs are fun finger food for carnivores. There is something primal about holding a bone in your hand and pulling the meat off with your teeth. Some people can do this with such style and panache that it becomes sensual.

In Spain, *costillas* are sold in shops pre-marinated with paprika and garlic, ready to be taken home and cooked. They are brilliant when slowly chargrilled — as are these pork ribs. This is a recipe we developed recently, a smoky rich marinade that clings to sweet gelatinous ribs.

METHOD

Preheat the oven to 200°C (400°F/Gas 6).

Put the rib racks in a large bowl. Season them with the sea salt then add the garlic, extra virgin olive oil, lemon juice, paprika, honey, sherry, white wine, mustard and parsley. Mix thoroughly, making sure the ribs are carefully covered in the marinade. Marinate for at least 1 hour.

In a large roasting tin, pour in 500 ml (17 fl oz/2 cups) hot water and the sherry vinegar. Place the ribs in the sherry water, meaty side down, and pour the marinade over the ribs. Roast in the oven for 30 minutes, basting every 10 minutes. Turn, meaty side up, and cook for 1 hour, or until very tender.

To serve, cut the ribs apart into single bones with a sharp knife and serve warm.

INGREDIENTS

200 g (7 oz) day-old *pasta dura* or other firm
   crusty bread, very finely sliced

200 g (7 oz) fillet steak

4 tablespoons very finely chopped
   red onion

few drops of Tabasco sauce, to taste

2 pinches of Spanish sweet smoked paprika,
   to taste

½ teaspoon dijon mustard

1 tablespoon finely diced cornichons
   (*see Note*)

1 teaspoon extra virgin olive oil

1 teaspoon chopped flat-leaf (Italian) parsley

pinch of sea salt flakes

sea salt flakes, extra, to serve

extra virgin olive oil, extra, to serve

1 quail egg yolk (optional), to serve

TAPAS 12, MEDIA RACIÓN 3

BISTEC ALEMÁN
MOVIDA STEAK TARTARE

This is our version of the international raw meat starter, named after the Tartars who loved their raw meat. We use wagyu topside steak because of its sweet nuttiness. If you can buy wagyu, and can afford its rather steep price tag, please do. When making tartare be conservative with your spices as you don't want to kill the flavour of the beef. With such a small amount of meat, one slip of the wrist and you could end up with Tabasco-flavoured mince!

METHOD

Preheat the oven to 180°C (350°F/Gas 4).

To make the croutons, put the bread slices on a baking tray and bake for 5–10 minutes until crisp and golden.

Make sure the meat is chilled and the knife, chopping board and your hands are very clean. Using a very sharp knife, cut the meat into very tiny dice.

Put the meat, onion, Tabasco sauce, paprika, mustard, cornichons, extra virgin olive oil, parsley and sea salt in a bowl and mix thoroughly. Serve in a bowl with a sprinkle of sea salt flakes, a little drizzle of extra virgin olive oil, the raw egg yolk on top, if using, and croutons to one side. Mix the raw egg into the mince and spoon onto the croutons to eat.

Note: Cornichons are pickled baby cucumbers.

INGREDIENTS

3 kg (6 lb 12 oz) oxtail (*see Notes*)

60 ml (2 fl oz/¼ cup) olive oil

fine sea salt

2 brown onions, diced

4 carrots, diced

3 garlic cloves, chopped

4 bay leaves

6 ripe tomatoes, peeled, seeded and diced (*see page 33*)

750 ml (26 fl oz/3 cups) fino sherry

1 teaspoon black peppercorns

4 whole cloves

2 tablespoons chopped flat-leaf (Italian) parsley

MEDIA RACIÓN 8, RACIÓN 6

RABO DE TORO

OXTAIL BRAISED SLOWLY IN FINO SHERRY

Oxtail is just that — a collection of vertebrae with a thin covering of meat. It is, however, perhaps the most succulent meat in the world. There is so much connective tissue in relation to the amount of red meat that when slowly cooked with aromatic vegetables, herbs and sherry, you have a rich gelatinous jus. In Spain they use the tail of *toro* — yes, a bull. In Australia it is more likely to be yearling steer. The flavour will be slightly lighter but, to misquote Shakespeare, 'Oxtail by any other name would taste just as sweet'.

METHOD

Cut away any excess fat from the oxtail, especially from the larger pieces. Leave the silver skin on, as this cooks down during the long cooking process.

Heat the olive oil in a large heavy-based saucepan over medium–high heat and brown the oxtail in two batches. Cook for 3–4 minutes each side to ensure the meat is evenly browned and season each side with fine sea salt. Once all the meat has been browned, remove and set aside. Add the onion, carrot, garlic and bay leaves to the pan. Cook for 1 minute, stirring occasionally. Reduce the heat to low–medium and cook gently for 15–20 minutes until the vegetables have browned. Add the tomato and cook for another 15 minutes until pulpy.

Add the fino sherry and stir with a wooden spoon, scraping up any cooked-on bits from the bottom of the pan. Return the meat to the pan with the peppercorns and cloves. Cover well with water and simmer for 3–4 hours, depending on the age of the oxtail. The meat is ready when it comes away easily from the bone. Spoon off any fat sitting on the surface of the sauce. If necessary, remove the meat from the pan and reduce the sauce over high heat until it thickens to a light coating consistency. Return the meat to the sauce, heat for several minutes on low then serve, sprinkled with parsley.

Notes: Ask your butcher to cut the oxtail through the joints.

If making the day before, reheat in a moderately hot oven, in a large ovenproof frying pan and bring the pan to the table to serve.

VEAL AND PORK RISSOLES WITH SHERRY SAUCE

This is my comfort food. This is the dish I asked mum to make for me when I was growing up. She learned the recipe from her mum. It's a cheap and delicious way to feed a family using cheaper cuts of meat, bulking it up with some bread and giving it a delicious flavour with the sherry sauce. But you don't think of that when you're 10 years old, hungry and have just come home from football practice; you think of getting out of your wet jumper and tucking into those moist spicy meatballs and hot rich sauce.

METHOD

To make the rissoles, soak the bread in the milk for 5 minutes. Squeeze as much of the milk as you can out of the bread. Discard the milk. Break apart the bread into fine pieces and put into another bowl.

Add the veal and pork to the bread. Mix together well with very clean hands. Add the garlic, parsley, nutmeg, wine, eggs and 1 tablespoon each of salt and freshly ground black pepper. Mix well with your hands until the mixture is of uniform consistency.

Shape into 16 rissoles — each should weigh roughly 120 g (4$^1/_4$ oz) and measure about 8 cm (3$^1/_4$ inches) in diameter and 2.5 cm (1 inch) in height. Lightly coat each rissole in the seasoned flour.

INGREDIENTS

200 g (7 oz) 2-day-old *pasta dura* or other firm
  crusty bread, crusts removed and torn
  into chunks

250 ml (9 fl oz/1 cup) milk

1 kg (2 lb 4 oz) minced (ground) veal

500 g (1 lb 2 oz) minced (ground) pork

3 garlic cloves, finely chopped

1 handful flat-leaf (Italian) parsley,
  roughly chopped

1 tablespoon freshly grated nutmeg

80 ml (2½ fl oz/⅓ cup) white wine

2 eggs

seasoned plain (all-purpose) flour, to coat

100 ml (3½ fl oz) olive oil

2 brown onions, finely diced

6 bay leaves

1 tablespoon Spanish sweet paprika

2 garlic gloves, extra, finely chopped

3 carrots, diced

500 ml (17 fl oz/2 cups) fino sherry or dry
  white wine

300 g (10½ oz/2 cups) peas, blanched

MEDIA RACIÓN 16, RACIÓN 8

Heat half of the olive oil in a large heavy-based saucepan over medium–high heat. Cook the rissoles for 2–3 minutes each side until browned, seasoning each side. Put on a tray or plate, cover with foil and set aside.

Once all the rissoles have been browned, add the remaining oil to the pan with the onion, bay leaves, paprika and extra garlic. Cook for 5 minutes, or until the onion has softened, stirring occasionally. Add the carrot and cook for 15 minutes, or until the carrot has softened slightly and is starting to brown, stirring occasionally.

Increase the heat to high, add the sherry and stir with a wooden spoon, scraping up any cooked-on bits from the bottom of the pan. Allow the sherry to boil for 1 minute then add 1.5 litres (52 fl oz/6 cups) water and bring to the boil. Reduce to a gentle simmer, place the rissoles in the pan, cover and cook for 45 minutes. Add the peas and cook for a further 5 minutes.

Remove the rissoles from the pan, cover with foil and set aside. Increase the heat to high and cook the sauce for 30 minutes until thickened to a coating consistency. Return the rissoles to the pan and cook for a few minutes to heat through before serving.

one 500 g (1 lb 2 oz) rib eye fillet, on the bone

fine sea salt

1 tablespoon thyme leaves

extra virgin olive oil, to serve

sea salt flakes, to serve

MEDIA RACIÓN 2

CHULETÓN

SPANISH RIB EYE

Twice a week we get some of the best beef in Australia delivered to our door. We have a hotline to a supplier in Sydney who finds us the very best beef and dry ages it for us in a humidity-controlled aging room. Although fiercely passionate about Spanish produce, I am proud to say that the beef we have in Australia is consistently better. Although in Asturias, northern Spain, they appreciate good quality, full-flavoured beef from older animals, the southerners sparingly eat yearling, which is not known for its great quality. *Chuletón* is a single, big rib eye steak on the bone that is traditionally cooked over charcoal, rested, sliced and shared. If you have a butcher who carries dry-aged beef, ask for it specifically.

METHOD

Allow the steak to come to room temperature.

To cook your steak medium–rare, preheat the barbecue grill or grill (broiler) to medium–high. Season the steak on both sides with a generous pinch of fine sea salt, some freshly ground black pepper and a sprinkle of thyme leaves.

Put the steak on the grill for 5 minutes. Turn the steak 90 degrees to get even crosshatch markings and cook for 3 minutes. Season the steak again then flip it. Season it again with a little more sea salt, pepper and thyme and cook it for 5 minutes. Allow to rest, uncovered, somewhere warm for 5–10 minutes.

Remove the fillet from the bone, reserving the bone, and slice the meat into 1 cm (½ inch) thick slices. To serve, lay the slices like a deck of cards on the bone, on a warmed plate. Dress with the very best extra virgin olive oil and sea salt flakes.

INGREDIENTS

1 kg (2 lb 4 oz) beef shin

150 ml (5 fl oz) olive oil

2 brown onions, diced

3 garlic cloves, chopped

4 bay leaves

1 red capsicum (pepper), seeded, membrane removed and chopped

1 green capsicum (pepper), seeded, membrane removed and chopped

6 tomatoes peeled, seeded and diced (see page 33)

500 ml (17 fl oz/2 cups) white wine

3 nicola potatoes, click cut into 2.5 cm (1 inch) cubes (see page 105)

4 carrots, chopped into 2.5 cm (1 inch) pieces

2 pinches of saffron threads

2 tablespoons Spanish sweet paprika

MEDIA RACIÓN 6, RACIÓN 4

ESTOFADO

BEEF SHIN BRAISED WITH CARROTS, TOMATOES, WHITE WINE AND SAFFRON

This is a simple and slow-cooked braise, typical of home cooks across the Spanish nation. In winter, at any one time there would be hundreds of thousands of *estafodos* simmering on stovetops across Spain. In the south they might use pork neck and shoulder and artichokes, while in the north they might use beef shin and runner beans. It's always slow cooked on the stovetop or in the oven and served in the one dish with plenty of bread to mop up the sauces.

METHOD

Trim the beef shin of any obvious tendon. Cut into 4–5 cm (1½–2 inch) chunks. Heat 100 ml (3½ fl oz) of the olive oil in a large heavy-based saucepan over medium–high heat. Brown the meat, in batches, for 2–3 minutes each side, seasoning while cooking. Remove and set aside.

Reduce the heat to medium and add the remaining oil to the pan. Cook the onion, garlic and bay leaves for 10–15 minutes, stirring occasionally, until the onion has browned.

Reduce the heat to low–medium and add the capsicum. Cook gently for 15–20 minutes. Add the tomato and cook for another 20 minutes until the sauce is well reduced. Increase the heat to high and add the white wine, stirring with a wooden spoon to scrape up any cooked-on bits from the bottom of the pan. Add the meat and enough cold water to cover the meat. Bring to the boil then reduce to a simmer. Simmer gently for 30 minutes then add the potato and carrot. Skim the surface to remove any foamy residue and excess oil.

Put the saffron in a cup and pour a few tablespoons of the hot broth over the threads. Leave to infuse for 1 minute then add the saffron mixture to the pan. Add the paprika, stir and season to taste. Cook for 1–1½ hours, or until the beef is very tender (but not falling apart) and the sauce has thickened. Bring the pan to the table and allow people to serve themselves. Serve with fresh bread.

CALLOS A LA MADRILEÑA

OX TRIPE WITH A SPICY CHORIZO
AND CHICKPEA SAUCE

Tripe is one of my favourite dishes — although perhaps not a sadly missed part of the Anglo cooking culture, I am led to believe. I hear many stories from older customers who balk at the idea of eating tripe after years of being traumatized by parents forcing them to eat rubbery tripe with white sauce. A true pity. My tripe is never rubbery and will not traumatize anyone — that's a promise. It is a rich and gelatinous dish, enriched with *jamón* and chorizo, sharpened with tomatoes and white wine, with the added bonus of chickpeas which, I believe, are good for you. This is very moreish and the sauce is delectably sweet. Order pre-cooked tripe from the butcher, as uncooked tripe takes 8–10 hours to cook.

INGREDIENTS

60 ml (2 fl oz/¼ cup) olive oil

3 brown onions, diced

4 garlic cloves, sliced

5 bay leaves

1 dried red chilli

2 red capsicums (peppers), seeded, membrane removed and finely diced

200 g (7 oz) *jamón*, thickly sliced and diced into 5 mm (¼ inch) cubes (*see page 20*)

four 150 g (5½ oz) chorizos, cut into 1 cm (½ inch) thick slices (*see page 28*)

8 tomatoes, peeled and diced (*see page 33*)

750 ml (26 fl oz/3 cups) dry white wine

1 pig's trotter, cut in half lengthways

2 kg (4 lb 8 oz) cooked ox tripe

3 tablespoons Spanish sweet paprika

600 g (1 lb 5 oz) cooked chickpeas, drained (*see page 16*)

MEDIA RACIÓN 6, RACIÓN 4

METHOD

Heat the olive oil in a large saucepan over medium heat and cook the onion, garlic, bay leaves and chilli for 5 minutes, or until the onion is soft. Add the capsicum and cook for a further 5 minutes.

Add the *jamón* and chorizo and cook for 5 minutes to brown the outside of the sausage. Add the tomato and cook for 5 minutes until soft. Increase the heat to high and add the white wine, stirring with a wooden spoon to scrape up any cooked-on bits from the bottom of the pan. Allow the wine to come to the boil.

Carefully add the pig's trotter halves and pour in enough cold water to cover them. Bring to the boil. Skim the surface to remove any foamy residue and excess oil. Add the tripe and enough water to cover well. Bring to the boil. Skim again. Add the paprika and boil for about 3 minutes then reduce to a simmer.

Cover and cook for 3–6 hours until soft and gelatinous (see Note). You may need to add more water during cooking. When the tripe feels soft enough for your liking, add 250 ml (9 fl oz/1 cup) cold water to the pan and add the chickpeas. Continue to cook, uncovered, for a further 20–30 minutes. The sauce should have a rich but light, coating consistency. Extend with a little stock if too thick or continue cooking to reduce.

Notes: Cooking time for the tripe can vary greatly and will be determined by the time that it has already been cooked by the butcher.

If making the day before, reheat in a moderately hot oven, in a large ovenproof frying pan and bring the pan to the table to serve.

INGREDIENTS

2 ox tongues (about 2 kg/4 lb 8 oz)

4 carrots

1 brown onion

12 bay leaves

2 tablespoons black peppercorns

1 handful flat-leaf (Italian) parsley, stalks and
    leaves separated, leaves chopped

10 whole cloves

60 ml (2 fl oz/¼ cup) olive oil

1½ brown onions, extra, finely diced

3 garlic cloves, finely sliced

2 green capsicums (peppers), seeded,
    membrane removed and diced

6 tomatoes, peeled and roughly chopped
    (*see page 33*)

500 ml (17 fl oz/2 cups) fino sherry

sea salt flakes, to sprinkle

MEDIA RACIÓN 10. RACIÓN 6

LENGUA ESTOFADA

TWICE-COOKED OX TONGUE WITH SHERRY, CARROT AND PARSLEY

Lengua estofada is my favourite dish, because it brings me so much joy and satisfaction to work with what is basically a very ugly piece of meat and transform it into a succulent dish with a rich sauce of sherry and carrot. I also get great satisfaction when people tell me, 'I don't eat tongue' then they go and eat a whole plate and say 'that wasn't tongue, that was great!'

METHOD

Soak the tongues in a large bowl of salted water overnight in the refrigerator. Drain well.

Put the tongues in a large saucepan and cover with water. Add two of the carrots, the onion, eight of the bay leaves, 1 tablespoon peppercorns, the parsley stalks and five of the cloves. Bring to the boil then reduce to a simmer and cook for 2–3 hours until tender. The tongues are done when the skin peels off easily. Strain the stock and reserve. Discard the onion, carrots, herbs and spices.

Remove the tongues from the dish, allow to cool slightly then peel while still warm. Remove any rough pieces of connective tissue at the root of the tongue. Cut the tongues into 1.5 cm (⅝ inch) thick slices. Preheat the oven to 160°C (315°F/Gas 2–3).

Heat the olive oil in a flameproof casserole dish over medium heat and cook the diced onion, remaining bay leaves and garlic for 5 minutes, stirring occasionally. Add the capsicum and cook for 10 minutes until soft, stirring occasionally. Dice the remaining carrots, add to the dish and cook for 15 minutes, or until browned. Add the tomato and cook for a further 5 minutes.

Increase the heat to high. Add the sherry, stirring with a wooden spoon to scrape up any cooked-on bits from the bottom of the pan. Bring to the boil then add 700 ml (24 fl oz) of the tongue stock and bring to the boil. Skim the surface to remove any foamy residue and excess oil.

Add most of the chopped parsley, reserving a little for garnish. Put the remaining peppercorns and cloves in a piece of muslin (cheesecloth), tie off and add to the casserole. Continue cooking for 5 minutes. Reduce the heat to medium. Add the tongue slices and enough extra stock to make sure all the slices are covered. Remove from the heat and cover with the lid.

Put the casserole dish in the oven and cook for 45 minutes. Remove the cover, increase the heat to 180°C (350°F/Gas 4) and continue cooking for 20 minutes. The tongue is done when almost falling apart. Discard the peppercorns and cloves.

The sauce should have a light, coating consistency. If necessary, remove the tongue and reduce the sauce over medium–high heat until thickened slightly. Serve on a plate then spoon over a little sauce and sprinkle with the reserved parsley and sea salt flakes.

INGREDIENTS

6 rabbit legs, cut at the joint

6 garlic cloves

6 thyme sprigs

1.5 litres (52 fl oz/6 cups) olive oil

about 300 g (10½ oz) 2-day-old *pasta dura* or other firm crusty bread

2 tablespoons thyme leaves, chopped

1 large handful flat-leaf (Italian) parsley, chopped

100 ml (3½ fl oz) chicken stock (*see page 42*)

100 g (3½ oz) butter, roughly chopped

MEDIA RACIÓN 6, RACIÓN 4

CONEJO CONFITADO

CONFIT RABBIT LEG WITH BREAD AND THYME SAUCE

About half an hour from my house is a great bluestone mansion sitting by the banks of the Barwon River. Some Einstein in the nineteenth century thought it would be a nice idea to have a few rabbits run about the front paddock. So they brought them over from England. Those few rabbits bred up into a plague of biblical proportions and virtually ate Australia to the ground.

Ever since we moved to Geelong my family has been doing our bit to save Australia from this vermin. Dad was a mean shot, mum a good cook and my sister and I were hungry, growing kids. Rabbit is lean, flavoursome and surprisingly easy to cook. At MoVida, we love to confit rabbit. It cooks all the flesh without drying it out.

This dish creates its own bread sauce. The breadcrumbs on top become crisp and brown and the ones that fall into the roasting tin absorb the stock, cooking juices and flavour of the rabbit and thyme.

METHOD

Preheat the oven to 140°C (275°F/Gas 1).

Lay the rabbit leg pieces and the garlic in a roasting tin, just large enough to comfortably fit the rabbit. Place a sprig of thyme on each leg and cover with the olive oil. Cover the dish with foil and cook for 2–3 hours, or until the meat comes away from the bone.

Meanwhile, make coarse breadcrumbs by breaking up the bread into a food processor then blending on high for several minutes. Add the thyme, parsley and a pinch each of salt and pepper and mix in the food processor for 20 seconds.

When the rabbit is cooked, remove from the oil and drain on paper towel. Put in a clean roasting tin, just large enough to comfortably fit the rabbit, pour in the chicken stock and cover with the breadcrumb mix. Place small pieces of butter on the breadcrumbs above each leg.

Increase the oven to 180°C (350°F/Gas 4) and cook for 20 minutes, or until the breadcrumbs are brown. To serve, place a rabbit leg on a warm plate and serve the sauce to one side.

INGREDIENTS

2 kg (4 lb 8 oz) venison shin

125 ml (4 fl oz/½ cup) olive oil

3 brown onions, finely diced

1 garlic bulb, cut in half crossways

3 bay leaves, crunched up

2 tablespoons thyme leaves, chopped

3 carrots, diced

750 ml (26 fl oz/3 cups) Pedro Ximénez sherry

375 ml (13 fl oz/1½ cups) red wine

MEDIA RACIÓN 8, RACIÓN 6

VENUADO CON PEDRO XIMENEZ

VENISON SLOWLY BRAISED WITH PEDRO XIMENEZ SHERRY

This is a big, full-flavoured and slow-cooked dish that marries the sweet barrel flavours of Pedro Ximénez sherry with the lean gaminess of venison. Choose a cut from the leg that has done plenty of work, such as shin. The powerful muscles and connective tissue will take a long time to slowly cook, allowing the flavours to meld, change and sweeten.

METHOD

Clean the venison by cutting away any tendon. Leave on the silver skin as this will cook down. Cut the venison into 6 cm (2½ inch) cubes.

Heat 60 ml (2 fl oz/¼ cup) of the olive oil in a large, wide, heavy-based saucepan over medium–high heat. Cook the onion, garlic, bay leaves and thyme for about 15 minutes, stirring occasionally, until the onion is golden brown. Add the carrot and continue cooking for 30 minutes until the carrot is brown. Remove the vegetables from the pan and set aside.

Increase the heat to high and add the remaining oil. Lightly season the venison and cook, in batches, for 3–4 minutes on all sides until browned.

Add the sherry and red wine, scraping up any cooked-on bits from the bottom of the pan. Return the meat and vegetables to the pan with enough water to cover the meat and bring to the boil. Reduce the heat to low and simmer gently for 2 hours, skimming off any foamy residue that rises to the surface. Add 1 litre (35 fl oz/4 cups) water, or just enough to cover the meat. Continue simmering for another 1½–2 hours, or until the meat is very tender but not falling apart.

Remove the cooked venison, cover with foil and keep warm. Reduce the sauce until it has a light, coating consistency by cooking over high heat for 15 minutes. Season to taste.

To serve, strain the sauce through a fine sieve, place the meat on a plate and spoon the sauce over the meat.

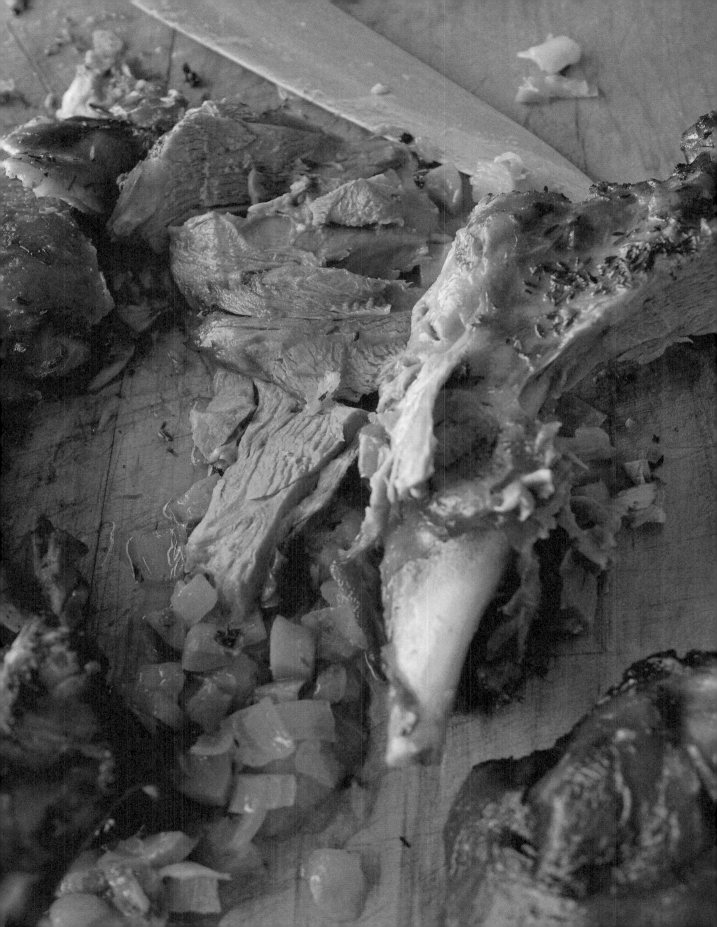

INGREDIENTS

forequarter of a 3–6 month old goat (about 1.5–2 kg/3 lb 5 oz–4 lb 8 oz), cut into 4 pieces

750 ml (26 fl oz/3 cups) fino sherry

150 ml (5 fl oz) extra virgin olive oil

2 tablespoons thyme leaves, chopped

8 bay leaves, gently crushed

2 carrots, roughly chopped

2 brown onions, roughly chopped

1 garlic bulb, peeled and roughly crushed

4 pinches of sea salt flakes

MEDIA RACIÓN 6, RACIÓN 4

CABRITO ASADO

BABY GOAT ROASTED ON A BED OF AROMATIC VEGETABLES

There are a lot of restaurants in Spain with a *horno de leña* (wood-fired oven) at its heart. The fires are lit first thing in the morning and go well into the day. All day and night whole suckling pigs, half lambs and pieces of goat are cooked in giant terracotta trays. The steady heat cooks the meat evenly, slowly easing the meat off the bone, and the embers give the flesh a slightly smoky quality.

If you have a wood-fired oven this is the perfect excuse to light it up. A mate of mine cooks this in his camp oven, on his bush block down the Great Ocean Road. He puts a shovelful of embers on the heavy metal lid and leaves it cooking for hours. The slow cooking melts the flesh and the coals give it a gentle fragrance. You can use very lean lamb if you can't find goat.

METHOD

Marinate the goat by putting it into a bowl with the sherry, extra virgin olive oil, thyme, bay leaves, carrot and onion. Rub the crushed garlic into the goat pieces and put the remains of the garlic in the marinade. Baste the goat with the marinade several times, cover tightly and refrigerate overnight.

Preheat the oven to 180°C (350°F/Gas 4).

Remove the goat from the marinade and set aside. Pour the marinade into a roasting tin, making a bed with the vegetables. Lay the goat on top of the vegetables and season with the sea salt. Put in the oven and cook for 1 hour. Turn the meat over and cook for a further 1–1½ hours, or until the meat comes away from the bone.

Remove from the oven and allow to rest for 10 minutes. Carve the meat and serve with a little of the cooking juices and some of the vegetables.

DAILY BREAD ...

Every day at MoVida we start the shift by baking bread. As dawn breaks the first chef arrives, unlocks the doors, turns on the lights, switches on the coffee machine and lights the ovens — in that order.

Our bread is made by hand, literally. There are no weights or measures. Just the deft judgment of chefs who make bread every day of their working lives, who measure yeast, salt and sugar by the handful.

The first bread into the oven is the sourdough, which has been proving overnight. It's made in small paella pans to give it a lovely, round, crusty base. Next, the yeast bread is made from scratch. It's made in great sprawling, freeform flat loaves, drizzled with olive oil and punctuated with sprigs of rosemary or dusted with Spanish smoked paprika.

It's funny but the bread is always better when it has been made by the same chef for several days in a row. They get into a groove and improve every day. But a humid day, an approaching storm or wintry morning will produce an entirely different loaf. I suppose this is because bread dough is alive, made up of thousands of growing yeast cells.

INGREDIENTS

35 g (1¼ oz) fresh yeast

1 heaped tablespoon salt

1 heaped tablespoon sugar

2 tablespoons olive oil

1.4 kg (3 lb 2 oz) strong plain (all-purpose) flour

olive oil, extra, to drizzle

sea salt flakes, to sprinkle

12 small rosemary sprigs

Spanish sweet smoked paprika, to sprinkle

MAKES 2 LOAVES

JIMMY'S MOVIDA BREAD

This is a very wet, sticky dough and is best made in a food processor or an electric mixer with a bread or dough hook.

METHOD

Break apart the yeast in a bowl and pour 1 litre (35 fl oz/4 cups) lukewarm water over the yeast. Whisk until the yeast has dissolved. Add the salt, sugar and oil then mix together and leave in a warm place for 30 minutes, or until the mixture starts to bubble.

Add the flour and stir to combine then place in a food processor or electric mixer and mix well, using the bread hook attachment, for 12 minutes. Rest for 5 minutes then mix again for 5 minutes. Remove from the food processor, cover with plastic wrap and leave to rise for 30 minutes.

Preheat the oven to 230°C (450°F/Gas 8). Heavily oil two 35 x 45 cm (14 x 17¾ inch) baking trays.

Divide the dough into two equal portions and, on a well-floured work surface, shape each portion into rough 25 cm (10 inch) rounds. Drop the rounds onto the trays, push the dough out towards the edges then drizzle with olive oil.

Prove once more in a warm place for 15–20 minutes. Drizzle both rounds with a little more olive oil and a generous sprinkle of sea salt flakes. Dot one round with rosemary sprigs, poking them in. Bake both rounds for 30 minutes, or until the bread sounds hollow when knocked with your knuckles. Sprinkle the plain loaf with the paprika as soon as it comes out of the oven. Cool both rounds on a wire rack. Serve the bread with every meal.

EMBUTIDOS

EMBUTIDOS

EMBUTIDOS
SMALL GOODS

At MoVida, we make hundreds of spicy chorizo and *morcilla* every week. We do it because we believe handmade sausages are the best. We also know what goes into every sausage and have strict control over their quality. I teach my staff that in a Spanish kitchen nothing is ever wasted — ever. When so much time, money and energy go into raising an animal for the table, it is just illogical to throw any part away. Spices and traditional recipes transform the undervalued cuts into true culinary delights. We use the lesser-loved cuts from the forequarter of the animal to make our *salchicha* (pork sausage) and chorizo.

As chorizo and *morcilla* are used in so many dishes in this book, I thought it would be improper not to give you my family recipes for them. When I asked my dad for the recipes he insisted that I give you his recipe for *salchicha* too. I don't imagine that every person who reads this book will rush out to make *morcilla* but I know several who will.

To make sausages you will need some ingredients that are not readily available from any other place than a butcher. Pork shoulder, back fat and sausage casings can be ordered from most butchers, but give them a week's notice. You can also ask them to grind the meat for you. Explain to them what you are doing and they will generally give you some good advice.

When making small goods, follow the three-word mantra: cold, clean and quick.

Cold — Make sure the ingredients are cold. This stops the fat from smearing the casing and making an unappealing sausage.
Clean — Cleanliness is essential. Scrub all tools and surfaces until they are very clean. Your hands must also be very clean.
Quick — Work fast, as this will prevent the ingredients from warming up.

Oh … and one other thing. Making small goods and sausages with friends and family — with the aid of the odd glass of wine — is truly traditional in all sausage-making cultures. So, go and make good *embutidos* and follow in the footsteps of centuries of Spaniards.

SALCHICHAS DE CERDO
PORK SAUSAGES

The Latin root of the Spanish word for sausage (*salchicha*), is the key to the importance that these little tubes of rich, spicy meat have always held for Spanish people. The root *sal* comes from *salus*, which means salted. Sausages were traditionally made by families at the end of autumn when a pig was slaughtered, cut up (fat and all), mixed with salt and spices and stuffed into its own intestines, then hung from the rafters and dried. The salt in those sausages — a thirst-inducing 3 per cent — helped to stop bacteria from spoiling the meat. One by one, the *salchichas* were taken down and incorporated into *cocidos* and other stews with salted pork and dried legumes. These stews sustained the family through the long lean winter. As the sausages in this recipe are to be eaten fresh, we have reduced the salt from the original recipe by half.

METHOD

Soak the sausage casing in fresh cold water for 12 hours, changing the water several times. When ready to fill, drain well.

Coarsely grind the pork shoulder and pork fat in a meat mincer or using the meat mincing attachment to a food processor. Tip into a large bowl, add the salt, sugar, peppercorns and 1 teaspoon freshly ground black pepper and mix together with very clean hands for about 5 minutes to ensure it is very well combined.

INGREDIENTS

1.5 m (4.9 feet) long, about 36 mm (1¼ inch) wide sausage casing

700 g (1 lb 9 oz) pork shoulder, cut into 2.5 x 5 cm (1 x 2 inch) strips (*see Note*)

300 g (10½ oz) pork back fat, cut into 2.5 x 5 cm (1 x 2 inch) strips (*see Note*)

2 teaspoons fine sea salt

1 level teaspoon sugar

1 teaspoon black peppercorns

MAKES 1 KG (2 LB 4 OZ) SAUSAGES

Slide one open end of the sausage casing onto the nozzle of the sausage attachment of a food processor. Alternatively, use a sausage pump or commercial pastry bag. Tie off the opposite end of the casing with kitchen string, as you would tie off a balloon, then fill the casing with the sausage mix. Make sure the skin is not too tight or the sausage will burst when it is tied off. Carefully pull the sausage casing off the filling tube and tie off that end. Twist into 10 cm (4 inch) links, twisting each new link in the opposite direction. Remove a shelf from the refrigerator and hang the sausages in a bundle from a hook. Place a plate underneath to catch any dripping fluid.

Cook within several days of making, or put the sausages in plastic bags and freeze for up to 1 month.

Note: Longer pieces of meat and fat work best in the auger of the mincer, as they pull through more easily. Square pieces can get stuck.

SPANISH BLOOD PUDDING FROM BURGOS

Light, delicate, perfumed with a touch of spices and with a melt-in-the-mouth texture, *morcilla* is *the* small good of Spain. Made by traditional small goods makers, *morcillas* hang from the ceiling in great rows of burgundy-coloured loops.

Sautéed and cooked with eggs, they make the most indulgent and fragrant *morcilla revueltos* (scrambled eggs with Spanish blood pudding, see page 128). Sliced thickly and roasted in a cast-iron pan in a 180°C (350°F/Gas 4) oven for 10 minutes, *morcilla* puffs up and becomes light and fluffy. With their mix of sweet, savoury and spice, *morcillas* are perfect with a little glass of *amontillado* wine.

Oh, and by the way, did I mention they are made with lard, pork fat and pig's blood?

METHOD

Soak the sausage casing in fresh cold water for 12 hours, changing the water several times.

Preheat the oven to 180°C (350°F/Gas 4). Place the unpeeled garlic in a small roasting tin and roast for about 30 minutes until very tender. Remove the skin and finely chop two of the cloves. (The remaining garlic can be used for making garlic butter, or other recipes that call for roasted garlic.)

Put the onion in a large saucepan, cover with cold water and place over high heat. Boil for 12 minutes until the onion is cooked but still a little firm. Drain well, as excess water in the onion will make the sausages too soft.

Put the rice into a large saucepan and add 500 ml (17 fl oz/2 cups) water. Bring to the boil then reduce to a simmer and cook for 12 minutes until the rice is cooked but still a little firm in the middle. Drain well and allow to cool.

INGREDIENTS

1.5 m (4.9 feet) long, about 36 mm (1¼ inch) wide sausage casing

1 garlic bulb, unpeeled

1.25 kg (2 lb 12 oz) onions, roughly chopped

250 g (9 oz) white short-grain rice

125 g (4½ oz) lard, at room temperature

375 g (13 oz) back fat, coarsely minced

250 ml (9 fl oz/1 cup) pig's blood

1 level teaspoon white pepper

1 tablespoon fine sea salt

½ teaspoon freshly grated nutmeg

pinch of ground cloves

pinch of ground cinnamon

1 tablespoon Spanish sweet paprika

2 teaspoons Spanish hot paprika

½ teaspoon dried oregano

MAKES FIVE 500 G (1 LB 2 OZ) MORCILLA

Put all the ingredients — except the sausage casing — in a very large bowl and season with 1 level teaspoon freshly ground black pepper. Mix well for 5 minutes, cover with plastic wrap then refrigerate for 3 hours.

Slide one open end of the sausage casing onto the nozzle of the sausage attachment of a food processor. Alternatively, use a sausage pump or commercial pastry bag. Tie off the opposite end of the casing with kitchen string, as you would tie off a balloon, then fill the casing with the sausage mix. Make sure the skin is not too tight or the sausage will burst when it is tied off. Tie off the other end of the casing and make 30 cm (12 inch) long sausages by twisting every 30 cm (12 inches) along the sausage. Twist each new link in the opposite direction. Tie the two ends together to form loops. Continue until all the mixture has been used.

Bring a very large saucepan of water to the boil then reduce to a simmer over medium heat. Drop the raw sausages into the pan, one or two at a time, and allow to simmer for 20 minutes to set the *morcilla*. Check to see if fully set by squeezing gently. They should feel spongy and not liquid.

Remove the sausages and allow to cool slightly over very clean tea towels (dish towels) on a table. Remove a shelf from the refrigerator and hang the sausages in a bundle from a hook. Place a plate underneath to catch any dripping fluid.

After a few days the *morcilla* will be ready to use. Use within a week of making or tightly cover with plastic wrap and freeze for up to 1 month.

INGREDIENTS

1.5 m (4.9 feet) long, about 36 mm (1¼ inch)
    wide sausage casing
1 kg (2 lb 4 oz) pork shoulder, cut into
    2.5 x 5 cm (1 x 2 inch) strips (*see Note*)
200 g (7 oz) pork back fat, cut into
    2.5 x 5 cm (1 x 2 inch) strips (*see Note*)

2½ teaspoons fine sea salt
4 tablespoons Spanish sweet paprika
1 level tablespoon Spanish hot paprika
3 level tablespoons dried oregano

MAKES 1 KG (2 LB 4 OZ) SAUSAGES

CHORIZO

This is my father's recipe for fresh chorizo. My dad says that sausages should not be made from offcuts and that they must be made from good quality pork shoulder. He makes about 10 kg (22 lb) at a time. He makes them with twice as much salt as this recipe so he can hang the rest to cure in the garage. He eats some fresh but the rest he hangs and dries and then cuts up and serves with a little *cerveza* (beer) or sherry.

METHOD

Soak the sausage casing in fresh cold water for 12 hours, changing the water several times. When ready to fill, drain well.

Coarsely grind the pork shoulder and pork fat in a meat mincer or using the meat mincing attachment to a food processor. Tip into a large bowl, add the salt, sweet and hot paprikas, and dried oregano and mix together with very clean hands for about 5 minutes to ensure it is very well combined.

Slide one open end of the sausage casing onto the nozzle of the sausage attachment of a food processor. Alternatively, use a sausage pump or commercial pastry bag. Tie off the opposite end of the casing with kitchen string, as you would tie off a balloon, then fill the casing with the sausage mix. Make sure the skin is not too tight or the sausage will burst when it is tied off. Carefully pull the sausage casing off the filling tube and tie off that end. Twist into 10 cm (4 inch) links, twisting each new link in the opposite direction. Remove a shelf from the refrigerator and hang the sausages in a bundle from a hook. Place a plate underneath to catch any dripping fluid.

They can be cooked as per regular sausages or used in recipes calling for chorizo.

Cook within several days of making or put the chorizo in plastic bags and freeze for up to 1 month.

Note: Longer pieces of meat and fat work best in the auger of the mincer, as they pull through more easily. Square pieces can get stuck.

SAUSAGES AT HOME

When mum and dad first arrived in Australia they didn't know where to get chorizo or *morcilla*, so the natural thing for them to do was to make their own. They'd get together with my dad's brother Paco and his wife, Carmen, and turn out metres and metres of rich, spicy sausages over the weekend. It was not just a chance to make small goods, it was a chance to come together, speak Spanish, drink wine and laugh. I think it eventually became an excuse to party. My dad, however, is still very serious about his sausage making. He still makes brilliant *morcilla* and some of the best *jamón* I have tried outside of Spain.

In Spain, women rarely make sausages — it is men's business. Out of necessity mum and dad work together and mum knows the recipes almost as well as dad does! But dad still knows the secrets of hanging and maturing and bit-by-bit he is slowly passing them on to me, so I can, in turn, pass them on to my son, Pepe.

POSTRES

DESSERTS

The Spanish sweet tooth is one of our great inheritances from the Moors. Centuries after their departure, the Spanish are left with a love of cinnamon, citrus and all things sweet. Desserts in Spain can be cooling, soothing, refreshing or outright decadent. Some of the spices used may reprise flavours from the main meal, but a dessert is not a crescendo, it is a segue — a sweet moment to move on to the next part of the day. Desserts are always seen as complementary to the main meal. After a big *cocido* we only eat a little fresh fruit, perhaps some figs or pears, perhaps a little cheese. Desserts need to respect both the flavours of the previous dishes and the constitution of the people eating them.

One of my favourite sweet flavours of Spain is *merengada*. It is a simple and beautiful concoction of sweetened milk, which has been infused with citrus and cinnamon. *Merengada* pulls together the core pillars of the nation's cuisine — the fruits of the land, the fruits of labour, the spices from the ancient trade routes and sugar from Spain's more recent colonial era. *Merengada* has so much flavour and is so easy to prepare.

Although chocolate has been consumed in Spain and Spanish colonies since the days of the conquistadors, it was generally always drunk. But if food is a conversation between cooks around the world then chocolate is a constant talking point, and it is no wonder that a classic French dish like rich chocolate ganache has entered the Spanish vocabulary, *ganacha*, and now has a permanent position on our dessert menu at MoVida.

Ultimately, sweet dishes in Spain are associated with special occasions. With sugar being so expensive until the late 1700s and not until quite recently cheap and abundant, it was traditionally saved to make cakes and sweets for family occasions, such as marriages and religious festivals. The recipe for *torrija* (see page 314) in this chapter is my mother's recipe and it is as simple as it is addictively delicious. *Torrija* in Spain is only ever eaten at Easter, but here in Australia, untied from the bindings of tradition, we are free to make this and other festive desserts at any time of the year.

CHOCOLATE CON CHURROS

SPANISH DOUGHNUTS DUSTED WITH CINNAMON AND SERVED WITH RICH DRINKING CHOCOLATE

The secret to *churros* is in the making of the dough. You might need a few goes to get it right but as the raw ingredients are cheap and readily available — just flour and water — the practice is affordable. The objective is to make dough that is firm, smooth and sticky. You can buy the *churrería*, the thick plastic tube with a screw that extrudes the dough, in good food shops and Spanish stores. You can also use a star nozzle on a piping bag, but this requires a lot of muscle power.

METHOD

Make cinnamon sugar by sifting the sugar and cinnamon together in a small bowl. Set aside.

Bring the milk just to the boil over high heat in a saucepan then reduce the heat to a simmer. Add the chopped chocolate and stir until the chocolate has melted and there are no lumps. Make a paste with the cornflour and 2 tablespoons cold water then stir into the chocolate milk mixture. Continue stirring for about 12 minutes, or until the mixture thickens and easily coats the back of the spoon. Remove from the heat and cover with baking paper (cut into a circle big enough to cover the pan). Covering the chocolate milk mixture with baking paper will keep it warm and prevent a skin forming on top of the milk.

INGREDIENTS

180 g (6¼ oz) caster (superfine) sugar

2 tablespoons ground cinnamon

1 litre (35 fl oz/4 cups) milk

250 g (9 oz) dark couverture chocolate, chopped

2 tablespoons cornflour (cornstarch)

125 g (4½ oz/1 cup) plain (all-purpose) flour

125 g (4½ oz/1 cup) self-raising flour

2 tablespoons olive oil

435 ml (15¼ fl oz/1¾ cups) boiling water

sunflower or other light oil, for deep-frying

**MAKES 30 CHURROS AND ABOUT
1.25 LITRES (44 FL OZ/5 CUPS)
HOT CHOCOLATE**

To make the *churros*, sift the plain four, self-raising flour and a pinch of salt into a heatproof bowl. In a separate bowl add the olive oil to the boiling water and pour over the dry ingredients. Mix with a wooden spoon for 30 seconds — the dough should be fairly soft and sticky to touch.

Fill a deep-fryer or large heavy-based saucepan one-third full of oil and heat to 170°C (325°F), or until a cube of bread dropped into the oil browns in 20 seconds.

Roll the *churros* mixture into a cylinder shape slightly smaller than the *churrería*. Place a tight layer of plastic wrap over a tray and squeeze out 15 cm (6 inch) long *churros* onto the tray. Deep-fry the *churros,* in batches, for 2 minutes then turn and fry for a further 2 minutes, or until golden. Drain on paper towel and sprinkle with the cinnamon sugar.

Meanwhile, return the chocolate to the stovetop over low heat and gently reheat, stirring regularly. To serve, pour the hot chocolate into cups, and dunk the *churros* into the chocolate.

INGREDIENTS

875 ml (30 fl oz/3½ cups) pouring
   (whipping) cream
1 vanilla bean

175 g (6 oz/¾ cup) caster (superfine) sugar
8 egg yolks

MAKES 1 LITRE (35 FL OZ/4 CUPS)

HELADO DE VAINILLA
VANILLA ICE CREAM

This is a good stock-standard recipe for vanilla ice cream. You can replace the vanilla bean with the zest of a lemon and an orange and a few cinnamon sticks to make *helado merengada*.

METHOD

Pour the cream into a heavy-based saucepan. With a sharp knife cut open the vanilla bean lengthways and scrape the seeds into the cream, then add the bean.

Over medium heat infuse the vanilla into the cream by heating until just before it comes to the boil. Remove from the heat and allow to cool for 10–15 minutes. Remove the vanilla bean.

In a bowl gently whisk the sugar into the egg yolks until it is just mixed in. Very slowly add 250 ml (9 fl oz/1 cup) of the warm cream to the eggs while you gently whisk together.

Very slowly add the remainder of the cream and gently whisk together. Strain the cream and eggs into a clean saucepan and stir continuously over low–medium heat for 10–12 minutes, or until the cream thickens enough to coat the back of the spoon.

Allow to cool for 20 minutes then place into an ice cream maker and follow the manufacturer's instructions. Alternatively, transfer to a shallow metal tray and freeze, whisking every couple of hours, until the ice cream is frozen and creamy in texture. Freeze for 5 hours or overnight. Soften in the refrigerator for 30 minutes before serving.

INGREDIENTS

4 lemons

2 litres (70 fl oz/8 cups) milk

450 g (1 lb) sugar

2 cinnamon sticks

6 egg whites

1 teaspoon lemon juice

16 fresh figs, peeled and halved, or 1 kg
  (2 lb 4 oz) fresh cherries (*see Note*)

100 ml (3½ fl oz) anis liqueur

ground cinnamon, to dust

SERVES 8

LECHE MERENGADA CON HIGOS Y ANIS

FROZEN CITRUS AND CINNAMON SOFT SERVE ICE CREAM WITH FRESH FIGS IN ANIS

Leche merengada is a quick frozen dessert made with milk prepared with the holy trinity of citrus, cinnamon and sugar. This recipe makes a wonderful, sweet soft serve ice cream, which is at its very best when freshly made. We have teamed this with fresh figs and anis liqueur, but it is just as good with other sweet ripe fruit, especially cherries. You may have a little left over, but that is a bonus for the chef!

METHOD

To make the *leche merengada*, peel the lemon rind into very wide strips, carefully avoiding any pith. The larger you make the pieces of rind the fewer you will have to remove at the end.

Pour the milk into a large saucepan and add the lemon rind, 400 g (14 oz) of the sugar and the cinnamon sticks. Place over low heat and bring to a simmer very slowly. Remove from the heat and allow to cool to room temperature. Pour the milk into a 28 x 34 cm (11¼ x 13½ inch), 10 cm (4 inch) deep freezer proof dish and freeze overnight.

Whisk the egg whites in a large bowl until soft peaks form then add the remaining sugar and the lemon juice and whisk through until the sugar has dissolved. Turn out the frozen milk into a large stainless steel bowl. Using a metal spoon break up the frozen milk into very small pieces. Add half the beaten egg whites and whisk this into the frozen milk until it is very smooth, using electric beaters or a balloon whisk. Taste it to make sure it is creamy, without any large ice crystals. Continue whisking until it is very smooth. Gently fold in the remaining egg white then very quickly pour into the cleaned freezer proof dish and place in the freezer immediately. Freeze for several hours or until it has the consistency of soft serve ice cream.

Meanwhile, sprinkle the figs with the anis. Serve within 24 hours for the best result. Serve the figs in a bowl, topped with the *leche merengada* and dusted with ground cinnamon.

Note: If using cherries, remove the stems and stones. Put the cherries in a bowl, add the anis and 200 g (7 oz) icing (confectioners') sugar and mix.

CREMA CATALANA
BAKED CITRUS AND CINNAMON CUSTARD

Some food scholars argue that *crème brûlée*, a rich, cool cream custard with a crisp topping of fresh toffee is a French invention. Others claim it came from Trinity College in Oxford, where the crest of the college was emblazoned into the top with a hot branding iron. Aurora, the mother of the owner of Bodega Pepe in Aragon, however, insisted that it was a Catalán invention.

It doesn't matter who was first, what matters to me is that it is a great dessert. This is all about citrus and cinnamon and a smooth texture. In Spain, they have a special iron, in the shape of a coil, like a branding iron, which they use to burn the sugar on the top. We use a kitchen blowtorch — these are cheap, available from good food stores and give the best result. If you're pyrophobic you can make the toffee crust by putting the *crema catalana* in a baking tray filled with chilled water to stop the custard from overcooking then placing them under a hot grill (broiler).

METHOD

The day before serving, make the custard base. Start by peeling the lemon and the orange rinds into very wide strips, carefully avoiding any pith.

Pour the milk and cream into a large heavy-based saucepan. With a sharp knife cut open the vanilla bean lengthways and scrape the seeds into the milk and cream then add the bean and cinnamon.

INGREDIENTS

rind of 1 lemon

rind of 1 orange

250 ml (9 fl oz/1 cup) milk

750 ml (26 fl oz/3 cups) pouring
  (whipping) cream

1 vanilla bean

2 cinnamon sticks

200 g (7 oz) caster (superfine) sugar

8 egg yolks, at room temperature

230 g (8¼ oz/1 cup) caster (superfine)
  sugar, extra

1 tablespoon anis liqueur, to drizzle

MAKES 6

Put over medium heat and watch the saucepan carefully. Just before the milk and cream boil, reduce the heat to low and simmer very gently for 10 minutes then remove from the heat and leave to cool for 10 minutes, to allow the flavours to infuse.

Preheat the oven to 160°C (315°F/Gas 2–3).

In a separate bowl, gently mix the sugar with the egg yolks. Remove 125 ml (4 fl oz/½ cup) of the milk and cream and slowly strain it through a sieve into the egg and sugar mixture as you gently whisk together. Slowly strain the rest of the milk through the sieve and gently whisk together. Discard the citrus rind, cinnamon sticks and vanilla bean.

Pour the egg and cream mixture into a clean saucepan. Return to the stove over low–medium heat and gently cook for 10–12 minutes, or until the mixture coats the back of a spoon, stirring constantly.

Place six 200 ml (7 fl oz) shallow ovenproof dishes in two roasting tins. Pour the mixture into the individual dishes. Pour enough hot water into the tins to come halfway up the dishes. Cook in the oven for 30 minutes until just set. When done the custard should wobble slightly. Remove from the oven and allow to cool slightly then cover with plastic wrap and refrigerate overnight.

Sprinkle 2 tablespoons of the extra caster sugar evenly over the top of each custard. Apply the heat of a kitchen blowtorch, holding at a 45 degree angle, to the top of the custards until the sugar melts into toffee. Drizzle with a little anis and serve immediately.

INGREDIENTS

unsalted butter, softened, to brush

plain (all-purpose) flour, to dust

350 g (12 oz) dark couverture chocolate
(*see Note*)

4 eggs, at room temperature

125 ml (4 fl oz/½ cup) pouring
(whipping) cream

50 g (1¾ oz) unsalted butter, at room
temperature, cut into 1 cm (½ inch) cubes

MAKES 6

GANACHA

HOT GANACHE CHOCOLATE PUDDING

This is a good chocolate dessert. It is also a good excuse to eat Spanish nougat, which goes so well with the chocolaty pudding, and is thankfully now sold in Spanish shops in Australia.

Last time we were in Spain it was Christmas, the time to eat and serve nougat. Vanessa and I decided to pack the spaces in our suitcases with enough Spanish nougat to see us through when we got back to Melbourne. As soon as the shops opened after Christmas we marched in to buy boxes and boxes of the stuff. We had, however, forgotten just how traditional Spain still is. To our dismay the shop staff had hauled all the nougat off the shelves and loaded it onto a pallet and were wrapping it in plastic wrap. When we asked for some they replied something along the lines of, 'Nougat? After Christmas? Are you crazy? No one buys nougat after Christmas'. Please feel free to make this *ganacha* and serve it with Spanish or any good quality nougat — any time of the year you like. Cut or break up the nougat into small morsels and dot these around the plate with a good spoonful of vanilla ice cream.

METHOD

Using a pastry brush, grease six 125 ml (4 fl oz/½ cup) ramekins or dariole moulds with the softened butter using vertical strokes. Lightly dust with flour and refrigerate until ready to use.

Break or chop the chocolate into small pieces and melt in a heatproof bowl over a saucepan of barely simmering water for about 5 minutes, stirring regularly with a metal spoon until smooth and free flowing — make sure the base of the bowl does not sit in the water. Once the chocolate starts to melt, remove from the heat so the chocolate does not burn. Don't allow any water in the chocolate, as it will become granular.

While the chocolate is melting, break the eggs into a bowl and gently whisk together. Bring the cream to the boil in a small saucepan over medium heat. Once boiled, remove the pan immediately from the heat and set aside to cool for 5 minutes.

When the chocolate has melted, add several tablespoons to the egg and gently mix through. Slowly and gently mix through the rest of the chocolate. Add the cream and gently whisk through. Add the unsalted butter and gently mix until it has all melted. Cover with plastic wrap and allow to set in the refrigerator for 1 hour, or until the consistency of soft fudge. Spoon the mix into the chilled ramekins, filling almost to the top. Cover with plastic wrap and refrigerate for at least 30 minutes or overnight.

Preheat the oven to 200°C (400°F/Gas 6).

Evenly space the ramekins on a baking tray and bake for 15 minutes. When done, the edges will be cracked and the centre of the top will be just soft and dome shaped, and just unset. Remove from the oven and allow to cool for 3 minutes. Place a plate on top of the ramekins and gently upturn. Serve with vanilla ice cream and small pieces of Spanish nougat.

Note: Buy chocolate with the highest percentage of cocoa that you can find.

INGREDIENTS

500 g (1 lb 2 oz) caster (superfine) sugar

500 ml (17 fl oz/2 cups) milk

500 ml (17 fl oz/2 cups) pouring
  (whipping) cream

2 whole eggs, at room temperature

9 egg yolks, at room temperature

MAKES 6

FLAN DE NATA
SPANISH RICH CRÈME CARAMEL

This is the most popular of all Spanish desserts. Its similarities to French *crème caramel* are obvious — a rich baked milk and cream custard sitting on top of a layer of bittersweet caramel. But the French connection has never stopped the Spanish from making this classic dessert.

Almost every little local restaurant I have stepped into in Spain has had this on the menu — almost like Australia in the late 1980s when sticky date pudding appeared on our menus. And probably for the same reason, because they are both so bloody good!

This recipe in front of you is the king of *flan* recipes. It actually makes seven servings, but one is a test *flan*. Serve with *pestiños* (see page 328).

METHOD

Caramelize 300 g (10½ oz) of the sugar in a heavy-based frying pan over high heat for 5 minutes, swirling occasionally until it starts to pool with golden liquid. Reduce the heat to medium and cook for another 1–2 minutes, without stirring, until golden. Be careful not to burn the sugar.

Quickly spoon 2 tablespoons of caramel into the bottom of seven 200 ml (7 fl oz) ramekins or dariole moulds (remember — one is a test flan). Place the moulds in a roasting tin.

Pour the milk and cream into a large heavy-based saucepan over medium heat. Just before the milk boils, remove from the heat and allow to cool for 10 minutes. Preheat the oven to 170°C (325°F/Gas 3).

Combine the whole eggs, egg yolks and the remaining sugar in a metal bowl and whisk very lightly until combined.

Gradually pour 250 ml (9 fl oz/1 cup) of the milk and cream mixture onto the egg and sugar while you gently whisk (this ensures that you don't aerate the mixture too much). Slowly add the remainder of the milk and cream and mix together. Once combined, pour the mixture back into a clean, heavy-based saucepan and place over low–medium heat.

Stir the mixture for 10–12 minutes with a wooden spoon until it is thick enough to coat the back of the spoon. Using a ladle, pour the mixture immediately into the prepared ramekins, filling to the top.

Pour enough hot water into the roasting tin to fill up to 1 cm (½ inch) from the top of the ramekins. Cook in the oven for 1 hour. Test only one of the custards to see if done by inserting a knife in the centre to the bottom. Pull to one side and if the caramel rises, it is done. Allow to set overnight in the refrigerator.

To serve, run a knife around the edge and carefully invert each ramekin onto six individual serving plates.

TORRIJA

FRIED MILK PUDDING DUSTED WITH CINNAMON AND HONEY

Torrija is extreme French toast — beautiful, golden slices of fried bread soaked in a cream and citrus infusion and slathered in honey and sherry syrup.

This is Easter food. Every year mum makes a huge batch of *torrijas* and piles them up high, her intention being that there will be enough to last all through Easter. But every year my sister and I, my dad and other family members eat them up and the pile is gone by the afternoon. Mum makes a *jarabe* (syrup) that is intense and sticky. I prefer mine a little less sticky. If you are making these for yourself, please feel free to bend the rules and eat with some vanilla ice cream and a little glass of Pedro Ximénez sherry.

METHOD

Put the milk, cream, orange and lemon rind, sugar and two of the cinnamon sticks in a large saucepan over low heat and simmer gently for about 30 minutes. Remove from the heat and allow to cool to lukewarm (this should take 30–45 minutes).

Strain the lukewarm milk mixture into a shallow bowl, large enough to hold all the bread. Soak the bread in the milk for 30 minutes.

INGREDIENTS

1 litre (35 fl oz/4 cups) milk

1 litre (35 fl oz/4 cups) pouring
  (whipping) cream

rind of 2 oranges, cut into large strips

rind of 2 lemons, cut into large strips

175 g (6 oz) caster (superfine) sugar

4 cinnamon sticks

2 loaves 2-day-old *pasta dura* or other firm
  crusty bread, cut into 2.5 cm (1 inch)
  thick slices

480 g (1 lb 1 oz/1⅓ cups) honey

500 ml (17 fl oz/2 cups) oloroso sherry

2 tablespoons ground cinnamon

180 g (6¼ oz/¾ cup) caster (superfine) sugar,
  extra

6 eggs

100 g (3½ oz) unsalted butter

SERVES 8-12

In another saucepan make the *jarabe* by heating the honey, sherry, remaining cinnamon sticks and 250 ml (9 fl oz/1 cup) water over high heat. Just before boiling point, reduce to a simmer and cook for 45 minutes. The syrup should still be quite runny, but thickened slightly.

Make cinnamon sugar by sifting the cinnamon and extra sugar together in a small bowl. Set aside.

Lightly beat the eggs in a shallow bowl. Melt half the butter in a large frying pan over low—medium heat. Lift the bread from the milk and drain for a few seconds before placing it into the beaten egg. Cover the bread very well, as this will form a seal and keep the flavoured milk and cream in the bread when fried.

Cook the bread, in two batches, for 2 minutes each side, or until golden, adding more butter as needed. Remove the bread from the pan and briefly drain on paper towel. Dust the fried bread with cinnamon sugar. Place in a non-metallic tray in a single layer and cover with the *jarabe* while still warm.

When ready to serve, pile the *torrijas* high on a serving plate and spoon over a little of the residual *jarabe*.

Note: This recipe make a lot of *torrija*, but it is a traditional family dish — for a large family!

INGREDIENTS

6 eggs, separated, at room temperature

820 g (1 lb 13 oz) caster (superfine) sugar

1 tablespoon fresh yeast

125 g (4½ oz/1 cup) plain (all-purpose) flour

70 g (2½ oz) unsweetened cocoa powder

350 ml (12 fl oz) brandy

150 ml (5 fl oz) white rum

100 ml (3½ fl oz) dark Jamaican rum
  (optional)

rind of 2 oranges, cut into large strips

rind of 2 lemons, cut into large strips

1 whole star anise

1 litre (35 fl oz/4 cups) milk

3 cinnamon sticks

100 g (3½ oz) Calasparra rice, rinsed
  and drained

SERVES 6

BORRACHUELO CON SALSA DE ARROZ
SWEET BRANDY-SOAKED CHOCOLATE SPONGE WITH RICE PUDDING SAUCE

Borrachuelo means drunkard. It refers to the amount of rum and brandy-flavoured *jarabe* (syrup) this chocolate sponge soaks up. This is a good recipe for sponge, as it is lightened by egg whites and leavened by yeast, which also gives it a nutty richness.

When making the sponge, make sure the equipment is really clean because any fat or oil will stop the egg whites from fluffing up. The other little tip is to always think light when making a sponge — a gentle touch will help keep the sponge nice and airy.

The other delight is the rice pudding sauce. It is remarkably easy to make and so delicious. If you keep on cooking it and reduce the milk it becomes rice pudding! This dish is also excellent with some fresh goat's curd or a little drizzle of leatherwood honey.

METHOD

Preheat the oven to 180°C (350°F/Gas 4). Line a 22 x 26 x 5 cm (8½ x 10½ x 2 inch) cake tin with baking paper then brush with a little melted butter.

Gently whisk the egg yolks and 90 g (3¼ oz) of the sugar together in a bowl for 2 minutes until the consistency of thick, foamy cream.

Break the yeast into small pieces then add to the egg yolks and sugar. Mash the yeast with the back of a fork until there are no lumps and whisk to mix through.

In another bowl, whisk the egg whites until they keep their shape but before they form soft peaks. Gradually add 90 g (3¼ oz) of sugar to the whisked eggs, continuing to whisk gently, for 2 minutes, or until the sugar dissolves. Continue whisking until the egg whites form soft peaks.

Add a third of the beaten egg white to the egg yolk mixture and whisk together to just combine then very gently fold the remaining whites through the yolks until just combined. There should be no white lumps, but be careful not to beat out the air.

Sieve the flour and cocoa together into a large bowl then sieve onto the egg mixture, one-third at a time, gently folding each addition through. Pour the mixture into the prepared tin and bake for 20–25 minutes, or until a skewer inserted into the centre of the cake comes out clean. Turn out onto a wire rack, remove the baking paper and allow to cool completely.

Meanwhile, to make the syrup, put 500 g (1 lb 2 oz) of the sugar, the brandy, rums, half of the lemon and orange rind strips, star anise and 1 litre (35 fl oz/4 cups) water in a saucepan over high heat. Stir until the sugar has dissolved and bring to the boil. Reduce the heat to a simmer and cook for 1 hour, or until reduced by half. Remove from the heat and allow to cool until just warm.

Using a long serrated knife, carefully cut off and discard the thin layer of upper 'crust' on the sponge, to help soak up some of the *jarabe*. Cut the sponge into six equal portions and put these into a 22 x 26 cm (8^1/$_2$ x 10^1/$_2$ inch) non-metallic dish. Pour most of the warm *jarabe* over the sponge. Using the back of a spoon gently 'push' the *jarabe* into the cake. Cover with plastic wrap and allow to soak for several hours, occasionally spooning over the remaining *jarabe*.

To make the rice pudding sauce, put the milk, remaining orange and lemon rind, the cinnamon sticks and remaining sugar in a heavy-based saucepan over medium heat. Stir until the sugar has dissolved then, as soon as the milk starts to boil, add the rice. Return to the boil then reduce to a simmer and cook for about 30 minutes, or until the rice is tender. Remove from the heat and allow to cool just a little before removing and discarding the orange and lemon rind and cinnamon sticks. Blend in a food processor for several minutes until smooth.

To serve, place the soaked sponge pieces onto a plate and spoon over any residual *jarabe* and then the rice pudding sauce.

INGREDIENTS

200 ml (7 fl oz) strained blood orange juice (about 6–8 small blood oranges) (*see Notes*)

7½ gelatine leaves (5 g/⅛ oz each) (*see Notes*)

8 granny smith apples, unpeeled, cored and chopped

80 ml (2½ fl oz/⅓ cup) sweet green apple liqueur

125 g (4½ oz) caster (superfine) sugar

2 egg whites

SERVES 6

ESPUMA CUAJADA DE MANZANA CON GELATINA DE NARANJA SANGUINA

FRESH GRANNY SMITH MOUSSE WITH BLOOD ORANGE JELLY

Realistically, most Spanish meals finish with fruit. To make this healthy Spanish habit into something more elevated for a restaurant or special dinner party, I invented this dish using some modern techniques favoured by modern Spanish chefs. This recipe requires a lot of whisking and is unapologetically dependent on the brawn of the electric hand mixer.

METHOD

Heat the blood orange juice in a saucepan over high heat and remove from the heat just before it boils. Soften two gelatine leaves in a bowl of cold water for 30 seconds. Drop the leaves into the hot orange juice and stir until the gelatine has dissolved. Allow to cool then pour into six 150 ml (5 fl oz) pre-chilled serving glasses. Refrigerate.

Purée the apple in a food processor. Strain the apple purée through a fine sieve and discard the solids. Pour 500 ml (17 fl oz/2 cups) of the juice into a saucepan. If there is not enough juice, purée more apples or extend the fresh juice with bottled juice. Add the liqueur and caster sugar and boil over high heat for 5–10 minutes until the liquid has reduced to 500 ml (17 fl oz/2 cups).

Soften the remaining gelatine leaves in a bowl of cold water for 30 seconds and then drop into the hot apple liquid and stir until the gelatine has dissolved. Pour the apple and gelatine mixture into a bowl that is sitting on top of an ice bath. After 10 minutes it should be cold enough to start beating into a mousse. The ice bath needs to sit under the apple mixture for the duration of the beating. Using electric hand beaters, beat for 10 minutes and as the mixture starts to set (it should be around room temperature), add one egg white and continue beating for 10 minutes, or until it is noticeably thicker. Add the other egg white and beat for a further 10 minutes until the volume has tripled.

When ready the apple mousse will form soft peaks. Pour over the top of the orange jelly and refrigerate for 2 hours before serving.

Notes: If blood oranges are out of season, buy blood orange juice from the supermarket or delicatessen.

Use gelatine leaves which are 23 x 7 cm (9¾ x 2 inches) in size.

QUESO

CHEESE – FOUR OF SPAIN'S MOST POPULAR

QUESO MAHÓN
Although many Australians will remember the Balearic Islands for the antics of Christopher Skase, for centuries the island of Menorca has been better known for its *Mahón* cow's milk cheese. It's moulded into a square and rubbed with paprika to give it a lively orange tinge. A versatile cheese, it can be eaten when fresh, semi-cured or aged. Young *Mahón* is sweet and milky but as it ages it becomes nuttier and has been likened to real cheddar. It is traditionally eaten with olive oil drizzled over the top, black pepper and freshly chopped tarragon.

QUESO DE MURCIA AL VINO
Made in the hot, arid Murcia region on the southeast coast of Spain, this goat's milk cheese is washed in high tannin red wine to develop the rind, which gives it a lovely red tinge. It is matured for 3 months, during which time it develops a floral aroma, a mild fruity flavour and a smooth buttery texture.

QUESO VALDEÓN
Valdeón cheeses are a blend of 90 per cent cow's and 10 per cent goat's milk. Like many blue cheeses, Valdeón is pierced to allow blue mould to develop. When mature the cheeses are wrapped in sycamore leaves. It is an aromatic cheese with the lingering tang of blue mould and is slightly fruity with a creamy paste.

QUESO MANCHEGO D.O.
This is Spain's best-known cheese and is made in Don Quixote territory in Castille–La Mancha, from Manchega sheep's milk. It comes in wheels imprinted with a zigzag pattern and has a sweet nutty character and, like Italian parmigiano, it develops little crunchy 'flavour crystals'. It can be eaten young at 4 months but many prefer it aged to 12 months or more.

REPOSTERÍA

REPOSTERÍA
PASTRIES

In Spain, every decent-sized town has a convent run by nuns who make sweets and pastries. I remember my Great Aunt 'Cha Cha' Pepa taking me to a whitewashed convent on the outskirts of Aguila de la Frontera. We went to buy some biscuits but it felt more like we were leaving a baby there, to become an orphan. There was a slightly clandestine air to the way we had to leave our money in a rotating door in the convent wall. We put in our money and spun the door around. There was a little noise of our coins being taken and then we opened the door again to find a box of *polvorones* (individually-wrapped little almond and lard biscuits). They are called *polvorones* after the Spanish word *polvo* (dust). They were so light and delicate that they almost turned to dust when you picked them up. Unfortunately, the nuns kept their recipes tightly to themselves and I have never found a recipe for *polvorones* that comes close to theirs.

It is this shortness and lightness of many Spanish pastries that has always intrigued me. Unlike Northern European baked goods, which are shortened with butter, a lot of Spanish pastries use olive oil or lard to stop the gluten forming when making pastry. This makes Spanish pastry very crumbly and sometimes very brittle. Olive oil and lard add lightness to pastry that butter, which tends to enrich and moisten, doesn't seem to achieve.

When making any of the olive oil pastries in this book make sure you use olive oil that has been processed. This removes a lot of the colour and flavour. Do not use extra virgin olive oil, as this is far too strong. Good olive oil is labelled as such and is available in supermarkets. Lard has a wonderful taste all of its own that seems to enhance sweetness. Lard is available in some supermarkets and sold in 250 g (9 oz) blocks, like butter.

INGREDIENTS

1 lemon	250 g (9 oz) goat's curd
185 g (6½ oz) caster (superfine) sugar	1½ tablespoons caster (superfine) sugar, extra
2 tablespoons ground cinnamon	1 quantity *pestiño* pastry (*see Note*)
70 g (2½ oz) dried muscatel grapes	1 egg, lightly beaten
60 ml (2 fl oz/¼ cup) Pedro Ximénez sherry, or	sunflower oil, for deep-frying
other very sweet fortified wine	

MAKES 16

FLOAN

SWEET PASTRY HALF MOONS WITH PEDRO XIMÉNEZ AND FRESH GOAT'S CURD

Floan are from the north of Spain. Vanessa and I saw them in a *pastelería* (pastry shop) and had to try them. We liked them so much that we kept on having to try them. It is amazing just how much you can eat in the name of research. To make things easier, we are using the *pestiños* pastry recipe from page 328. Most Spaniards would turn in their graves if they knew we were using *pestiños* pastry, but it is so versatile and so tasty that it is worth bending the rules. Any leftover pastry can be used to make *pestiños*, to have on standby for coffee or dessert.

METHOD

Remove and finely chop the zest from the lemon. To make the cinnamon sugar, combine the caster sugar and ground cinnamon in a bowl. Set aside until ready to use.

Pluck the muscatels from the stalks, place in a bowl and pour over the sherry. Cover and leave overnight — the muscatels will absorb the sherry and become plump.

To make the filling, whisk the goat's curd with the extra sugar until well combined. Add the lemon zest and the muscatels along with half of the sherry that remains from soaking the muscatels.

Roll the pastry out on a well-floured surface to 2–3 mm (1/16–1/8 inch) thickness. With a 10 cm (4 inch) round pastry cutter cut the pastry into 16 circles. Put 3 teaspoons of filling on one half of a circle. Brush one edge of the pastry with some beaten egg. Fold over and crimp the edges together with a fork. Repeat with the remaining pastry and filling.

Fill a deep-fryer or heavy-based saucepan one-third full of oil and heat to 170°C (325°F), or until a cube of bread dropped into the oil browns in 20 seconds. Deep fry, in batches, for 2 minutes each side, or until golden brown. Remove from the oil and drain on paper towel. Allow to rest until cool enough to handle then dust with the cinnamon sugar.

Note: Make the *pestiños* pastry (see page 328) up to the point of resting for 10 minutes.

INGREDIENTS

90 g (3¼ oz) caster (superfine) sugar

1 tablespoon ground cinnamon

500 g (1 lb 2 oz) plain (all-purpose) flour

1 teaspoon bicarbonate of soda (baking soda)

pinch of fine sea salt

1 tablespoon ground cloves

185 ml (6 fl oz/¾ cup) olive oil

1 tablespoon fennel seeds

185 ml (6 fl oz/¾ cup) fino sherry

sunflower oil, for deep frying

MAKES ABOUT 60

PESTIÑOS
SHERRY PASTRIES FLAVOURED WITH FENNEL, CLOVES AND CINNAMON

This is an exciting recipe to make but much care is needed as the hot oil and cold sherry makes plumes of smoke and steam. Anyone entering the kitchen while you're making them could suspect you of practising alchemy! Although *pestiños* are traditionally a Christmas treat, they are good any time of the year and excellent with good black coffee. Or serve them with a few scoops of vanilla ice cream and Pedro Ximénez sherry, as a quick and easy dessert. This recipe makes a large quantity of *pestiños*, but they store well in an airtight container and will keep for weeks.

METHOD

To make the cinnamon sugar, combine the caster sugar and ground cinnamon in a bowl. Set aside until ready to use.

Sieve the flour, bicarbonate of soda, sea salt and ground cloves in a large heatproof bowl and combine well. Form a well in the centre.

Put the oil and the fennel seeds in a frying pan and fry the seeds over medium heat for a few minutes until the seeds brown and release their flavour. Remove from the heat.

Pour the hot oil into the well in the dry ingredients then immediately and very carefully add the sherry. Allow to bubble for 10 seconds and when the bubbles subside, mix together with a wooden spoon, until the mixture forms a soft pastry. Bring together into a loose ball with your hands. Allow to rest for 10 minutes.

Roll out the dough on a well-floured surface until about 3 mm (⅛ inch) thick. (A large chopping board is good, as you can take the pastry directly to the deep-fryer.) Cut the dough into 1 x 8 cm (½ x 3¼ inch) strips using a crinkle-cut pastry cutter.

Fill a deep-fryer or large heavy-based saucepan one-third full of oil and heat the oil to 170°C (325°F), or until a cube of bread dropped into the oil browns in 20 seconds. Deep-fry the *pestiños* in batches for a few minutes until golden. Drain on paper towel. Allow to rest until cool enough to handle then sprinkle with the cinnamon sugar.

INGREDIENTS

120 g (4¼ oz) dark chocolate, chopped

145 g (5¼ oz/⅔ cup) caster (superfine) sugar

350 g (12 oz/1 cup) honey

500 g (1 lb 2 oz) blanched almonds

250 g (9 oz) whole dried figs

165 g (5¾ oz/1⅓ cups) plain (all-purpose) flour

4 tablespoons good quality unsweetened cocoa powder

2 tablespoons ground cinnamon

MAKES 1 LOAF

PAN DE HIGOS

SPICY CHOCOLATE AND FIG BREAD

This is more an after dessert sweetmeat than bread. It is dark, sweet, thick and dense. *Pan de higos* is similar to the Italian *panforte* but simpler and easier to make. You can slice it very thinly using a sharp bread knife and serve it with coffee.

METHOD

Grease and flour a 22 x 12 x 6 cm (8½ x 4½ x 2½ inch) loaf (bar) tin, tipping out any excess flour. Preheat the oven to 180°C (350°F/Gas 4).

Gently melt the chocolate in a bowl over a saucepan of simmering water for 5 minutes, stirring occasionally — make sure the base of the bowl doesn't touch the water. In a separate saucepan melt the sugar and honey over low heat for 10 minutes until the sugar has dissolved.

Meanwhile, combine the almonds, figs, flour, cocoa and cinnamon in a large bowl. Pour the melted chocolate and the honey and sugar mixture over the dry ingredients and mix well. You should end up with a stiff, slightly sticky mass. Spoon into the prepared tin and use lightly dampened hands to smooth over.

Bake for 25 minutes, or until it is dry but still yields to the touch on top. It will seem rather underdone; however the bread will continue to cook and firm up once out of the oven. Let cool in the tin for 5 minutes then run a knife around the edge and turn out onto a wire rack. Allow to cool completely; this will take several hours.

To serve, cut into 3 mm (⅛ inch) slices. *Pan de higos* can be refrigerated, unsliced and covered, for up to 2 weeks.

TARTA DE SANTIAGO
SAINT JAMES TART WITH QUINCE

Santiago de Compestela is not just home to a magnificent twin-spired medieval cathedral but is also the birthplace of a wonderful tart. *Tarta de Santiago* is always filled with ground almonds and egg in a buttery short pastry. (Butter is more common in the greener, wetter north where dairy cows thrive.) After baking, the cross of the knights of Saint James (Santiago means Saint James) is placed on top of the tart and then it is dusted with sugar, leaving the sign of the cross on the tart. At this tart's core is a square of quince paste, surrounded by an almond filling sweetened with Pedro Ximénez sherry, and then encased in buttery, shortcrust pastry flavoured with lemon. I think you'll agree it was worth the trip.

METHOD

To make the pastry, cut 250 g (9 oz) of the butter into 1 cm (½ inch) cubes. Using your fingertips, rub the butter into the flour until the mixture resembles fine breadcrumbs. Add 325 g (11½ oz) of the caster sugar, the lemon rind and a pinch of salt and mix in well with a wooden spoon. Mix in the egg yolk and then two of the eggs, one at a time. Mix together for 1 minute until a soft dough forms. Roll the dough into a ball, wrap in plastic wrap and refrigerate for 2 hours.

To make the filling, blend half the almonds in a food processor for 2 minutes until finely crushed. Add the remaining almonds and blend for 30 seconds until very roughly crushed. The idea is to have a mix of finely crushed and roughly crushed almonds.

Mix together the almonds, remaining sugar, sherry and orange rind in a bowl. Add the remaining six eggs, one at a time, and mix well.

INGREDIENTS

300 g (10½ oz) unsalted butter, at room
    temperature

500 g (1 lb 2 oz/4 cups) plain (all-purpose)
    flour

480 g (1 lb 1 oz) caster (superfine) sugar

rind of 2 lemons, finely grated

1 egg yolk, at room temperature

8 eggs, at room temperature

350 g (12 oz) blanched almonds

60 ml (2 fl oz/¼ cup) Pedro Ximénez sherry

rind of 1 orange, finely grated

1 egg, extra, lightly beaten

500 g (1 lb 2 oz) quince paste

icing (confectioners') sugar, to dust

MAKES 12

Melt the remaining butter and mix thoroughly into the filling. Cover with plastic wrap and refrigerate for 1 hour.

With a little butter grease, then flour, twelve 10 cm (4 inch) diameter flan tins.

Cut the pastry into four portions and roll each one out on a clean, well-floured bench to about 2 mm (¹⁄₁₆ inch) thick. Cut out three 12 cm (4½ inch) circles from each portion of pastry and line the tins with the pastry. Prick each base several times with a fork. Trim the edges. Cover with plastic wrap and let rest in the refrigerator for 1 hour.

Preheat the oven to 160°C (315°F/Gas 2–3).

Line each pastry case with baking paper and a layer of baking beads or dry beans and bake for 15 minutes. Remove the paper and beans and brush the base of the tart with a little of the beaten egg and return to the oven for a further 5 minutes, or until lightly golden. Remove from the oven.

Divide the quince paste into 12 equal slices. Place a slice of quince paste into each pastry shell and cover with the filling. Bake in the oven for 20 minutes, or until firm to the touch. Remove from the oven and allow to cool. Dust with icing sugar.

INGREDIENTS

310 g (10¾ oz/1½ cups) caster
    (superfine) sugar

2 tablespoons ground cinnamon

2 eggs, at room temperature

250 ml (9 fl oz/1 cup) pouring
    (whipping) cream

250 ml (9 fl oz/1 cup) freshly squeezed
    orange juice, strained

zest of 1 lemon, very finely chopped

125 ml (4 fl oz/½ cup) pure olive oil

850 g (1 lb 14 oz) self-raising flour

sunflower oil, for deep-frying

MAKES ABOUT 24

ROSQUILLAS
SWEET LEMON DOUGHNUTS

Rosquillas are the best and easiest doughnuts to make in the world. When I make them with my mum, she laughs and says my hands are too big to form them properly. She has a wonderful knack of rolling out the dough in one perfect, gentle movement. The dough itself is a one-step process and is shortened with olive oil and flavoured with lemon rind to make the shortest, lightest and tastiest doughnuts. The temptation is to dust them with icing sugar and eat them straight away. Don't. Wait until they cool down. They are so much better when cool.

METHOD

To make the cinnamon sugar, combine 185 g (6½ oz) of the caster sugar and the ground cinnamon in a bowl. Set aside until ready to use.

Put the eggs, cream, orange juice, lemon zest, olive oil and the remaining sugar in a bowl and mix well. Sift in the flour, stirring until a soft dough is formed. Knead for 1 minute on a lightly floured work surface. It should be the consistency of loose bread dough.

Roll pieces of the dough in the palms of your hands into balls just smaller than golf balls. You should have about 24 balls. Then on a cold, lightly floured work surface, roll each ball into a cylinder 15 cm (6 inches) long. Bring the ends together to make little doughnut-shaped rings and pinch together to seal.

Fill a deep-fryer or heavy-based saucepan one-third full of oil and heat to 180°C (350°F), or until a cube of bread dropped into the oil browns in 15 seconds. Deep-fry the *rosquillas* for 2 minutes then turn and deep-fry for a further 2 minutes, or until golden. Drain on paper towel. Allow to rest until cool enough to handle then coat with cinnamon sugar.

Note: *Rosquillas* are best eaten on the day that they are made, but they will keep for a couple of days — when they will be best suited to dunking in morning coffee.

INGREDIENTS

50 g (1¾ oz) blanched almonds, roasted
(*see page 14*)

2 eggs

125 ml (4 fl oz/½ cup) pure olive oil

115 g (4 oz/½ cup) caster (superfine) sugar

250 g (9 oz) lard, at room temperature

340 g (11¾ oz/2¾ cups) plain
(all-purpose) flour

rind of 1 lemon

60 ml (2 fl oz/¼ cup) anis liqueur

1 egg, extra, lightly beaten

icing (confectioners') sugar, to dust

MAKES 36

MANTECADOS DE ALMENDRA
RICH CHRISTMAS ALMOND BISCUITS

Someone once asked me if butter instead of lard could be used to make *mantecados* and I answered, 'No. Of course not! Make shortbreads if you like butter!' I must have been feeling quite unseasonably belligerent that day, as *mantecados* are a traditional Christmas treat. But lard is the traditional shortening to make *mantecados*. Lard is rendered pork fat and is still popular in Spanish cooking. Lard has only very recently disappeared from Anglo-Saxon cooking and it is interesting to note that suet (kidney fat) is still used in some Christmas pudding recipes. Lard gives a great depth of flavour and another dimension to pastries. It highlights the sugar and the spice and, despite any preconceptions people might have, it leaves the palate feeling cleaner than if butter were used. My family never makes this biscuit at any other time of the year, so when I taste that lard flavour with the almonds and the hint of anis it can be no other season. In my mind, without lard there could be no *mantecados*. Without *mantecados* there would be no Christmas. It would be like New York without snow or Bondi Beach without backpackers. Yes of course you could make this recipe with butter but you would not be making *mantecados*, you'd be making almond shortbread.

METHOD

Line a baking tray with baking paper. Preheat the oven to 180°C (350°F/Gas 4).

Coarsely grind the almonds in a blender or using a mortar and pestle. Put the almonds into a bowl with the eggs, olive oil, caster sugar, lard, flour, lemon rind and anis and mix well to combine. Roll into 36 balls, slightly smaller than a golf ball, then flatten to discs approximately 1 cm (½ inch) thick. Pat around the edges to make sure the sides are straight.

Place on the baking tray and brush the *mantecados* with the lightly beaten egg. Bake for 25 minutes, or until lightly browned and cooked through. Allow to cool on a wire rack then roll the *mantecados* in icing sugar.

CHRISTMAS IN A SPANISH HOUSEHOLD

It's funny, I look back on the Christmases from my childhood and I seem to remember a lot of legs. Legs of uncles and aunties who'd come around to our place on Christmas Eve to party. In Spain, the exchanging of presents happens on 6 January, Three Kings Day. When we moved to Australia this was amalgamated into Christmas Eve, so the traditional dinner and party and presents were all combined, which helped fuel the children's excitement. We'd have a meal of *pinchitos muronos* (chargrilled Moorish lamb skewers, see page 246) and do the Aussie thing and have some *gambas a la plancha* (grilled garlic prawns, see page 141) which dad would usually cook on the barbecue. We would also have Russian Eggs, which are boiled eggs stuffed with their own yolk and mayonnaise. We were allowed to stay up well past midnight.

Some time during the night, Uncle Rebola, who was considered by many to be quite an accomplished flamenco singer, would put on a performance and sing soulful *cante hondo* (deep and emotional songs). Mum would bring out her *mantecados de almendra* and dad poured liberal shots of anis liqueur and brandy. However, the focus was never on the food. It was always on the family. Special attention was paid to the very young and our grandparents.

But the food was a constant. As a child, it seemed like it was never-ending, like magically self-replenishing plates.

It was only when I was older that I realized how much hard work mum and dad put in; every year the food was consistently good and tasted just as good as it did the year before. It's just the people who changed. This year was the first year our son Pepe spent Christmas with his grandparents. Mum's *mantecados* were exactly as I remember them and dad was just as liberal with his shots. But the smiles our little boy brought to their faces — sometimes I think mum and dad were going to burst they were smiling so much. I don't think I can remember seeing them so happy.

BEBIDAS

BEBIDAS
DRINKS

Although I have been closely associated with drinking for many years this is not my area of expertise. I hand the reins over to bar manager, Andy McMahon, and sommelier, Dante Ruaine.

SPANISH DRINKS CULTURE

There is no set time for drinking in Spain. There is no cultural ethos that limits the time of day when you can or cannot drink. The day may start with a shot of brandy or anise-based spirit and finish with another at 2 am after a night strolling the warm streets. Because it is not considered a taboo, drinking did not get condensed into compact legal drinking hours as it did in Australia, where the phenomenon of 6 o'clock closing led to binge drinking. The consumption of alcohol in Spain is spread out, interspersed with lots of walking and lots of sobering tapas.

At MoVida we open at midday so we don't experience the early morning side of Spanish culture, but we share the same respect for our food and drink. Drinking and eating are fun; drinking very good wine, beer and sherry and eating great food are even better.

BEER – CERVEZA

There is a notion that when you go out to dine you should drink wine. But Spanish food is salty. Spain has a hot climate and so does Australia. So what should you do? You should drink beer. Beer quenches thirst, and is a fun drink. When eating Spanish food, think Spanish and order what you *feel* like drinking, not what you are *supposed* to be drinking. It doesn't even need to be Spanish. A good Australian lager might be a perfect drink with the *almendras saladas* (salted almonds, see page 66); a Spanish beer with the *salmorejo cordobes* (Córdoba's thick tomato and bread soup, see page 88); or perhaps a German *weissebier* (white beer) with *gambas a la sidra* (prawns cooked in apple cider, see page 145).

WINE – VINO

In Australia we are fortunate in having strong representation of Spanish wines, covering key varietals. In MoVida's little bar we offer a compact list, which explores wines from all over the world and back again to our local producers here in Victoria.

Our wine list takes into consideration the food being served but still provides interesting and funky options for the customers.

Following is a list of wines in order from lightest whites to heaviest reds with a brief description and some recipe suggestions.

ALBARIÑO

Albariño wine is native to the cool, damp province of northwestern Spain, Galicia. It is rich and racy and a lot of people talk about its pear, citrus fruit and floral aromas. With its spritely acid structure it matches a broad range of light dishes, particularly seafood.

Pimientos de piquillo con ajoarriero (see page 81)
Deep-fried red *piquillo* peppers stuffed with salt cod
Vieiras con vino y migas de pan (see page 138)
Scallops baked in their shells with white wine and breadcrumbs.
Espinacas a la andaluza (see page 178)
Spinach and chickpeas slowly cooked with spices and sherry vinegar

VERDEJO

This spicy, slightly unctuous white wine is grown in Rueda, a high altitude region 2 hours from Madrid. With its wonderful texture, tropical fruit aromas and long, ripe, gentle acidity, it's a particularly good partner to many Spanish dishes that may have a bit of oomph, so require a subtle wine match.

Sopa de picadillo (see page 91)
Jamón and pasta soup with mint
Pargo al fondo (see page 160)
Whole snapper baked on potatoes and capsicums

TEMPRANILLO

A perfumed and often spicy red, *tempranillo* is Spain's primary indigenous grape variety, which is now being planted enthusiastically all over Australia. It has lovely, gentle and earthy tannins and a food-friendly, meaty–earthy aspect. It has been described as having similar qualities to Barolo and Burgundy and goes well with meat, mushrooms and dishes with a little spice.

Habas con jamón (see page 185)
Braised broad beans with ham and mint
Cocido (see page 104)
Chickpea and meat broth
Cordero al chilindrón (see page 247)
Pyrenees lamb with white wine and paprika sauce
Cerdo asado (see page 252)
Roast pork belly with quince *alioli*

GARNACHA

Garnacha is the Spanish version of the variety otherwise known as Grenache. It originated in Spain, and makes everything from light, fruity-dry *rosados* to powerful, rich full-bodied reds. Either way, it's a variety with lovely raspberry, earthy and herb aromas, fresh acid, and is very versatile with regard to food.

Rabo de toro (see page 258)
Oxtail braised slowly in fino sherry
Chuletón (see page 264)
Spanish rib eye
Estofado (see page 265)
Beef shin braised with carrots, tomatoes, white wine and saffron

SHERRY — JEREZ

Sherry is an Anglicization of Jerez, the central wine town in the southwest corner of Andalusia. Four hundred years of British merchant influence has celebrated, entrenched and refined the production of this diverse group of lightly fortified wines, which today we call 'sherry'.

Sherries come in sweet and dry, rich and elegant styles. They are made from predominantly white, but also brown, grapes. But what they all share is an extended period of barrel maturation (4 years minimum for decent wines) in the solera system.

In our opinion, sherry is the best aperitif in the world because the acidity activates the taste buds, prepares the palate and gets the digestive juices flowing. Thankfully, sherry is undergoing a renaissance — after an extended period of being in the dark ages because of a long association with alcoholics, grandmothers and alcoholic grandmothers!

For a first timer, sherry can be quite a puzzling drinking experience, particularly when trying fino and manzanilla for the first time, as they are bone-dry and nutty. But the moment you put sherry with food it makes complete sense.

MANZANILLA AND FINO
Cool, crisp and kept in the fridge

Manzanilla
Manzanilla is made on the coast near Jerez and is bone-dry, floral, salty and crisp. People have linked the proximity of the manzanilla vineyards to the coast with the sherry's shell-like characteristic, which makes it the perfect match for oysters, sardines, fried whitebait and mussels.

Fino

Fino is made 15 kilometres (9 miles) inland. It's made from the same grape variety and has the same method of production, but it has a fuller, nuttier and yeastier style and lacks the coastal influence. It goes just as well with seafood but can cut through oily dishes such as mackerel *escabeche*. The old blokes in Spain will drink it before lunch with a little *jamón*, chorizo or a bowl of olives flavoured with thyme, fennel and orange.

AMONTILLADO AND OLOROSO
Pantry-dwelling midfielders

Amontillado

This is a light brown starter kept in the pantry to start off any meal or conversation. It has great aromas of honey and roasted nuts, a crisp finish and a wonderfully lingering flavour of almonds. We believe it was made for serving with salted almonds. It is also a perfect foil for the *raya con avellanas* (skate with hazelnuts and lemon, see page 158), as it matches the hazelnuts and cuts through the butter.

Oloroso

Oloroso is the Johnny Cash of the sherries, walking the line between sweet and dry. It has rich, deep walnut characteristics dotted with caramel, toffee and wood spice. It also has a refreshing acidity, balanced with a lovely textural richness. With its savoury and glycerol elements it goes well with *Manchego* cheese and *Tarta de Santiago* (Saint James tart with quince, see page 332).

PEDRO XIMÉNEZ
Dark, sweet and sticky

This is the grandfather of sherries — a thick, dark chocolate-brown liquid with a syrupy texture and aromas of figs, dates, prunes, sultanas and Christmas cake spices. We use it a lot to flavour dishes but is perfect drizzled over ice cream or a chocolate ganache. It can also be brought out at the end of the meal, before it's time for the spirits and pool cues. A nice little glass of chilled PX (as the funky young people like to call it) sets off the night.

TAKING A SEAT AT THE BAR ...

When MoVida first opened, the culture of sitting at a bar and eating good food and drinking good wine was not very well appreciated. We always offer the same food and wine at the bar as we do at the tables, but there is a stigma attached to eating at a bar — it reminds people of cheap pub meals. People walk in to our fully booked room, are offered a great seat at the bar and then storm out saying, 'I don't take second best!' But to those who understand bar culture, our bar has the best seats in Melbourne. The food is just as good and the wine the same but during the course of the night the vibe swells, the customers are up close with the staff, the conversation moves and flows and you can forget about cutlery and table manners — it's the place to eat, drink and let your hair down. Hollywood types, politicians, European royalty, American musicians — they all come to eat at our bar. Sitting in the restaurant is like going to a Bach recital, but taking a seat at the bar is like groovin' with James Brown.

SANGRÍA – THE PARTY ANIMAL OF THE IBERIAN PENINSULA

Sangría is all about chilling cheap booze and having a laugh. As soon as you put wine together with lemonade and citrus fruit you know that no-one is taking anything seriously. It's about the beach, party and fun. As such, we can't resist occasionally serving it up in summer. It is the easiest cocktail in the world to make. The more rough and ready the red wine you use, the better your sangría will be. I reckon you should use cooking wine, because any trace of subtle French oak will be obliterated! You can't get sangría wrong. There is no real recipe. It is based on what you have in the refrigerator at the time.

INGREDIENTS

310 ml (10¾ fl oz/1¼ cups) red wine

125 ml (4 fl oz/½ cup) brandy

1 cinnamon stick

60 ml (2 fl oz/¼ cup) Licor 43, or other sweet liqueur

1 banana, cut into 1 cm (½ inch) thick slices

2 plums, stoned and chopped

4 lemon wedges

150 g (5½ oz) cherries, if in season

500 ml (17 fl oz/2 cups) orange soda or lemonade, chilled

MAKES ABOUT 1 LITRE (35 FL OZ/4 CUPS)

SANGRÍA
RED SANGRÍA

Combine all the ingredients except the orange soda in a 2 litre (70 fl oz/8 cup) pitcher. Cover with plastic wrap and refrigerate overnight. Fill four large tumblers with ice. Pour the orange soda into the pitcher and mix. Pour the sangría over the ice.

INGREDIENTS

310 ml (10¾ fl oz/1¼ cups) white wine

1½ teaspoons red wine

125 ml (4 fl oz/½ cup) white rum

60 ml (2 fl oz/¼ cup) Cointreau

seeds from 1 pomegranate

4 lemon wedges

lime wedges

500 ml (17 fl oz/2 cups) soda water
  or lemonade, chilled

6 mint sprigs, leaves only

MAKES ABOUT 1 LITRE (35 FL OZ/4 CUPS)

SANGRÍA BLANCA
WHITE SANGRÍA

Combine the wines, rum, Cointreau, pomegranate seeds and lemon wedges in a pitcher and mix. Cover with plastic wrap and refrigerate overnight. Fill four large tumblers with ice and add four lime wedges into each glass. Pour the soda water into the pitcher then pour the sangría over the ice. Garnish with mint leaves.

ÍNDICES
INDEX

Page numbers in **bold** indicate recipes.

ACKNOWLEDGMENTS

Mr and Mrs Camorra Senior
Cornelius McMahon
Peter Bartholomew
David Mackintosh
Jimmy and the kitchen crew for all their dedication
and loyalty
Andy Mac and the irrepressible front-of-house team
Alice de Sousa from Casa Iberica — the woman who
kept this food alive in Melbourne
Jane Lawson
Laila and Stella
Pepe and Aurora (Bodega de Pepe)
Tomas Robles

Stephen Parker (Mount Moriac Olives)
Scott Wasley (Spanish Acquisition)
Simon Johnson (Fitzroy)
Tim and Amanda White (Book for Cooks)
Max Allen
Simon Field
Tiffany Treloar
Natalie Lleonart
Travis Jeffreys (stoneware)
Mr Loc Lam, Little Saigon Shopping Centre
Footscray Market Management
Cheeses supplied by Will Studd (Fromagent)

PUBLISHED IN 2007 BY MURDOCH BOOKS PTY LIMITED

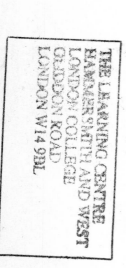

Murdoch Books Australia
Pier 8/9
23 Hickson Road
Millers Point NSW 2000
Phone: +61 (0) 2 8220 2000
Fax: +61 (0) 2 8220 2558
www.murdochbooks.com.au

Murdoch Books UK Limited
Erico House, 6th Floor
93–99 Upper Richmond Road
Putney, London SW15 2TG
Phone: +44 (0) 20 8785 5995
Fax: +44 (0) 20 8785 5985
www.murdochbooks.co.uk

Chief Executive: Juliet Rogers
Publishing Director: Kay Scarlett

Design Manager: Vivien Valk
Project Manager and Editor: Rhiain Hull
Concept and design: Reuben Crossman
Photographer: Alan Benson
Food Editor: Jane Lawson
Production: Maiya Levitch

National Library of Australia Cataloguing-in-Publication
Data
Camorra, Frank.
Movida : Spanish culinary adventures. Includes index.
ISBN 9781921259395 (hbk.). 1. Cookery, Spanish. 2.
Spain - Social life and customs -21st century.
I. Cornish, Richard, 1967-. II. Title. 641.5946

A catalogue record for this book is available from the
British Library.

Printed by 1010 Printing International Limited in 2007.
PRINTED IN CHINA.
Reprinted in 2008 (twice).

The Publisher would like to thank Simon Bajada for
lending equipment for use and photography.

IMPORTANT: Those who might be at risk from the
effects of salmonella poisoning (the elderly, pregnant
women, young children and those suffering from
immune deficiency diseases) should consult their
doctor with any concerns about eating raw eggs.

CONVERSION GUIDE: You may find cooking times vary
depending on the oven you are using. For fan-forced
ovens, as a general rule, set the oven temperature to
20°C (35°F) lower than indicated in the recipe. We
have used 20 ml (4 teaspoon) tablespoon measures.
If you are using a 15 ml (3 teaspoon) tablespoon, for
most recipes the difference will not be noticeable.
However, for recipes using baking powder, gelatine,
bicarbonate of soda (baking soda), small amounts of
flour and cornflour (cornstarch), add an extra teaspoon
for each tablespoon specified.